Instrumentation and Control
for the
Process Industries

JOHN BORER

ELSEVIER APPLIED SCIENCE PUBLISHERS
LONDON and NEW YORK

ELSEVIER APPLIED SCIENCE PUBLISHERS LTD
Crown House, Linton Road, Barking, Essex IG11 8JU, England

Sole Distributor in the USA and Canada
ELSEVIER SCIENCE PUBLISHING CO., INC.
52 Vanderbilt Avenue, New York, NY 10017, USA

British Library Cataloguing in Publication Data

Borer, John
    Instrumentation and control for the process
    industries.
    1. Process control   2. Engineering instruments
    I. Title
    670.42'7   TS156.8

ISBN 0-85334-342-X

WITH 259 ILLUSTRATIONS

© ELSEVIER APPLIED SCIENCE PUBLISHERS LTD 1985

Printed in Great Britain by Galliard (Printers) Ltd, Great Yarmouth

Preface

The term 'process control' embraces a wide range of activities which include, but are not limited to, the measurement or automatic regulation of process variables. Control of any industrial process also includes the actions taken by the operators, and the setting and reviewing of objectives relating to energy balances, production rates, efficiency, etc. The ability to do any of these things, however, rests on the ability to measure the variables which describe these criteria, and for this reason any engineer who wishes to address himself to the science and art of control must first have a clear understanding of the principles and practice of measurement. More and more the design and synthesis of control systems is being recognised as the province of the systems engineer whilst the traditional instrument engineer's role is associated with the instruments used to measure and regulate variables, leaving the process engineer to decide how the process shall be controlled. The control engineer's function today in the process industries combines these two areas of technology. Clearly the control engineer must know as much as possible about process design and equipment design as well as measurement and systems engineering: in other words, a competent control engineer must have a very wide engineering knowledge indeed.

This book is an attempt to put into one volume the essential basic knowledge required by a control engineer in the process industries. Such a book cannot possibly be comprehensive and no pretence is made that this one is. The first half of the book describes the established measuring techniques and practices for the most fundamental measurements (which comprise 90% of all process measurement): the remainder of the book is devoted to the design of measuring systems, regulating systems and finally control systems. No attempt has been made to cover on-stream analysis, batch control, or the design of advanced control systems, but these may well form the subject matter for a second volume at a later date.

JOHN BORER

Acknowledgements

Thanks are due to the following for permission to reproduce previously published material:

American Meter Co. Inc. for Fig. 4.35;
British Rototherm Co. Ltd for Fig. 6.2;
Ferranti plc for Fig. 7.14;
Flo-tran Inc. for Fig. 4.31;
Foxboro Great Britain Ltd for Figs 2.8, 7.5, 7.7, 7.8, 7.9 and 9.5;
Gervase Instruments Ltd for Fig. 4.19;
KDG Flowmeters for Fig. 5.13;
Kent Process Control Ltd for Figs 4.11, 4.24 and 9.26;
Kistler Instruments Ltd for Fig. 2.12 (left);
Measurement Technology Ltd for Fig. 7.26;
Moore Products Co. (UK) Ltd for Figs 4.30, 9.11, 9.12 and 9.17;
The Open University for Figs 2.9 (left), 2.10, 2.12 (right), 4.23, 4.25, 6.9, 6.10, 6.17, 6.24, 6.36, 6.37, 6.38, 7.13 and 7.15;
Rosemount Engineering Co. Ltd for Figs 6.19, 6.29 and 6.30;
Taylor Instrument Companies for Fig. 4.5;
Thorn EMI Datatech Ltd for Fig. 2.9 (right);
Voest-Alpine AG for Figs 2.1–2.3, 3.5, 3.6, 3.19–3.23, 8.3–8.10;
Whessoe Systems and Controls Ltd for Fig. 3.8.

Contents

CHAPTER 1

Principles of Industrial Measurement

1.1 GENERAL

In order to operate chemical plant processes, e.g. chemical reactions, petroleum distillation, etc., it is essential to know the values of physical states of the process fluids, such as pressure, temperature and density, as well as rates of flow and often analytical data. Industrial instruments have been developed to measure all these parameters and in turn the instruments themselves depend on physical laws. Before we can use any tool (and instruments are tools for measuring) we need to know its capability. It is necessary to define limits of performance for any measuring instrument or system, and before we can do this the terminology used needs to be defined.

1.2 INSTRUMENT PERFORMANCE

It is important to determine with what precision measurements can be made using the instrument or system, but this will depend on many factors. Because of slack in linkages, friction and many other imperfections, repeated measurements made with the same system will only give the same result within a certain *error band*. This limitation on performance of a measuring system is referred to as *repeatability*. No matter how repeatable the results there will be a limit on the *resolution* with which they can be indicated or recorded. The measuring system will have a range or *span* over which it can work, and ideally a graph of the relationship of measured variable to instrument indication (or recording) will be a straight line (Fig. 1.1). In fact this will never be the case, and *accuracy* will be defined as the limit of confidence which can be placed in a measurement, taking all the factors into account (Fig. 1.2).

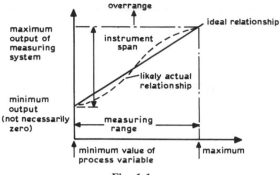

Fig. 1.1.

1.3 RANGEABILITY

Any industrial measurement system should give information of sufficient accuracy to facilitate control of the process operations over a *range* of operating conditions. It is often forgotten, however, that many of the causes of error are related to the maximum of the measuring range. Manufacturers usually quote errors in terms of FSD (full scale deflection). If a process variable is to be measured it is implied that it varies in the course of normal process operation; to allow for such variation the range of the measurement system will normally be selected so that the normal operating value of the variable represents about 70% of FSD. Thus, if, typically, a range of process variable of 3 to 1 is to be measured and the system accuracy is $\pm 1\%$ FSD then the errors to be expected at the lower end of the range will be

$$(1 \times \tfrac{1}{0 \cdot 70} \times \tfrac{1}{3}) = \pm 5\%$$

1.4 ASSESSMENT OF ERRORS

It is easier to say how the performance of a measurement system is determined, than to determine it in practice. Whilst the instrument technician at a refinery or chemical plant will rarely, if ever, be asked to carry out such an evaluation experimentally, it is, nevertheless, essential that he understand how this is done. Sometimes the errors caused in the different ways outlined above will cancel one another out; sometimes they will add up and so reinforce each other. Thus the actual error which occurs

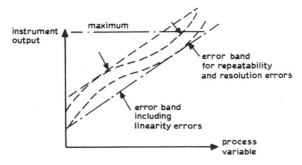

Fig. 1.2.

in any particular measurement is *randomly* determined; only the *probability* that the error will be greater or less than a certain size can be determined. Therefore the accuracy of a measurement system is always quoted in statistical terms, that is the size of error which has, say, a 90% probability of occurring; it cannot be quoted in any other way.

To establish this statistical data, experiments must be made repeatedly with the measuring system under test, so that the error is found on a sufficient number of occasions to allow the data to be reliably grouped; the probability of the occurrence of errors of different sizes can then be evaluated. This is obviously a very time-consuming method.

1.5 CALIBRATION

Industrial measuring devices and systems must be robust and easily maintainable, and to some extent accuracy is sacrificed to these ends. Any experiment to assess the error of measurement requires that there exists some other means of establishing the true value of the process variable being measured. Since such experiments are carried out under laboratory conditions, a more accurate instrument is often available so that the measurements can be made simultaneously on this and the industrial instrument under test. Such high accuracy instruments are known as *substandard*, and are usually at least one order of magnitude better in terms of accuracy (that is ten times more accurate). If such substandard instruments are not available, some fixed physical phenomenon, such as the boiling point of a liquid, must be used to evaluate the accuracy, at least at certain fixed points on the instrument range.

1.6 ZERO AND SPAN

As the range of the process variable will be different for each individual application, industrial instruments are almost always made in such a way that the *span* can be adjusted to suit each application within a wide range, so that sensitivity, accuracy and other sources of error are proportional to the span. In the course of normal operation the span of the instrument can change owing to vibration, heat, physical blows or any number of other causes, as can the zero setting. These two adjustments must therefore be checked (and if necessary corrected) frequently, often whilst the instrument remains in its installed position on the plant. Obviously it is not possible in most cases to use substandard instruments or other laboratory techniques, and such 'on plant' checks are usually made by 'injecting' known test inputs using special test equipment.

1.7 DRIFT

A very important aspect of the performance of industrial measuring systems is their propensity to 'drift'. Either span or zero may change gradually because of the ageing of components (this is very important in the case of electronic equipment) or other forms of slow deterioration. Such drifting is common in new equipment and for this reason span/zero checking should be carried out more frequently immediately after installation. However, if an instrument should be found to drift continuously, long after its installation, it should be returned to the manufacturer as unsatisfactory. Unfortunately this type of failure often goes undetected and manufacturers rarely provide data on drift as part of performance specifications.

1.8 RESOLUTION

This term applies to the precision with which the measurement can be displayed, recorded, or logged. If the measuring system presents the results of the measuring process to the operator in the form of an indicated figure then the size and length of the indicator scale will inevitably limit the size of the smallest unit which the human eye can 'discriminate'; however, there would be little point in supplying a larger indicator if the size of unit which could then be read is smaller than the limit of accuracy of the measuring system itself. Thus, the indicator or recorder should have a scale size which is consistent with the limits of accuracy of the measuring system.

A different situation arises in the case of digital displays which are becoming very popular; discrimination depends on the number of digits used to represent the measured value, regardless of the size of the display, and the precision of the electronic circuitry which converts the measurement into the digital quantity displayed (or recorded).

1.9 HYSTERESIS

A common cause of error in many measurement systems is hysteresis, caused by friction or by any one of a multitude of directional effects in mechanical, pneumatic, hydraulic or electrical mechanisms. These result in a different measurement being obtained if the process variable has increased to the measured value from some previous lower value, or alternatively has decreased from some previously higher value.

1.10 DIRECT/INDIRECT MEASUREMENT

For the most part the techniques used in industrial measurement are inferential or indirect. For instance, in order to measure the temperature of a process fluid, the pressure of a liquid or gas sealed into a metal container may be measured, and the temperature 'inferred' from the pressure according to certain known relationships. Some techniques, however, are 'direct', e.g. the measurement of flow rate of a fluid by the positive displacement technique, in which the meter actually transfers a 'package' of process fluid from one place to another, depending on mechanical seals to prevent any of it returning. Such techniques are usually more accurate though much more expensive than inferential techniques.

1.11 SAMPLING

It is necessary to ensure that the measurement made, though it may be perfectly accurate, is representative of the measurement required. For instance, the flow rate or temperature of a fluid may vary across the diameter of the pipe if the flow is not sufficiently turbulent to ensure good mixing. Again, even if flow is sufficiently turbulent, the flow rate or temperature may vary with the passage of time. Temperature or pressure may vary at different places in a large tank either in a regular manner, and therefore predictably, or in a random manner, and therefore unpredictably. In such cases it may be necessary to make more than one measurement in order to determine the mean value of the variable. If the 'distribution' of the variable in time or position is predictable (as, for instance, the distribution of fluid flow across a pipe) this may not be difficult: if however the distribution is random it will only be possible to make a number of measurements (as many as is practicable) and hope that their average is a close approximation of the true mean value of the variable. The probability that this is the case increases with the number of such measurements made and decreases with the differences in the measurements across the distribution in time or position. The calculation of a suitable tolerance is statistically based and will depend upon the degree of certainty which is considered adequate (there can never be absolute certainty in such cases); for instance, there may be a 90 % certainty that the average of the measurements is within $\pm 1 \%$ of the true mean value.

CHAPTER 2

Measurement of Process Pressure

2.1·DIRECT PRESSURE MEASUREMENT

Deadweight testers are the most accurate calibration instruments in use for pressures above those which can reasonably be measured using a manometer. Pressure is provided by weights acting on a piston which fits very closely into a cylinder containing oil (Fig. 2.1(a)); the pressure developed in the oil is equal to the weight divided by the cross-sectional area of the piston, and this pressure is applied to the inferential instrument under calibration:

$$p = \frac{W}{A}$$

Friction between the piston and the cylinder is the only source of error and in a well-made instrument this is negligible.

To obtain very high pressures the piston is stepped as shown in Fig. 2.1(b) and a second gland added. This has the effect that the area over which the weight is distributed is the difference of the cross-sectional areas of the two sections of the piston, and thus the pressure generated by even quite a small weight can be very high indeed:

$$p = \frac{W}{(A_1 - A_2)}$$

The ring balance manometer comprises a tube bent into a circle and supported on a knife-edge pivot so that it can rotate (Fig. 2.2). Pressures p_1 and p_2 are isolated from each other by a partition on the one hand and liquid fill on the other. Because of the difference in pressure across the partition (which is fixed to the tube) a turning moment is applied to the tube; this is balanced by a turning moment produced by a counterweight and the angle of rotation is a measure of the pressure applied. For very low

7

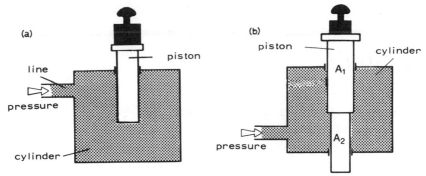

Fig. 2.1.

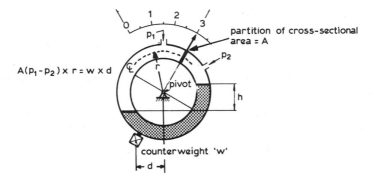

Fig. 2.2.   Ring balance gauge.

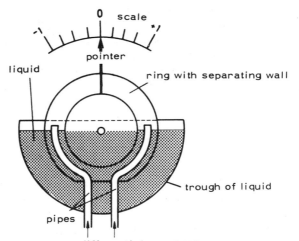

Fig. 2.3.   'Bell' ring balance gauge.

pressures the 'bell' ring balance gauge (Fig. 2.3) provides a solution to the errors caused by the stiffness of the tubes connecting p_1 and p_2 to the process.

2.2 INDIRECT PRESSURE MEASUREMENT

The commonest instrument used to measure pressure in a process plant is the pressure gauge. This is normally mounted close to the point of measurement and connected to it by an 'impulse' pipe, so that the process fluid is brought up to, and in most cases, into the gauge. Elastic deformation of a suitable measuring element is translated into motion of a pointer across a scale by mechanical gearing.

The commonest form of measuring element used is the 'Bourdon' tube which is a tube formed into an arc of a circle as shown in Fig. 2.4. Increasing internal pressure causes the tube to deform elastically in such a way that it straightens out. Different cross-sectional shapes are used for different pressure ranges and applications.

The Bourdon tube exhibits hysteresis error and the zero is often indeterminate and may change with use and ageing. Wear in the linkage also produces deadband error and expensive gauges use jewelled bearings; however, the most serious source of error is temperature variation. The Bourdon tube changes shape in response to variations in temperature unless made of a material which has a near zero coefficient of expansion, such as Ni-Span-C. Cheaper gauges are made from copper or brass, whilst for very high pressures, hardened steel solid drawn Bourdon elements are used.

The form of Bourdon tube shown in Fig. 2.4 is known as the 'C' type, but

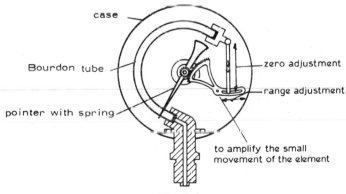

Fig. 2.4.

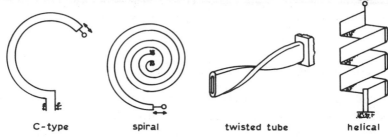

| C-type | spiral | twisted tube | helical |

Fig. 2.5. Bourdon tubes.

other forms are used to obtain greater movement from the same pressure change (Fig. 2.5). The movement of a Bourdon element is proportional to the angle through which it is bent: the 'C' form is bent through approx. 200° whilst a spiral or helical element can be bent through 1000°. The helical form is used for higher pressures as the radius of curvature and therefore the stress is uniform over the whole length of the element, which is not the case for the spiral form.

The Bourdon element is very sensitive to vibration and is prone to fatigue failure if subjected to fluctuating pressure. It is also prone to corrosion in some cases owing to the fact that the process fluid enters the element. All these problems can be overcome by using a diaphragm element. The diaphragm can be protected against overpressure by limiting its possible movement as shown in Fig. 2.6; it can also be effectively protected against corrosion by coating with silver or plastic.

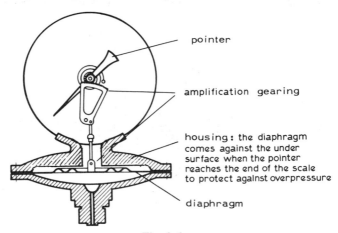

pointer

amplification gearing

housing: the diaphragm comes against the under surface when the pointer reaches the end of the scale to protect against overpressure

diaphragm

Fig. 2.6.

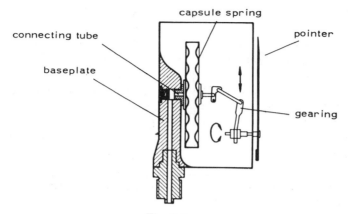

Fig. 2.7.

The capsule measuring element (Fig. 2.7) consists of two metal diaphragms soldered together to form a closed capsule. When the pressure rises the capsule expands and thus operates the pointer mechanism. Capsules are used to measure absolute pressures because they are easily 'evacuated' and can be made very sensitive to small pressure changes.

Stiff diaphragms are 'stacked' to produce measuring units with much greater movement than a single capsule. One of the best known measuring devices which uses stacked diaphragms is the 'Barton' meter (Fig. 2.8). This unit is used to measure small differential pressures where the background pressure is high. It can withstand overpressures because each diaphragm is

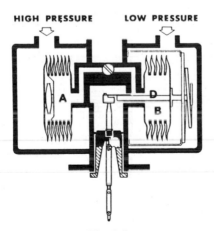

Fig. 2.8.

shaped to fit into the next in such a way that when the 'stack' is fully compressed it is 'solid' and resists any further deformation.

The two stacks are filled with liquid, and increasing pressure in the high pressure chamber compresses stack A, thus displacing liquid into and expanding stack B and moving the pointer arm, D. Reduction of pressure in the low pressure chamber has the same effect, whilst an increase in this chamber or a decrease in the high pressure chamber moves the pointer in the opposite direction. The spring, C, adds to the elastic resistance of the diaphragm stacks to the applied pressure and thus allows the instrument to be calibrated to respond over the desired range.

Corrugated bellows are often used in place of stacked diaphragms as they can be made more easily by a single pressure-forming operation (stacked diaphragms involve soldering each pair of diaphragms).

2.3 MEASUREMENT BY ELECTRO-MECHANICAL METHODS

All the measuring elements described so far depend on the elastic properties of metals to provide a force which is proportional to the process pressure: in every case the elastic *movement* of the metal element is measured, in many cases after amplification by mechanical gear and lever mechanisms. An electrical response can be used very easily to cause a pointer or recorder pen to move across a scale or chart. Such instruments produce an electrical current or voltage in response to pressure, by virtue of a change of capacitance, inductance or resistance.

All electrically conductive materials show a change in resistance if stressed, and this 'piezo-resistive' phenomenon is used to produce the 'strain gauge'. Strain gauges are fixed to a diaphragm or other mechanically deformed measuring element, and instead of measuring the movement under pressure, the change in resistance of the strain gauge is measured. 'Strain' being the change of length of an elastic element which accompanies the stress set up by pressure on the diaphragm or other mechanical measuring element, the movement which is necessary to cause an adequate (for measuring purposes) response from a strain gauge is very much less than that which could be properly measured by mechanical means. This in turn enables 'stiffer' and therefore more robust measuring elements to be produced, which is particularly important when considerable 'over-pressure' may have to be tolerated by the measuring element, or when measuring very large pressures or forces (pressure being force per unit area, the measurement of force and pressure are almost the same).

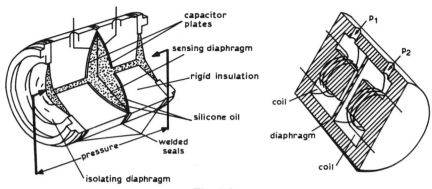

Fig. 2.9.

Capacitance or inductance can be changed by small deflections of a sensing diaphragm, thus providing alternative ways to measure the deflection by electrical means (see Fig. 2.9).

Using any of these methods it is necessary to translate the change in electrical resistance, capacitance or inductance into an electrical force capable of moving the pointer or pen of the indicating or recording device

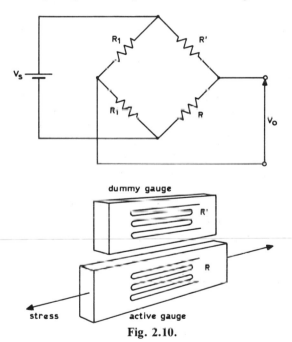

Fig. 2.10.

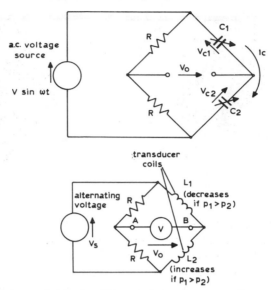

Fig. 2.11. (a) An a.c. bridge for differential capacitance measurement. (b) An a.c. bridge circuit used to detect the relative changes in the inductances L_1 and L_2.

in the measurement system. This is achieved by using a 'bridge' as shown in Figs 2.10 and 2.11.

The 'bridge' operates on the principle that the input voltage is divided across the two fixed reference resistors in the left-hand 'leg' and across the two measuring resistors, capacitors or inductances in the right-hand leg, in proportion to the values of these components. Thus, the two reference devices are of equal value, as are the two measuring devices at zero reading; as the pressure changes, however, the two measuring devices are no longer of the same value and the voltage between them changes and is no longer the same as that between the two reference devices. This difference produces a voltage, V_0, at the output which with power derived from the 'bridge' source drives a pen or pointer. This power source must be alternating in the case of inductance or capacitance bridges and can be either direct or alternating in the case of resistance (strain gauge) devices.

2.4 MEASUREMENT BY ELECTRICAL METHODS

If quartz crystal is 'squeezed' between two parallel faces, it responds by generating a voltage across those faces proportional to the pressure applied

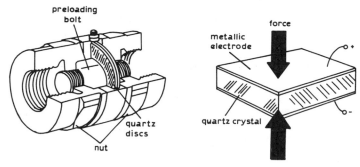

Fig. 2.12.

(Fig. 2.12). This 'piezo-electric' effect can be used to generate power to drive a pen or pointer directly by means of a special electronic circuit called a 'charge amplifier' without any mechanical motion at all. Thus, the piezo-electric sensing element is a true electrical device.

The electrical charge produced by a piezo-electric measuring element is proportional to the *change* in pressure applied, and, however perfect the charge amplifier, the charge will decay in time. For this reason it cannot be regarded as a viable method of measuring relatively steady pressures since no reliable zero can be established. It is used in fact to measure very rapidly fluctuating pressure where the fluctuation rather than the mean pressure is important (the mean can be established by a separate electro-mechanical instrument). Thus piezo-electric sensing elements find little application in process operations.

2.5 SELECTION OF MEASURING ELEMENT

The most common form of pressure measuring element used in plant processes is the Bourdon tube. Pressure gauges, i.e. indicating instruments mounted directly on the process pipe or vessel, almost invariably incorporate a Bourdon tube. The exceptions to this rule are found where the process fluid is highly corrosive, requiring the use of construction materials for the measuring element which are more suitable to a diaphragm than a Bourdon tube; or when vibration might be a problem, since a diaphragm is less liable to fatigue failure than a Bourdon tube in these circumstances. The diaphragm or 'Shaffer' gauge is also more suited to measuring fluctuating pressure for the same reason and can be made more sensitive than a Bourdon tube for measuring pressures lower than 1 bar. For highly corrosive applications the diaphragm can be coated with such materials as PTFE or silver. The Bourdon tube, however, in its simple 'C' form, and manufactured in a variety of materials from phosphor-bronze to chrome–molybdenum steel, is used to measure pressures from 1 bar up to at least 5000 bar.

In the spiral or helical forms the Bourdon tube is used in instruments which require greater movement than can be obtained from a 'C' form, e.g. circular chart recorders. This eliminates the need for a quadrant and pinion gear which is the cause of deadband error and lack of sensitivity in the cheaper 'C' element.

For measuring small pressures the sensitivity and lack of temperature dependence of the capsule element makes it ideal, either in the single form, or, where greater movement is required, in the stacked form used in the Barton meter. The measurement of small differential pressures at high static pressures can be achieved in this way, and often bellows are used instead of stacked diaphragms.

Piezo-electric measuring elements are not normally used in process plant because they only measure the change in pressure and not the total pressure. Electro-mechanical elements do have the advantage that they can be made much stronger than elements which must distort enough to operate a linkage, and also that deadband error, which increases as pivots and bearings wear, is avoided. However, the precautions which must be taken to avoid risk from incendiary sparks is a serious drawback. This is less serious when electrical transmission of signals is used.

2.6 CALIBRATION OF SENSOR ELEMENTS

In general the 'direct' methods are used to calibrate sensors which operate on the 'indirect' (inferential) principles. This is because the direct methods, i.e. 'U' tube or single leg manometers, deadweight testers, etc., are capable of higher accuracy whilst at the same time being too cumbersome for use on the plant. Measuring elements which depend on the stress set up in an elastic material (which is the case with all the elements described) must be checked periodically to see if their span or zero setting has 'shifted' owing to slight non-elastic behaviour of the material; this is the main disadvantage of indirect methods. Calibration checks will also be necessary if the instrument has been subjected to overload, sustained fluctuations or severe vibration in service. Calibration checks, as well as the original calibration, must be made by comparison of readings taken from the instrument under test against readings taken on a substandard instrument when both are subjected to the same pressure at the same time. The substandard must be 10 times more accurate, and this is achieved by using a device which is capable of greater accuracy and which can be expected to maintain that greater accuracy over long periods (if this were not the case, the substandard instruments would require calibration checking as often as the 'field' instruments). Periodically, and also in the event of any possible damage, the substandard instrument will have to be checked in its turn; this is usually achieved by sending it to an organisation that specialises in calibration because the precision required to achieve the even greater accuracy in the 'reference' standard device is normally beyond the capability of a plant instrument workshop.

The extent of calibration checks vary with the instrument and its application; a simple low accuracy pressure gauge will have only zero calibration adjustment—it is assumed that the range (span) will not change outside the performance limits set (some cheap gauges may not even have zero setting adjustment). Nevertheless, calibration checks are usually necessary in order to ensure that the gauge is indeed still within calibration. Most instruments will have adjustable spans as well as zero settings; periodical checking will discover if the instrument is drifting in respect of either. Hysteresis is normally a feature of the instrument and errors from this cause would not normally change during use. However, deadband is often caused by slack in mechanical movements and can be expected to increase with use in instruments which rely on gears, pivots, etc. Linearity is usually a feature of the instrument, but may be changed by 'softening' of springs or bellows after considerable use.

Calibration checks on field instruments are normally a matter of comparing readings on the instrument under test and the 'substandard' at about 10 points up *and down* the range. For especially accurate 'field' measurement systems (which are fortunately rare) it may be necessary to adopt a 'statistical' approach and make a large number of such tests. From such data the 'norm' and the 'standard deviation' of repeated readings can be calculated, and these may be a better guide to the performance (and its possible deterioration) than a single set of results.

2.7 SEALS AND PURGES

In many applications the process fluid cannot be allowed into the measuring element. There are many reasons for this; the fluid may solidify

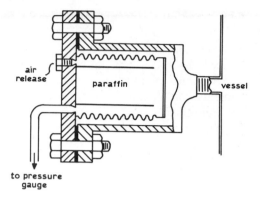

Fig. 2.13.

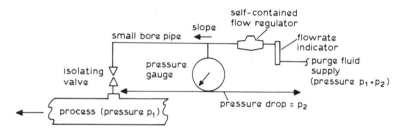

Fig. 2.14.

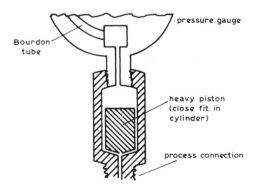

Fig. 2.15.

at the temperature of the measuring element, deposition may occur in the element, or the fluid may be corrosive. In all these cases it may be necessary to interpose a 'seal' between the process and the measuring element. A typical seal is shown in Fig. 2.13.

The space between the seal and the measuring element is filled with a liquid that will not vaporise and all air and gas is removed by bleeding. Care must be taken that the seal and impulse lines are not subjected to changes in temperature to the extent that expansion of the fluid 'fill' (or contraction) would bring the bellows up to their limit stops; provided this precaution is taken and the 'spring rate' (or resistance) of the bellows is negligible compared to the pressure to be measured, the pressure will be transferred from the process to the 'fill' fluid. Such a seal would serve for a clean fluid that would be likely to solidify in impulse lines, provided the seal itself was well lagged. It would not be suitable for use with a dirty fluid which would allow sludge to gather in the bellows corrugations, or a process fluid which would deposit solid matter. For such applications a plain or corrugated diaphragm would replace the bellows. More likely, however, a purge system would be engineered for such an application.

The principle of a purge system is that a fluid (liquid or gas) is allowed to flow into the process fluid through a narrow bore tube at such a rate that the process fluid itself is prevented from entering; thus if the process fluid is dirty, corrosive, or likely to deposit solid matter on the measuring element, a purge will enable measurement to be made nevertheless. However, it is not always acceptable to introduce another fluid into the process line, so the purge technique cannot always be used. A purge system is illustrated in Fig. 2.14, the self-contained flow regulator ensures that the correct flow rate is maintained whatever the pressure in the process stream, provided the supply pressure in the purge line is at an appreciably higher pressure than the highest process pressure possible. The purge fluid may be a gas, such as air or nitrogen, or a liquid, such as water or paraffin.

2.8 DAMPING

One of the main dangers in measuring pressure is that surges may overpressure the instrument, or that rapid fluctuations may cause fatigue fracture in the measuring element. Such dangers are avoided by using dampers (or 'snubbers') such as the one shown diagrammatically in Fig. 2.15. The inertia of a relatively heavy piston fitted in a chamber between the process and the instrument in the vertical plane absorbs the energy of surges or fluctuations.

2.9 HYDROSTATIC HEAD CORRECTION

The measuring element will not normally be located at the same level as the pressure tapping in the process pipe or vessel, as considerations such as access for service and reading tend to dictate the location. If, therefore, the process fluid is a liquid, the hydrostatic head must be allowed for in calibrating the instrument; often this will mean that routine zero/span calibration checks will be made in the field, the substandard instrument being taken to the field instrument instead of the latter to the workshop. If the process pressure is relatively low, care is necessary in selecting a position for installation to ensure that the hydrostatic head correction is within the scope of the zero adjustment available.

2.10 PROCESS PRESSURE CONNECTIONS

Whilst the impulse piping from the pressure connection on the process pipe or vessel to the measuring instrument must obviously be rated to withstand the maximum pressure to which it may be subjected in the course of operation, there are many reasons why it may not be necessary or even desirable to follow the process piping or vessel specifications beyond the first isolating valve. For one thing, should a leak occur, the impulse line and instrument can be isolated and repaired without affecting the process operation, whereas this may not be possible in the case of the process pipework or vessels. Consequently the first isolating valve has a special significance; the outlet is taken as the boundary beyond which 'instrument' rather than 'piping' specifications apply. The valve should always be located as close to the tapping point as possible.

2.11 SAFETY

Measuring instruments vary in their capacity to withstand pressures above those which they are designed to measure; this will always be a feature of the design of the instrument. Instruments may on the other hand have to withstand 'overpressure' for a variety of reasons, the most obvious being that pumps have a higher 'no flow' head than that developed at 'design' flow rate. It is not always possible to buy an instrument that will withstand the maximum pressure that can, under fault conditions, occur in the process; this will usually be set by a safety valve in the process line. It is essential, however, that the instrument should be able to withstand the highest pressure that can occur in *normal* operation.

Even if the instrument is never subject to overpressure, the measuring element (which is normally the weakest part) may still fail because of a manufacturing fault or, after considerable use, metal fatigue. For this reason the case in which the measuring element is housed will be provided with a 'blow-out disc' or some other means to relieve the flow of process fluid which could result from a catastrophic failure of the element. Care should be taken when installing the instrument not to obstruct such relief devices and also to see that they are directed away from positions where people are likely to stand, particularly if the process fluid is toxic, corrosive, hot, etc. The glass in recording or indicating instruments will be blown out if these relieving devices are restricted, causing another hazard. Finally, there must always be an isolating valve between the 'process' and 'instrument' piping because of these factors—as the measuring elements must operate within the 'elastic' region they cannot be made not to rupture under any circumstances. For such absolute safety strain gauge methods must be used.

CHAPTER 3

Fluid Level Measurement

3.1 DIRECT METHODS OF MEASUREMENT

The simplest method of measuring the liquid level in a vessel is the sight glass (Fig. 3.1). However, a sight glass behaves exactly the same way as a manometer and so the level in the glass is only an accurate measure of the level in the vessel provided the density of the liquid in the glass is the same as that of the liquid in the vessel. Therefore, when the temperature of the liquid in the vessel is much higher than ambient, as in the case of a boiler drum, or when it is much lower, as in the case of cryogenic plant, the level will not be correctly measured and a correction will have to be applied.

The other great drawback to the sight glass even for local indication is the fragility of glass. On the other hand, because it is such a simple device, and therefore there is little that can go wrong with it, sight glasses are required by law on such plant as steam raising boiler drums. To overcome the attendant risk of breakage, and consequent leakage of high temperature liquid at high pressure, automatic shut-off valves are built into the sight gauge as shown in Fig. 3.2.

To avoid the use of glass and to enable the measuring tube to be thermally insulated, magnetic followers are sometimes used with tubes made of non-magnetic material such as stainless steel (see Fig. 3.3). Strictly speaking this is not a sight 'glass' but the principle is the same.

The float and pulley method of level measurement has been used in various forms for a very long time (Fig. 3.4). The method in its simplest form depends on the weight of the float being counterbalanced by a weight at the other end of the pulley system (at the indicator), thus putting the wire (rope, or tape) into tension. At the same time the full weight of the float is partly diminished by its buoyancy in the process liquid. Thus, to reduce errors which would arise owing to changes in the density of the fluid (and

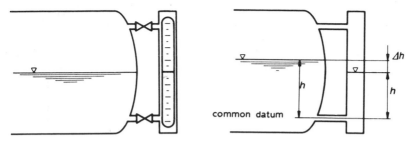

Fig. 3.1.

consequent changes in buoyancy) and also to friction in the pulleys, it is necessary for the float to have as large a cross-sectional area as possible, so that a small rise or fall in its position in the liquid will represent a large change in buoyancy force. Another source of error arises from the transfer of weight of the rope (wire or tape) from the float side of the system to the indicator side. A more accurate system is shown in Fig. 3.5; the rope is wound onto a drum as the float rises, and tension in a spring inside the drum reduces as the drum winds in the rope. The tension in the spring can

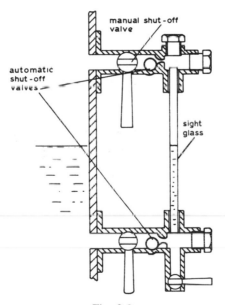

Fig. 3.2.

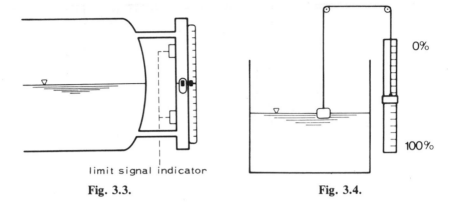

Fig. 3.3.   **Fig. 3.4.**

be made to equal the weight of the rope at all positions, either by the natural change in tension as the spring winds up or unwinds, or by changing the diameter of the drum and thus the length of the moment arm, as the rope coils onto the drum.

Very accurate measurement of the liquid level is required for inventory purposes in large storage tanks—accuracy of better than ± 2 mm *irrespective of the range of measurement*. This is not attainable in a mechanism which depends on the buoyancy of the float to provide the force to overcome pulley friction, etc.; a servo mechanism is used to supplement, if not replace, this driving force. A simple form of servo-assisted gauge is shown in Fig. 3.6. Part of the weight of the float and rope is supported by buoyancy and the rest by the spring. When the level changes this

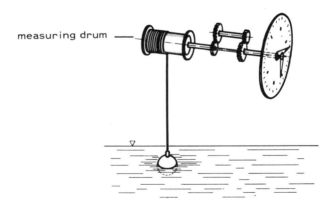

Fig. 3.5.

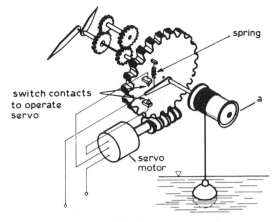

Fig. 3.6.

equilibrium is disturbed, with the result that one or other of the switch contacts is 'made', causing the servo motor to drive the float either up or down until equilibrium is again restored and the motor circuit broken. Because the motor, and not the float, provides the motive force, a large indicator can be used and also a remote indication system if desired.

The problems of rope/wire weight and the force required to drive an indicator mechanism can be overcome in another way, which provides even more accurate indication. A metal plate is lowered on the end of a metal tape until it is almost touching the liquid surface; the electrical capacitance

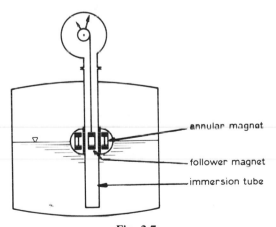

Fig. 3.7.

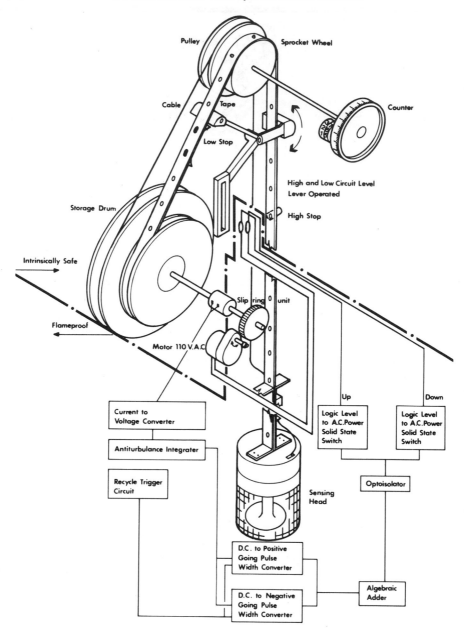

Pulley

Sprocket Wheel

Counter

Cable

Tape

Low Stop

High and Low Circuit Level
Lever Operated

Storage Drum

High Stop

Intrinsically Safe

Slip ring unit

Flameproof

Motor 110 V.A.C.

Up

Down

Current to
Voltage Converter

Logic Level
to A.C.Power
Solid State
Switch

Logic Level
to A.C.Power
Solid State
Switch

Antiturbulance Integrater

Recycle Trigger
Circuit

Optoisolator

Sensing
Head

D.C. to Positive
Going Pulse
Width Converter

D.C. to Negative
Going Pulse
Width Converter

Algebraic
Adder

Fig. 3.8.

between the liquid and this plate is measured, and a servo motor drives the plate up or down to maintain capacitance and hence the distance from the liquid surface at a constant value to within ± 1 mm. The indicator unit is mounted on top of, or at the side of, the tank, and this type of measuring system is used for accurate liquid level measurement in very large storage tanks. The servo unit is mounted in the indicator housing and the stainless steel tape runs over pulleys (as shown in Fig. 3.8) inside sealed pipes, thus making it suitable for use with tanks which are under slight pressure, e.g. petroleum storage tanks.

Servo gauge systems are electrically operated and precautions must be taken to ensure that they are safe to use in locations where there is an explosion or fire risk from petroleum vapour. To achieve this the servo mechanisms are invariably enclosed in flame-proof or explosion-proof enclosures; therefore, it is not possible to carry out maintenance or adjustments to the servo mechanisms in position, for which reason a special calibration 'rig' is essential even if the measurement range is 50 m or more. However, a limit stop is normally provided which gives a datum against which to compare the reading of the gauge; since it is the distance from this datum of the liquid surface which is being measured, there is normally no reason for the system to be out of calibration (it either works or it does not). Accuracy is effected by certain adjustments in the servo mechanism, and it is these adjustments which cannot safely be made in position, and which necessitate the gauge being removed to a workshop and installed in a special calibration rig.

Figure 3.7 shows a tanktop-mounted gauge which uses a magnetic follower so that the internal enclosure of the servo system can be isolated from the process environment. Figure 3.8 shows some details of a tankside gauge system using pulley and stainless steel tape.

3.2 INDIRECT MEASUREMENT BY HYDROSTATIC HEAD METHOD

Since pressure is force per unit of area, the pressure at the bottom of a tank of liquid depends on the height of the liquid above. The bottom of the tank is called the datum of measurement, and the level can be measured as the height of the liquid above this datum by inference from the pressure *at the datum*. The level in an open vessel is proportional to the gauge pressure at datum (Fig. 3.9). The pressure in a closed vessel is proportional to the

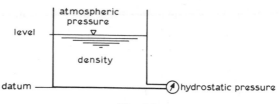

Fig. 3.9.

differential pressure between the datum and the space above the liquid (Fig. 3.10). Note that the level in the vessel is not normally the same as that of the fluid in the manometer; the manometer fluid may be of different density and temperature. The manometer measures hydrostatic pressure, *not* level.

The datum of measurement does not have to be the bottom of the tank and in fact rarely is. However, measurement of the level is always relative to the datum level, which can be anywhere at or above the bottom of the tank.

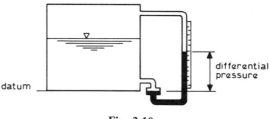

Fig. 3.10.

The level cannot be measured below the datum, which is fixed by the position at which the measuring gauge is connected into the vessel (see Fig. 3.11).

Liquids with low boiling points are those with boiling points which lie below the ambient temperature (e.g. liquid nitrogen). In order to measure such liquids the tank is insulated and its temperature maintained below the ambient temperature. The lower impulse line is not insulated, and, provided the vapour pressure at ambient temperature is higher than the hydrostatic pressure at the datum level, it will fill with vapour not liquid (Fig. 3.12). As any liquid entering would affect the measurement, the impulse lines are at a slight slope to the tank. It may be necessary to heat the lower impulse line to make sure it contains no liquid.

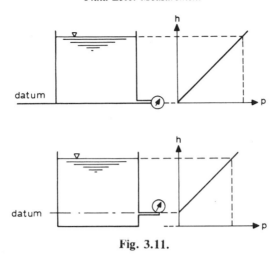

Fig. 3.11.

Condensation chambers are essential when measuring the liquid level of boiling liquids, because the vapour will condense in the upper impulse line which will be cooler than the inside of the tank (Fig. 3.13). The cross-sectional area of the condensation vessel is made large so that the level of the condensed fluid will not change significantly when the manometer liquid rises with the level in the tank. Any such rise will result in condensate draining back into the tank, whilst any fall will quickly be made good by further condensation. In fact, vapour will be condensing all the time and draining back into the tank. The measurement datum is the surface of the

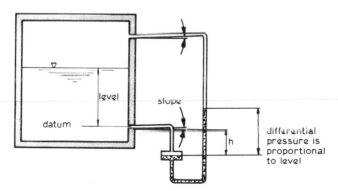

Fig. 3.12.

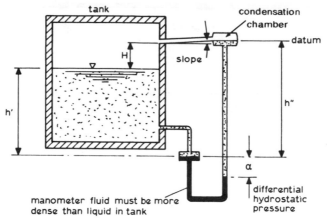

Fig. 3.13.

condensate in the condensation vessel, as this does not vary. The level of the liquid surface in the tank *below* the datum is (Fig. 3.13)

$$H = h'' - h'$$

and is proportional to the differential hydrostatic pressure α. Measurement of α must take into account the relative densities of the manometer fluid and the condensed process fluid.

If the process fluid is a viscous liquid it will not flow easily into impulse lines, and if it tends to crystallise or solidify it is likely to block them. In such

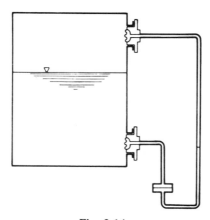

Fig. 3.14.

cases, and for slurries, seals will be used at each pressure tapping point as described in Chapter 2 (see also Fig. 3.14).

3.3. INDIRECT (INFERENTIAL) MEASUREMENT BY BUOYANCY TECHNIQUES

The *apparent* weight of a body which is immersed in a fluid is less than the actual weight by the weight of the fluid displaced. In the sensor shown in Fig. 3.15 the 'apparent' weight of the float is supported by the spring, which extends or contracts as the level of fluid in the vessel, and thus the apparent weight of the float, changes. The range of measurement is

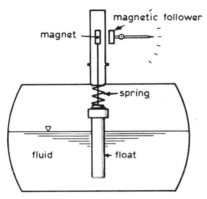

Fig. 3.15.

determined by the spring rate, and motion is amplified. The magnetic follower removes the need for a sealing gland. This is an inferential method of measurement, the apparent loss of weight of the float as the level rises depending on the density, as well as the volume, of the fluid displaced. Therefore, unlike the float/wire/pulley method the meter must be calibrated for a particular fluid, and changes of temperature will cause errors of level measurement. Other versions of this sensor use a torque tube and lever arm in place of the spring to transmit force (not motion) to a signal transmitting unit (see later).

3.4 THE USE OF 'BUBBLERS'

An alternative to the use of seals is the 'bubbler'. A gas is allowed to flow slowly through a vertical tube into the tank as shown in Fig. 3.16. In order

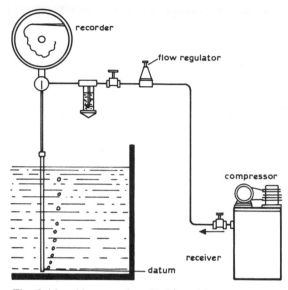

Fig. 3.16.   Air purge installation with compressor.

for this to happen the gas must be at the same pressure as the hydrostatic pressure in the tank at the point at which it comes out of the bubbler tube; the bottom end of the tube therefore determines the datum of measurement. A self-contained flow rate regulator is used to control the rate of gas flow so that it is the same at all levels of the liquid in the tank. The bubbler has the advantage that the measuring element can be located at any level; its position no longer determines the datum, as it is gas pressure not liquid hydrostatic pressure which is measured.

The gas can be instrument air or an inert gas such as nitrogen where necessary; it must not react with the liquid, the level of which is being measured. Instrument air must never be used to measure the level of petroleum in closed tanks because of the danger of forming an explosive mixture. As nitrogen is often used to 'blanket' such tanks, a bubbler system may be very appropriate.

3.5 THE USE OF 'LIMP' DIAPHRAGMS AND CAPSULES

The hydrostatic pressure at the datum level in a tank of liquid can be measured by a limp diaphragm sensing unit as shown in Fig. 3.17. The large 'pressure space' in the sensing element communicates via a small diameter capillary impulse tube with a bellows pressure sensing element of small volume, which may be mounted in any position, limited only by the length of the capillary. The gas (usually air) trapped in the pressure space is compressed until its pressure equals that of the hydrostatic head, the change of volume being accommodated by the 'limp' rubber diaphragm.

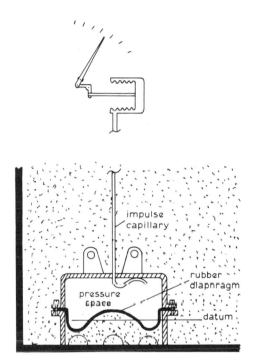

Fig. 3.17. Limp diaphragm sensing unit.

The bellows element measures hydrostatic pressure, and the gauge has to be calibrated to take account of the density of the fluid, and is subject to errors due to temperature effects (change of density).

The capsule type gauge shown in Fig. 3.18 operates in the same way except that the hydrostatic pressure is opposed partly by the stiffness of the sensing capsule itself. Calibration must take this into account, and whereas the 'limp' diaphragm of the previous gauge could be replaced without affecting calibration the capsule could not.

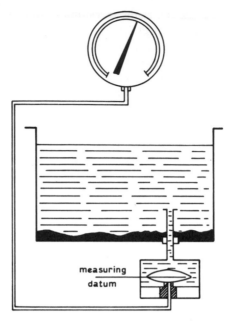

Fig. 3.18.   Capsule type gauge.

3.6 MEASURING LEVELS ELECTRICALLY

The measuring techniques described in this section depend on the different electrical properties of the fluid, the level of which is to be measured. They can only be used when these properties are suitable.

By capacitance (Fig. 3.19)
The insulated sensor (capacitive electrode) forms a capacitor with the container. The dielectric constant depends on the liquid being measured. If the level of the liquid changes then the capacitance also changes in proportion, provided that the dielectric constant of the liquid is much greater than that of air.

A high frequency voltage of constant frequency is used to measure the capacitance. The current flowing through the capacitor is proportional to the level. This high frequency current is converted to a standard output signal in the signal processing equipment.

The prerequisite for this measuring process is above all a stable dielectric

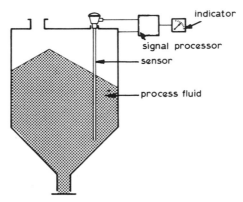

Fig. 3.19.

constant. This is not likely to be the case if the liquid is a mixture or two-phase, and in particular the presence of small quantities of water in petroleum causes serious errors in this type of instrument. When measuring water-based liquids very small quantities of dissolved solids cause serious errors. This type of measurement is most suitable for measuring the depth of powders in storage bins, as the dielectric constant is usually stable, and few other methods are available.

By conductivity (Fig. 3.20)
Two electrodes, immersed in the vessel, are at constant voltage. The area of cross-section between the electrodes increases as the level rises. The electrical resistance is reduced in the same ratio as the cross-section

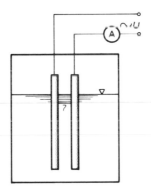

Fig. 3.20.

increases. The result is an increase in current, which is measured. The conductivity of most liquids changes with temperature, and the instrument must be calibrated for the particular liquid and compensated for temperature variation.

3.7 MEASURING LEVEL WITH SOUND PRESSURE

This technique is based on the measurement of the transit time of sound waves transmitted to, and reflected from, a surface. The velocity of sound is constant at constant temperature for any fluid.

The time elapse between transmission and reception is measured and used to determine the level.

The equipment should be mounted on the vessel so that the sound waves hit the material at right angles to the surface of the liquid, to ensure that they are reflected back to the receiver and not lost (Fig. 3.21). The method has the advantage that no contact is necessary between the sensor and the process fluid, and also that measurement is not dependent in any way on the properties of the process material (density, dielectric constant, conductivity, etc.) provided a reflection can be obtained. This depends on the density of the liquid or solid process material being much greater than air. The technique is dependent on the speed of sound pressure through air, and compensation must be made for the temperature of the air, since the speed of sound pressure varies slightly with temperature.

If the surface of the liquid is very disturbed or if it is a powder surface which is being measured, some of the reflected sound energy will be 'scattered' as shown in Fig. 3.22. This will tend to confuse the receiver since

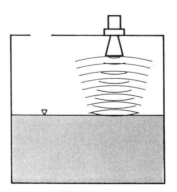

Fig. 3.21.

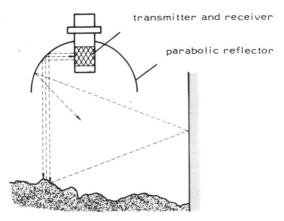

Fig. 3.22.

scattered sound pressure waves travel further than directly reflected energy and thus take longer in transit. To overcome this difficulty both transmitter and receiver can be mounted in a parabolic reflector which will reject reflected sound waves to a large extent.

The frequency of sound used depends on the distance of the transmitter/receiver from the surface of the liquid or powder and the range of measurement; the shorter these distances the higher the frequency used. For large ranges the lower frequency used is often within the range of response of the human ear and can easily be interfered with by other extraneous noises.

Apart from faulty temperature compensation, the calibration of the instrument cannot alter since it is not dependent in any way on the properties of the fluid or powder, the level of which is being measured. This means that a factory calibrated instrument can be used without 'proving' equipment. Dirt or condensation, scatter and interference will affect accuracy, but not calibration.

3.8 MEASURING LEVEL WITH RADIATION

This technique depends on the fact that gamma ray emission from a nuclear source is reduced in intensity as it passes through a solid or liquid in proportion to the density and the path length. A narrow beam of gamma radiation penetrates through both walls of the process vessel and the contents; the residual strength received at the detectors depends on the path

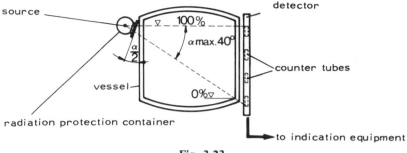

source

detector

100%

α max. 40°

counter tubes

vessel

0%

radiation protection container

to indication equipment

Fig. 3.23.

length through the contents which varies with the level in the vessel (the path length through the walls is constant and can be 'calibrated out'). Thus, provided that the liquid is much more dense than the air or gas in the space above and that the vessel walls are not excessively thick, the level can be determined from the variation in the rate of counting of gamma particles of the counter tubes.

The radiation protection container (with lead jacket) in which the radioactive source is situated, is mounted on the side of the vessel (Fig. 3.23). The detector is fixed on the opposite side of the vessel. A number of Geiger Müller Counter Tubes are installed, according to the level to be measured. The lowest counter tube will record the lowest count rate as the gamma particles reaching it will have passed through the greatest length of process liquid. The count rate will increase progressively towards the top until a level is reached where the radiation no longer passes through any process liquid. This point corresponds with the level in the vessel.

CHAPTER 4

Measurement of Fluid Flow Rate

4.1 GENERAL

Measurement of the flow rate of fluids through pipes and conduits is one of the important, if not *the* most important, branches of measurement in the process field: there are a great number of instruments on the market for this purpose and more are appearing all the time. As with all industrial measurements, these can be divided into two categories: direct (usually referred to as 'positive displacement') and indirect or inferential. Substandard instruments used for calibration are always of the direct type, as in the case of pressure measurement. A further important distinction must be drawn between the measurement of volume flow rate and mass flow rate, the former being the most commonly required.

Flow rate measurement is necessary for purposes of operating plant, but rarely for safety reasons. However, the transfer of process fluids into and out of tankage is often subject to commercial and customs (taxation) constraints, especially at points of delivery to a customer. Consequently, very high accuracy is often demanded of flow rate measuring systems, and calibration is of great importance. It is very important to be clear about the different ways of expressing accuracy which are used by manufacturers for different types of flow meter. In some cases it is expressed as a fraction or percentage of the 'full scale' or maximum flow which can be measured, whilst in others it is expressed as a fraction of the actual flow rate. In all cases the range of flow rates over which the quoted accuracy can be maintained should be given. The difference arises because of the principle of operation of the meter: in some cases the accuracy is a function of features related to the size of the sensing element, whilst in others the error is proportional to the amount of fluid flowing through the meter. A meter operating at 20% of its maximum capacity with an accuracy of $\pm 5\%$ of reading has exactly the same accuracy as another also operating at 20 % of its maximum with an accuracy of 1 % of full scale.

4.2 FLOW MEASUREMENT BY DIFFERENCE OF PRESSURE

Work has to be done on a fluid as it flows through a pipe, both to overcome the internal friction of the fluid (viscosity) as its molecules rub together, and to overcome the friction between the fluid and the pipe walls. However, aside from this gradual loss of energy, the fluid can neither gain nor lose energy as it flows. The total energy of the fluid at any point is made up of:

(a)   kinetic energy (or energy of motion),
(b)   potential energy (or energy of position (height)),
(c)   pressure energy.

If a restriction is placed in the pipe, reducing its cross-sectional area, the fluid will have to increase its velocity through this restriction, thus increasing the energy of motion. The energy of position cannot change suddenly, and so there must occur a reduction in pressure energy. This phenomenon, which is described by Bernoulli's energy equation, has long been used to measure the rate of flow. A restriction is made in the pipeline, and the difference of pressure measured upstream to that measured at the restriction where the flow velocity is increased has a fixed relationship to the increase in velocity. From the ratio of the cross-sectional area of the pipe to that at the restriction the ratio of the velocity of flow in the unrestricted pipe to that through the restriction can be calculated, and by equating the loss in pressure energy to the gain in velocity energy the flow rate can be calculated.

If the process fluid is a liquid (and therefore incompressible) it can be seen (Fig. 4.1) that the volume flowing past a point in the larger diameter pipe in a given time must be the same as that passing a point in the narrower pipe. Hence

$$A_1 \times V_1 = A_2 \times V_2 \qquad \text{or} \ \frac{V_1}{V_2} = \frac{A_2}{A_1} \qquad \text{or} \ V_2 = \frac{A_1}{A_2} \times V_1$$

where A_1 and A_2 are the cross-sectional areas of the pipe upstream and at the restriction, respectively, and V_1 and V_2 are the volumes flowing past points at these locations in a given time.

The energy of motion (kinetic) is proportional to the square of the

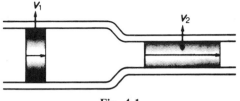

Fig. 4.1.

velocity of flow; therefore the reduction in pressure when the fluid enters the narrower pipe is proportional to:

$$(V_2)^2 - (V_1)^2 \quad \text{or} \quad (V_1)^2 \times \left[\left[\frac{A_1}{A_2} \right]^2 - 1 \right] \quad \text{or} \quad C \times (V_1)^2$$

Hence:

$$(P_1 - P_2) \equiv kC(V_1)^2$$

where k is a constant of proportionality and C is a constant depending on the ratio of cross-sectional area of the pipe upstream and at the restriction.

Naturally it is not practicable to reduce the diameter of the pipe for more than a short length in order to measure flow rate, since the energy absorbed by friction increases in proportion to the square of the velocity. The measuring restriction takes one of the forms shown in Fig. 4.2.

If the fluid is compressible (gas or vapour) it will decrease in density as its pressure falls and its velocity increases in order to flow through the restriction. Thus, a compressibility factor must be included in the relationship between pressure drop and velocity:

$$(P_1 - P_2) \equiv kCY(V_1)^2$$

where Y is the compressibility factor which will be unity for a liquid and greater than unity for any gas or vapour.

The value of the compressibility factor, Y, depends on the ratio of cross-sectional areas of the pipe and restriction, the ratio of pressures and the ratio of the specific heats at constant pressure and at constant volume (the 'adiabatic' constant). Hence, for any given fluid and any given restriction Y will be constant, and thus, for any fluid and any restriction:

$$(P_1 - P_2) = K(V_1)^2$$

where K is a constant which depends on: (i) the fluid, Y; (ii) the ratio of areas, C; (iii) the way in which the fluid behaves downstream of the restriction, k.

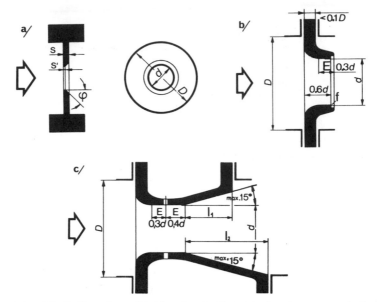

Fig. 4.2. (a) Orifice plate. (b) Nozzle. (c) Venturi: l_1, short venturi; l_2, long venturi.

Where the restriction is formed by a simple 'orifice plate' (Fig. 4.2(a)) the diameter of the restriction is not simply that of the orifice, as the fluid, having mass and therefore momentum, cannot change direction suddenly. For this reason k has to be found experimentally for orifice plates, but can be calculated from theory for a properly designed venturi (Fig. 4.2(c)).

As the process fluid reverts to a higher pressure state after the measuring restriction there is a tendency for energy-wasteful 'eddies' or 'swirls' to form near any sudden change of shape in the pipe wall. The venturi is designed to minimise this tendency and to ensure that the measurement of flow rate does not impose a large running cost on plant operation due to 'unrecovered' pressure loss; this is often a serious factor where the flows are very large, such as large gas compressor systems. Unfortunately, the large venturi is a very expensive piece of equipment, and often the 'short' venturi is used; these are less efficient in saving energy, but much better than the relatively cheap orifice plate, and cost considerably less than the venturi tube. The angle of the 'expansion' section of the venturi is chosen to enable the pressure in the fluid to 'hold' it against the pipe wall, even though the momentum will tend to make it continue in a straight line and thus leave the wall and form eddies. This does not affect the measurement, and where energy is not so important the 'nozzle' (Fig. 4.2(b)) will give similar accuracy. Both the venturi and the nozzle 'guide' the fluid into the restriction, so that there is no doubt where the low pressure tapping should be located.

The simplest form of restriction used, and by far the cheapest, is the orifice plate; the process fluid is not guided into the restriction and therefore its path is determined, not by the shape of the restricting element, but by the mass and velocity (momentum) of the fluid (see Fig. 4.3). The

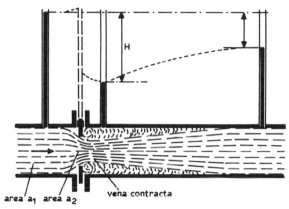

Fig. 4.3. Pressure relations for orifice installation.

narrowest cross-section occurs at the 'vena contracta' which is therefore the position at which the pressure differs most from the upstream pressure. The vena contracta occurs at approximately half a pipe diameter downstream of the leading edge of the orifice plate (which must be sharply defined for accuracy) and for maximum sensitivity for a given restriction the pressure tapping points are located half a diameter downstream and one diameter upstream (the so-called D and $D/2$ configuration), Fig. 4.4(a). Therefore, for a given differential measuring device this enables the energy loss to be minimised when using the cheap orifice plate.

The distance between the pressure tappings is such that these must be made on site, in the pipe wall, which makes it difficult to inspect; the cost of site labour is also high, and these facts have led to the use of 'flange taps' (Fig. 4.5) and 'carrier rings' (Fig. 4.4(b)). In the former case special flanges are supplied for the construction engineer to weld the pipe where orifice plates are to be installed: as these are always of the 'slip-over' type where the

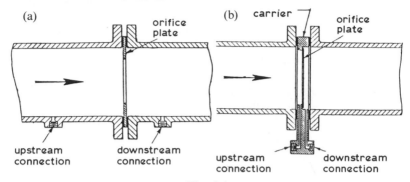

Fig. 4.4.

weld is made on the outside of the pipe the inspection problem is overcome, and no additional expensive site labour is used to install the orifice plate. Carrier rings are mounted between conventional flanges and are manufactured complete with tappings, isolating valves and a ring (in two halves) in which the orifice plate itself is mounted (allowing for standard manufacture and change of meter range).

The orifice plate itself is normally of the type shown in Fig. 4.2(a) with a 'sharp' edge facing upstream; in fact the accuracy of measurement depends on this edge remaining sharp. However, for relatively viscous fluids accuracy can be preserved at lower flow rates than would be possible with a sharp-edged orifice plate by using a quadrant or 'quarter circle' profile as shown in Fig. 4.5.

The reason for the importance of the edge profile of the orifice plate is that calibration of any restriction-type flow rate measuring system depends, not on comparison with a substandard (this type of meter is not usually provided with in-line proving equipment) but on known and very well documented data on the behaviour of fluids flowing in pipes. In particular, the data are only valid for certain values above a minimum of a non-dimensional number, known as Reynolds number. This number in turn depends on the density, velocity and viscosity of the process fluid.

In special circumstances the shape of the orifice can be other than circular, though the data relating flow rate to the measurement of pressure difference is not so well documented for other shapes; for this and other reasons accuracy will be low. Such a case is shown in Fig. 4.6: an orifice in the shape of a segment of the internal circular shape of the pipe allows dirt to pass freely, whereas a conventional orifice would not.

The accuracy with which flow rate can be measured by pressure

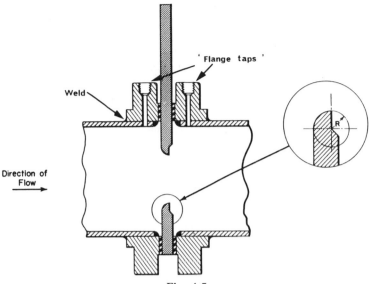

Fig. 4.5.

difference across a restricting element depends on the available data for density, compressibility, etc. and on the precision of measurement of the differential pressure. Obviously, it is important to employ a restriction which is sufficient to provide a readily measured pressure difference over the range of flow rates to be measured; however, a greater restriction than is necessary is very wasteful of energy. If the restriction element is properly

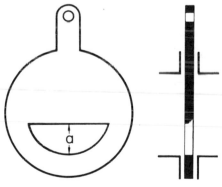

Fig. 4.6.

designed, accuracy is about $\pm 1\%$ of full scale over a range of flow rate of about 3:1. This low rangeability is the direct result of the square law relationship between flow rate and differential pressure: at 0·3 of maximum flow the pressure is $0·3^2 \simeq 0·1$ of maximum. However, the orifice plate can be replaced by another to change the range if this becomes necessary, and the range can be extended to approximately 10:1 by using three differential pressure measuring devices, each having a measuring range one tenth as large as the next.

In practice the orifice/pipe internal diameter ratio must be less than 0·55 for accurate measurement; at greater ratios (less restriction) the irregularities in the pipe surface seriously affect accuracy. The actual pressure drop will depend on the velocity of the flow in the pipe, i.e. on how generously the pipe has been sized for the flow it has to carry. Therefore, if three differential pressure measuring devices are used to measure over a range of 10:1 and the measuring span of the most sensitive is only about 5 cm W.G., the measuring span of the least sensitive will be 500 cm W.G. Using orifice plates, only about one half of this pressure drop will be 'recovered' when the fluid flow cross-sectional area 'expands' downstream of the vena contracta; in other words the pressure loss will be about 250 cm W.G., which represents a considerable energy loss. A much better recovery would be obtained using a nozzle or venturi, but these are expensive elements. Thus the orifice plate, although very cheap (especially in large sizes), is restricted in practice to applications where the range of flow rates to be measured is little greater than 2:1, or where energy loss is unimportant (such as the measurement of the flow rate of gas or crude oil from a producing well, where the natural pressure has to be dissipated).

Nozzles and venturis are very expensive in large sizes, while positive displacement meters are extremely expensive in large sizes, as well as absorbing a lot of energy. There is, therefore, a great incentive to find a less expensive meter, both in terms of capital cost and running cost (energy loss), which has the ability to measure accurately over a range of flow rates of about 10:1. A further grave disadvantage of any flow measurement system using a fixed restriction is that the response is very 'non-linear' because of the square law relationship between flow velocity and pressure drop. In addition to severely limiting the useful range of the system this means that the scale divisions on any indicator are much closer together at the low flow end of the scale than at the high flow end, making 'discrimination' more difficult. This factor also limits the accuracy of the signal produced by any transmitting device and has a seriously adverse effect when the measurement is used in an automatic control system.

4.3 MEASURING GAS FLOW RATES

If the meter is installed above the process line (Fig. 4.7), any liquid which may be carried along by the flowing gas, and which finds its way into the impulse lines can drain back into the process line; this prevents it from collecting in one or other of the impulse lines where it would cause a serious error because of the pressure exerted by a column of liquid. If, however the meter is installed below the process line, condensate traps of adequate capacity must be installed as shown in Fig. 4.8.

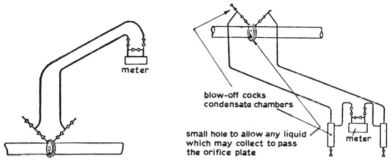

Fig. 4.7. Installation for clean non-corrosive gases meter above orifice.

Fig. 4.8. Installation for clean non-corrosive gases—meter below orifice.

4.4 MEASURING LIQUID FLOW RATES

If the meter is below the process line (Fig. 4.9), vent cocks must be fitted to allow gases and vapours to be released during commissioning and calibration. During normal operation, however, gases and vapours cannot enter the impulse lines as they are lighter than the liquid. If the meter is above the process line, gases and vapours can enter the impulse lines, and suitably sized traps must be installed (Fig. 4.10).

4.5 MEASURING VAPOUR (STEAM) FLOW RATES

If the process fluid is a vapour flowing at a temperature higher than ambient, which will condense at ambient, then because there is no flow through the impulse lines condensate will inevitably collect and fill the

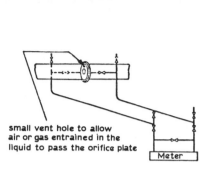

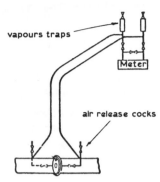

small vent hole to allow
air or gas entrained in the
liquid to pass the orifice plate

Fig. 4.9. Installation for clean
liquids—meter below orifice.

Fig. 4.10. Installation for clean
liquids—meter above orifice (necessary
pressure must be available to maintain
the liquid head to the meter).

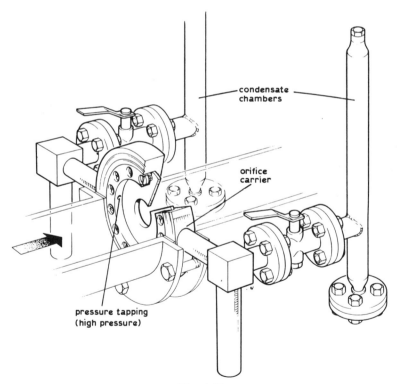

Fig. 4.11.

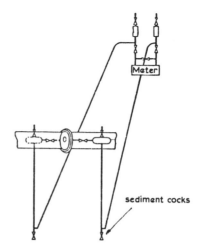

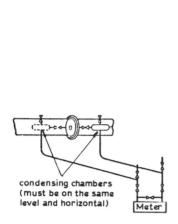

condensing chambers
(must be on the same
level and horizontal)

Meter

sediment cocks

Fig. 4.12. Installation for steam or other condensable vapour—meter below orifice.

Fig. 4.13. Installation for steam. Pressure of steam in the line must be sufficient to force condensate up to the level of the meter which is above the orifice.

impulse lines. Provided the head of liquid in each impulse line is exactly equal, no error will be introduced; for this reason the condensate chambers must be exactly level as shown in Fig. 4.11.

If the meter is below the process line (Fig. 4.12), cocks must be fitted to allow gas, which may have been dissolved in the condensate, to be vented. If the meter is above the process line, gas collecting traps must be added (Fig. 4.13).

4.6 MEASURING FLOW RATES IN CORROSIVE, TOXIC OR INFLAMMABLE FLUIDS

If the fluid is corrosive, seals may be used in the impulse lines; however, since the differential pressures generated by properly sized restriction elements are small, their use is not normally recommended. Either a diaphragm meter (see Chapter 2) constructed of suitably resistant materials or a transducer would be used. Seals would not normally be used for toxic or inflammable fluids.

4.7 ISOLATING/EQUALISING VALVE MANIFOLDS

In order to maintain, commission, or calibrate the flow measurement system, it must be possible to isolate the differential pressure measuring device from the impulse lines and to equalise the pressure on each side. A manifold of valves (capable of tight shut-off), often specially constructed as a single unit, is used (see Fig. 4.14).

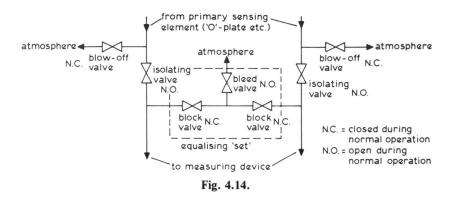

Fig. 4.14.

There must also be at least one shut-off (isolating) valve in each impulse line at the tapping point. The 'blow-off' valves allow each impulse line to be vented once the isolating valve at the tapping point is closed; the isolating valves then allow the measuring device to be removed. They also allow it to be 'equalised' using the 'block and bleed' equalising set for calibration purposes. In normal operation the two block valves are closed and the bleed valve is open; for equalising this is reversed. If either of the block valves leak the 'bleed' will be noticed, and flow will not take place in the impulse lines as it would if a single equalising valve were used.

4.8 INSTALLATION OF THE PRIMARY SENSING ELEMENT

The location of the orifice plate, etc., in the process line is critical. Bends, reducers or throttling valves will disturb the flow pattern on which the relationship between differential pressure and flow rate depends. In normal circumstances a straight length of pipe of 10 diameters upstream of the primary sensing element will be sufficient to allow such disturbances to subside, but this length depends very much on the cause of the disturbance.

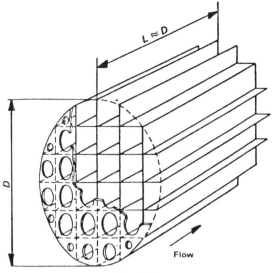

Fig. 4.15.

Fifty diameters may be insufficient if the cause is an almost closed throttling valve, as may be the case if the process lines are oversized. In such cases straightening vanes must be inserted in the pipeline (Fig. 4.15).

4.9 MEASUREMENT OF FLOW RATE BY VARIABLE AREA RESTRICTION METHODS

One solution to the difficulty of 'rangeability', implicit in measuring flow rate by measuring the pressure drop across a restriction, is to vary the cross-sectional area of the restriction rather than the differential pressure. Since the pressure drop is proportional to the ratio of the cross-sectional area of the restriction to that of the pipe, no square root is involved and the rangeability of flow measurement is not restricted as it is when using measurement of differential pressure across a fixed restriction. A simple 'variable restriction' measuring system is shown in Fig. 4.16(a).

A servo mechanism could be added to this system so that the 'gate' is driven to a position such that the differential pressure remains constant whenever flow rate changes. The disadvantage of this method is that the shape of the orifice, as well as its cross-sectional area, changes and in consequence it is not possible to obtain a reliable set of data on which to

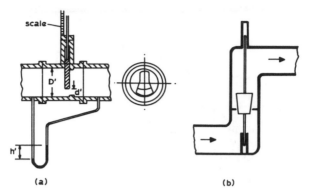

Fig. 4.16.   (a) Gate-type area meter; (b) orifice and plug meter.

base an accurate calibration of the system. Such systems cannot be used for accurate flow measurement.

The principle of variable area restriction is used extensively in the orifice and plug type of meter (Fig. 4.16(b)). Just as the positive displacement meter is in effect a pump, which, instead of driving the process fluid, is driven by it, so the orifice and plug meter is like a control valve, which, instead of regulating the flow by reason of the relative position of plug and orifice, is positioned by the flow.

One very big advantage of the plug and orifice type of meter is that it is

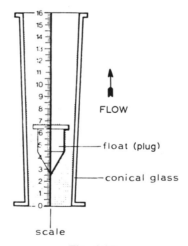

Fig. 4.17.

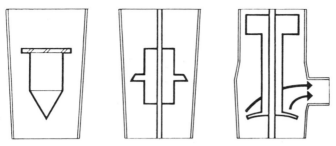

Fig. 4.18. Various shapes of float.

tolerant of dirt; the plug will move to open the orifice and allow dirt to pass through.

Modern versions of the instrument use a conical-shaped glass tube as the orifice, so that the 'plug' (float) moves up and down the whole length of the tube as flow rate changes from minimum to maximum (Figs 4.17 and 4.18). A magnetic follower can be used to operate an indicator pointer or transmitter mechanism.

This type of flow meter is capable of measuring to accuracies of about $\pm 1\%$ of full scale over a range of 10:1. However, in large sizes they are expensive as the measuring tube has to be the same diameter as the process line. Calibration depends entirely on construction of the glass tube which is made by special manufacturing processes.

The principles of differential pressure measurement and variable area measurement have been combined in the 'Gilflo' type of meter shown in Fig. 4.19. The plug or cone takes up a position in the orifice which is determined by the balance of forces generated by the spring on the one hand, and the differential pressure acting on the cone on the other. The position and shape of the cone together determine the size of the orifice; the shape of the plug is so arranged that the differential pressure generated is linearly related to flow rate and not, as in the case of a fixed restriction, to the square of flow rate. In effect the size of the orifice is varied to suit the flow rate; as a result the useful range of the meter is greatly extended.

The manufacturers claim a remarkable 100:1 range with a repeatability of $\pm \frac{1}{4}\%$ of maximum reading; however, this is to some extent of academic interest only, as at 1/100 of maximum flow rate the repeatability expressed as a fraction of actual flow rate is then $\pm 25\%$. At the lower limit of the range at which a turbine or positive displacement meter can reliably be used—20:1 (i.e. 5% of maximum)—the repeatability of the 'Gilflo' would be $\pm 5\%$, which does not compare favourably; however, at even lower flow

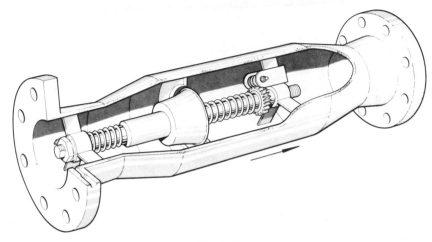

Fig. 4.19.

rates it would increasingly provide a better performance. In fact a turbine meter cannot be used at all at as low a flow as 1/100 of maximum, and it is doubtful if a positive displacement meter would operate at this sort of 'turndown'. This is a good example of the influence of the principle of operation on the performance of a flow meter; the 'Gilflo' is obviously a suitable meter to use where wide 'rangeability' is the most important requirement, but it would not be suitable for custody transfer applications.

The makers claim that this type of meter is insensitive to 'upstream conditions' (see Section 4.8) which represents a further advantage.

4.10 POSITIVE DISPLACEMENT METERS

This type of meter operates on the same principle as the vane, piston or gear pump, with the difference that it is driven by the flow of fluid whereas the pump drives the fluid. As shown in Fig. 4.20 a fixed *volume* of fluid is transferred from the inlet to the outlet for a given angle of rotation of the impeller shaft. Providing there is no leakage of the fluid past the sealing surfaces of the vanes, there is an exact relationship between the rotational velocity of the shaft and the fluid flow rate. A small amount of energy is absorbed in driving the rotor and this is provided by pressure difference between inlet and outlet. The same pressure difference will cause leakage across the seals if these are imperfect: hence the performance of a positive

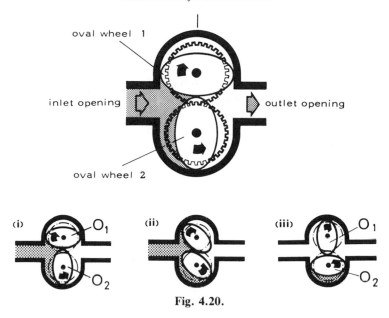

oval wheel 1

inlet opening

outlet opening

oval wheel 2

(i) O_1 (ii)   (iii) O_1

O_2 O_2

Fig. 4.20.

displacement (PD) meter depends on good seals and on minimising the friction losses in driving the meter. Gear type PD meters are typified by the meter shown in Fig. 4.20; the seal is made between the teeth of the gears, which are cut to provide a rolling rather than sliding action which is less likely to cause leaks. In addition to the sliding or rolling seals of the vanes or gears there must be a good seal at the ends of the impeller. There are many types of PD meter on the market, but all operate on the same principles: they can be built to stand very great pressure and are capable of staying within very accurate calibration for long periods of service when used to measure flows of viscous fluids (oils) which serve to lubricate the seals. Moreover, they are the only type of meter which is not only unaffected with respected to accuracy by increasing viscosity, but which actually becomes more accurate.

In the 'rotary piston' type of PD meter shown in Fig. 4.21 the central journal of the rotary piston travels around in the groove; the rotary piston itself is not free to rotate as the 'separating wall' slots through it. It therefore oscillates in the fashion which can be seen in Fig. 4.21 (i) to (iv) and by doing so transfers a volume of fluid equal to the capacity of volumes 1 and 2 from the inlet to the outlet port of the meter. This is accomplished as follows. In position (i) fluid enters both volume 1 and volume 2 spaces under the high upstream pressure, whilst fluid is still leaving volume 1 through the outlet port. High pressure acting on the separating wall and piston causes it to rotate. In position (ii) volume 2 space is full of liquid which has just entered from the high pressure upstream, and the inlet and outlet ports are both closed. In position (iii) fluid from volume 2 is leaving through the outlet port and has started to enter the rotary piston on the other side of the separating wall. High pressure on the piston and separating wall continues to cause rotation of the piston. In position (iv) volume 1 is full and about to discharge.

It should be noticed that the rotary piston does not in fact rotate, though

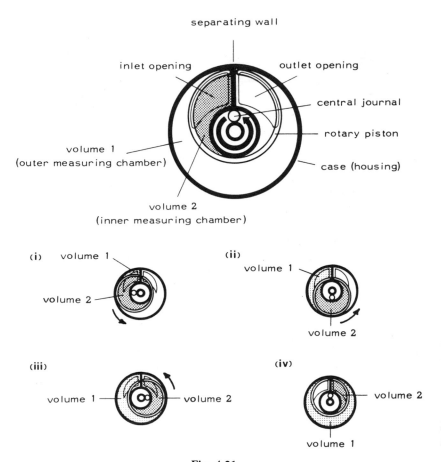

Fig. 4.21.

its central journal does; the piston itself moves from side to side and up and down, being constrained by the separating wall which separates the high upstream pressure from the lower downstream pressure. In one revolution the meter transfers a volume of liquid from the inlet port to the outlet equal to the combined volumes 1 and 2.

Another type of positive displacement meter known as the oval wheel meter is shown in Fig. 4.21. The distance between the spindles of the two 'oval wheels' is fixed, as is the sum of the major and minor axes of the oval (both 'wheels' are identical). They are geared to rotate together as shown in Fig. 4.21 (i) to (iii). In position it can be seen that a volume of fluid which has entered from the upstream high pressure has been trapped and will be delivered to the discharge port as the rotation continues. At all times the high pressure is sealed from the low pressure side and so this volume is delivered for each revolution of the meter, provided there is no leakage past the seals.

In all PD meters the mechanism should be as free as possible to rotate so that the difference in pressure between upstream and downstream is as small as possible, thus minimising leakage which will be proportional to pressure difference. For the same difference in pressure increased viscosity actually decreases leakage error.

4.11 TURBINE METERS AND IN-LINE PROVING

Turbine meters differ from PD meters in that there is no positive seal between the high upstream pressure and the lower downstream pressure. Like PD meters they are driven by this pressure difference, but unlike them any increase in the power required to drive the impeller will result in a change in calibration rather than an increase in pressure drop; therefore, any increased bearing friction, etc., affects accuracy in a way it does not in the case of the PD meter.

Turbine meters such as those shown in Fig. 4.22 have long been used to measure *and totalise* (see Chapter 5) the flow of utilities fluids—fuel oil, water, steam, etc. The impeller rotates at a speed which is proportional to the flow rate of the fluid, and it is easy to count the total number of revolutions in order to obtain a totalised flow measurement; thus, the rate of revolution provides a measure of the flow rate. The relationship is varied by any change in fluid viscosity, so that accuracy of these meters depends on the fluid viscosity remaining constant.

Positive displacement meters have been used for a long time in

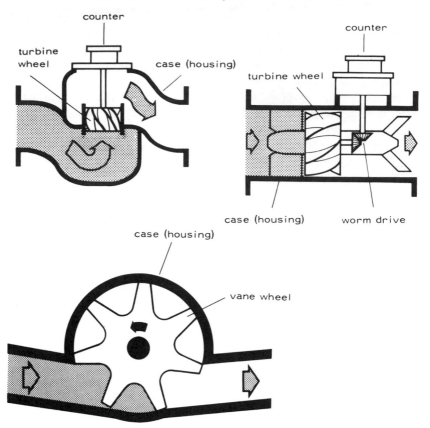

Fig. 4.22.

applications where very high accuracy is essential, e.g. custody transfer. In large sizes, however, they are very large and very expensive, and with the invention of the in-line prover, high precision turbine meters (Fig. 4.23) have taken their place, except for the measurement of high viscosity liquids. An impeller with blading similar to a gas or steam turbine is driven by the flow of fluid. The bearings of the impeller are almost frictionless, and the speed of rotation of the impeller is measured by electronic counting of the pulses generated by a small magnet embedded in the impeller as it passes the 'pick-up' coil. The energy absorbed by the metering element is very small, response is linear and with in-line proving equipment accuracy is comparable with that of a positive displacement meter over a 10:1 or

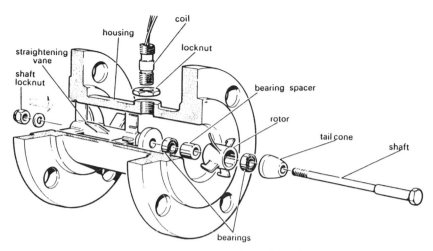

Fig. 4.23.   Component parts of a turbine flow meter.

greater range of flows. These meters are very much cheaper than positive displacement meters, especially in the larger sizes. When measuring clean fluids they compare favourably with venturi nozzles with regard to price and are more accurate over a much wider range. Performance deteriorates as viscosity of the process fluid increases; they cannot operate in dirty fluids as the bearings seize up. By their nature they operate electronically and must be certified safe to use in areas of the plant where there is fire/explosion hazard.

The installation of an in-line prover in addition to a flow meter makes it possible to check the calibration of the meter *whilst it is operating* as often as necessary, and with very little trouble. The greater susceptibility of the turbine meter to changes of calibration (as compared to the PD meter) is not an important factor therefore.

The meter prover is not itself a measuring device, but operates on the basis of stopping and starting a special counter, as a sphere, which is a close fit in the pipe and travels along with the process fluid, sweeps out an accurately known volume (Fig. 4.24). The counter counts the revolutions of the meter impeller and is started and stopped by 'detector' switches at the start and finish of the calibration run. The sphere stops in a section of pipe which is specially enlarged so that the fluid can flow past it: another calibration can be made by simply changing the position of the 4-way diverter valve so that the direction of flow through the calibrated section is reversed, carrying with it the sphere. The prover is itself calibrated by a

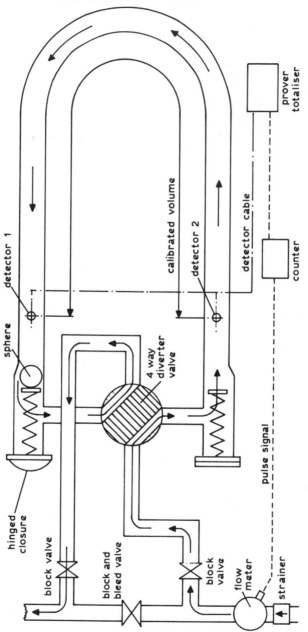

Fig. 4.24.   Diagram of bidirectional meter prover.

special calibrating service and, providing that it is not damaged, will not change over very long periods.

4.12 MAGNETIC FLOW METERS

This type of meter uses the process liquid as an electrical conductor, which by flowing through a magnetic field has an electric current induced in it. It consists of an electro-magnet wrapped around a length of process pipe, which is lined with an insulating material as shown in Fig. 4.25: electrodes are installed in the wall of the pipe on opposite sides, and these enable an electrical circuit to be formed through the liquid and the measuring device (a galvanometer). This type of meter imposes no energy loss as there is absolutely no obstruction to flow: it is very suitable for measurement in corrosive, abrasive, or very dirty liquids. It cannot be used to measure the flow rate of gases or low conductivity liquids (which unfortunately includes hydrocarbons) but is very suitable for most water applications. It also has the considerable advantage over most other flow meters that it is totally insensitive to flow profiles, turbulence, density or viscosity, as it measures the average velocity in the pipe and thus the true volume flow rate. If the process liquid deposits a film on the wall of the pipe which is significantly less conductive than the liquid itself, the accuracy will be affected as the electrodes/liquid resistance will increase. The range of the instrument has a lower limit because the velocity of the fluid must be great enough to cause a measurable electric current to flow, but it has no upper limit except that imposed by the current measuring instrument and the practical limits of flow rate in the process pipe (imposed by pumping pressure and frictional resistance). Accuracy of measurement is therefore largely a function of the electronic measurement of the electric current and of the magnetics of the meter; it is usually quoted by the makers as $\pm 1\%$ of the maximum flow rate recommended for the instrument.

4.13 ULTRASONIC FLOW METERS

Energy can be transmitted through liquid by alternating pressure waves in the same way that electrical energy travels through an electrical conductor; both travel at an exactly constant speed, though pressure waves travel many times slower than electricity. These facts are used to measure flow rate in liquids as shown in Fig. 4.26.

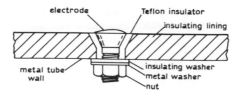

form of electrode

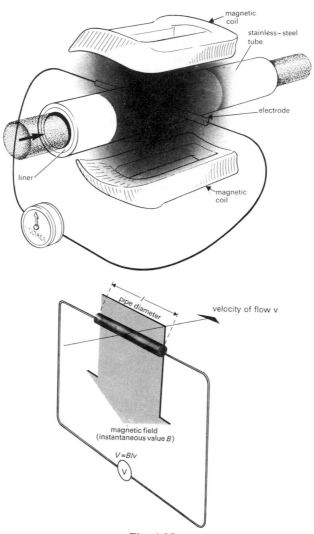

Fig. 4.25.

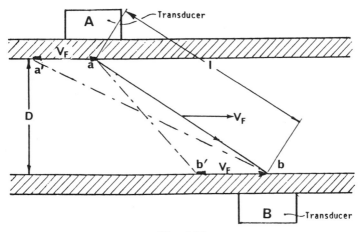

Fig. 4.26.

For energy to travel from transmitters/receivers A to B it must cover a distance ab; however, if the fluid is moving, the distance travelled through the fluid is ab' which is shorter. Energy travelling from B to A must also travel distance ab, or rather ba in this case, but since it travels against the direction of flow, the distance through the moving fluid is ba', which is longer. The transmitters/receivers A and B take it in turn to transmit short bursts of energy through the liquid, at the same time signalling the other transmitter/receiver by an electrical signal (which travels many times faster)

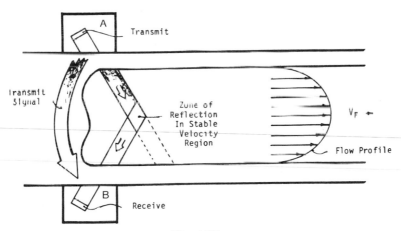

Fig. 4.27.

that it has done so. The 'time of flight' for ab' is compared with that for ba', the difference being proportional to the flow rate.

If the fluid contains a lot of solid matter the pressure energy is scattered, and little is received at the receiver. In such cases it is better to use the type of meter shown in Fig. 4.27. This type, called a 'Doppler shift' meter measures the 'phase shift' of signals received directly at B as compared with signals received by reflection (Fig. 4.28) (note that the beam has to be narrow). This phase shift is proportional to flow rate. This type of ultrasonic meter only works when there is plenty of dirt or air bubbles in the fluid to cause reflection.

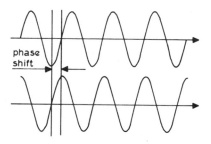

Fig. 4.28.

This type of meter offers no obstruction to flow, has no lower limit of flow beyond which it will not operate (unlike the magnetic flow meter) and will operate on almost any liquid. The makers claim rangeability of up to 200:1 and repeatability of $\pm 0.1\%$ of maximum flow rate, but only $\pm 2\%$ accuracy because this must depend on factory calibration (unless in-line proving equipment is installed). The cost does not depend on pipe size.

4.14 'VORTEX' METERS

This type of device uses a specially shaped obstruction, located in the centre of the pipe, to cause the formation of vortices in the same way that a protruding rock will sometimes do in a fast flowing stream. It has been found that when 'vortex shedding' occurs, the frequency with which vortices are 'shed' is extremely accurately related to the flow rate over a very wide range. The makers claim accuracy of $\pm 1\%$ of maximum rated flow over a range of up to 100:1. The shedding of a vortex is detected by a very

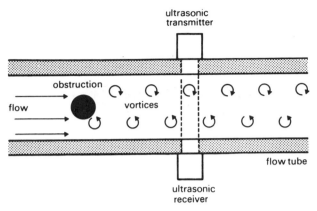

Fig. 4.29. Vortex flow meter.

sensitive temperature or pressure detector set into the obstruction or by a sonar type transmitter/receiver as shown in Fig. 4.29. The detectors set into the obstruction detect slight differences in pressure and temperature which occurs as a vortex is 'shed' first from one side and then from the other of the obstruction. The sonar type of detector relies on the signal at the receiver being disturbed as each vortex passes it. In both cases the pulses generated are counted by electronic circuits and the lower limit of the instrument range is set by the number of pulses generated by each unit of volume flow.

4.15 THE FLUIDIC FLOW METER

This type of meter is rather similar to the vortex meter in that it utilises the slight temperature difference which occurs when the flow of fluid across a sensitive thermistor element ceases. The principle of operation depends on the 'coanda' effect by reason of which a moving column of liquid, when faced with diverging pipe walls, will cling to one in preference to the other. As can be seen from Fig. 4.30, part of the flow is diverted through a passage on this side and serves to divert the main flow away from this wall, so that it then clings to the other wall; this action occurs repeatedly and the main stream oscillates rapidly from wall to wall. The frequency of oscillation is linearly proportional to the flow rate, accuracy being about $\pm 1\%$ over a range of flows which depends on the viscosity of the liquid, but may be as little as 3:1 or as much as 100:1. Detection of the flow/no flow change in the two bypasses is much more certain than with the vortex meter.

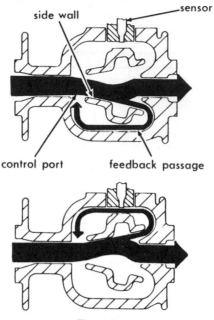

Fig. 4.30.

4.16 MASS FLOW MEASUREMENT

All the meters described so far measure the volume flow rate directly (positive displacement) or infer it from measurement of velocity. The mass flow rate is sometimes required, and can be obtained by computation from measurement of both volume flow rate and density. This is complex and expensive; however, for flow rates up to about 1000 kg h^{-1} of liquid it is possible to measure mass flow rate directly using the meter shown diagrammatically in Fig. 4.31.

This meter comprises a positive displacement pump and four carefully matched orifice plates, arranged in the form of a 'bridge' as shown. The differential pressure, measured across the pump, is linearly proportional to the mass flow rate Q. This is shown below.

Since the orifices are identical, the velocity of flow through orifices a and d are given by

$$(P_1 - P_2) = kC(V_a)^2 \times \text{density}$$

and

$$(P_1 - P_3) = kC(V_d)^2 \times \text{density}$$

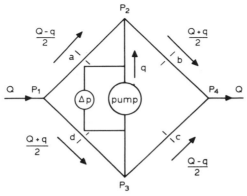

Fig. 4.31.

and since the pipe sizes are identical

$$(P_1 - P_2) = K\frac{(Q - q)^2}{4} \times \text{density}$$

and

$$(P_1 - P_3) = K\frac{(Q + q)^2}{4} \times \text{density}$$

or

$$\frac{(P_1 - P_2)}{\text{density}} = \frac{K(Q^2 - 2Qq + q^2)}{4}$$

and

$$\frac{(P_1 - P_3)}{\text{density}} = \frac{K(Q^2 + 2Qq + q^2)}{4}$$

By subtracting these equations we obtain

$$\frac{(P_1 - P_3) - (P_1 - P_2)}{\text{density}} = KQq$$

or

$$(P_2 - P_3) = KQq \times \text{density}$$

and since q is constant (positive displacement pump)

$$(P_2 - P_3) \propto Q \times \text{density (which is mass flow)}$$

Accuracy for this type of meter is quoted by the manufacturers as $\pm(0.5\%$ of actual flow rate $+0.02\%$ of maximum flow rate) over a range of 30:1.

4.17 STREAMLINE/TURBULENT FLOW AND VELOCITY PROFILE

The 'pattern' of flow of the fluid in the pipeline is very important and must be known when using most of the inferential methods (the only real exception being the magnetic flow meter). Depending on the velocity and viscosity, two very different patterns are possible—streamline or turbulent. Streamline flow takes place at low velocity and high viscosity, and is as the name implies a pattern in which each 'filament' of the flow travels in a straight line parallel to the axis of the pipe (Fig. 4.32). The pattern becomes

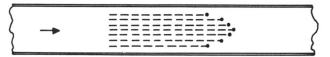

Fig. 4.32.   Streamline flow.

'turbulent' when the velocity increases to the point where these straight line 'filaments' break up into eddies and swirls. These eddies and swirls are initiated by small obstructions in the pipe, notably roughness on the pipe wall. If flow rate is increased smoothly in a pipe which is exceptionally smooth and without the normal obstructions found in process pipework, the onset of turbulent flow can be delayed, but normally it is a function of velocity and viscosity. The distribution of the velocity of flow across the pipe under streamline flow is as shown in Fig. 4.33(a)—almost stationary near the wall of the pipe and gradually increasing towards the centre. Such a pattern makes measurement of flow rate very difficult, for it will change (as shown by the dotted forms in Fig. 4.33(a)) as the flow rate increases or decreases making the generation of differential pressure across an obstruction or the speed of rotation of a turbine a function not only of the average flow velocity but also of the velocity distribution. For this reason flow rate measurement by these means is only possible when the flow pattern is *fully* turbulent, when the velocity distribution will be as shown in Fig. 4.33(b), more or less constant across the pipe diameter with only a very small 'transition' area close to the pipe wall. Even so most of the errors of measurement are associated with this region, which explains the reduction of accuracy at low flows using orifices and nozzles.

With certain exceptions, all inferential meters are liable to be adversely

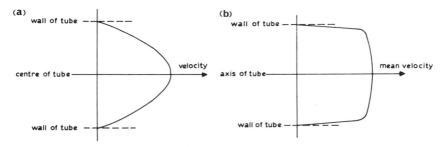

Fig. 4.33. (a) Streamline flow velocity distribution; (b) turbulent flow velocity distribution.

affected by anything upstream of the meter which will alter the normal flow of the fluid in the pipe. Anything which will impart a swirling motion to the fluid is to be particularly avoided, such as a sharp bend (Fig. 4.34) or a partly open valve (flow meters must *never* be located downstream of a control valve). Any sudden enlargement of the process line will also affect the flow pattern and cause errors in measurement. Orifice plates, nozzles and turbine meters are most seriously affected, whilst magnetic flow meters and variable area orifice meters are least affected (positive displacement meters are not affected at all). Minimum lengths of straight unobstructed pipe of constant diameter which must be provided in the piping design of the plant in order to avoid errors arising in this way are recommended in any standard on flow rate measurement (Fig. 4.35): these lengths vary from 10 diameters for a single 90° bend to 100 for a $\frac{3}{4}$-closed globe valve (most

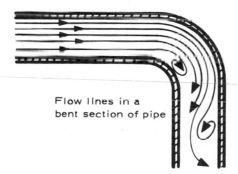

Flow lines in a
bent section of pipe

Fig. 4.34.

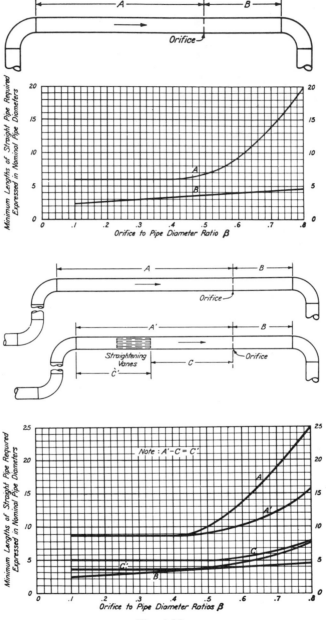

Fig. 4.35.

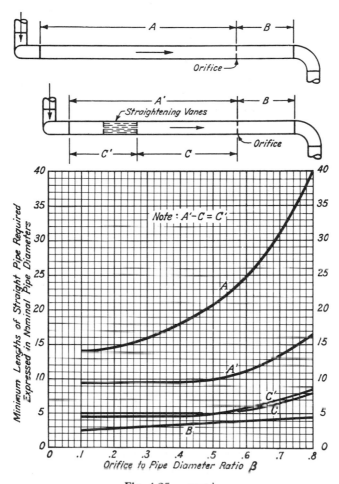

Fig. 4.35.—*contd.*

control valves are of the globe pattern). Where the problem is swirl, as in the case of two 90° bends in different planes, these lengths can be reduced by fitting into the process line a 'flow straightener' (which divides the pipe into a number of small passages over an appreciable length); in other cases this will not help.

These requirements may be an important factor in choosing the most appropriate meter, particularly in the case of retrofitting, since it is often very difficult to accommodate these requirements into the piping design.

4.18 SELECTING A FLOW METER

There are many considerations which determine the selection of a flow meter for a particular application:

accuracy and rangeability required;
nature of fluid: dirty or clean, corrosive, gas, vapour or liquid, temperature, pressure, conductivity, viscosity;
velocity of flow (pipe sizing);
restrictions on piping layout;
explosion and fire risk;
linearity;
energy conservation;
mass or volume flow rate;
cost and maintenance.

The accuracy of measurement of any of the meters described in this unit is better than $\pm 1\%$ of the maximum flow to be measured when the flow rate is actually greater than one third of this maximum. Positive displacement and turbine meters will provide much greater accuracy over a wider range, but are expensive; the Gilflo, fluidic and vortex types are not so accurate but all give very wide rangeability. Orifice plate meters are simple, relatively cheap and rugged, and can be changed to provide a different range, but are restricted to this performance. Magnetic and sonar types offer no restriction to flow and have no real upper limit; however, both require a certain lower limit of flow rate, which in practice may severely limit their range for some applications (depending on how generously the process line has been sized). On the other hand these types and to a lesser extent nozzles and venturis are not wasteful of energy. Magnetic flow meters cannot be used on petroleum fluids which are non-conductive electrically, and careful consideration must be given before using any of the electrical output types where there is a fire or explosion risk. Orifice and turbine types are particularly prone to error due to piping generated disturbances and viscosity changes in the fluid, as, to a lesser extent, are most other meters.

These are only a few of the comparisons that can be made and no firm rules can be given for the choice of meter.

4.19 INSTALLATION, MAINTENANCE AND CALIBRATION

Great care must be taken with the installation of any flow meter to ensure that nothing is done which may impair its operation; in this respect it is obviously essential to understand the principle of its operation.

Positive displacement meters depend for continued accuracy entirely on the maintenance of their sealing surfaces; it is obviously important therefore that they should never be installed without adequate upstream filters and strainers. What is adequate is a matter for decision by an engineer for each particular case, but it is worth remembering that it may be best to seek another type of meter if the flowing fluid contains very fine abrasive material. Turbine meters, too, will be damaged by fine abrasive material which can get into their bearings, and must be protected (by a strainer) from large solid particles which could damage their rotor blades. The energy loss which filters and strainers impose must be allowed for when the pumps and pipes are sized at the design stage; they must be cleaned regularly in use to prevent the pressure loss increasing to the point when it affects process operation.

Orifice plates, nozzles and venturis, and variable restriction devices are not capable of the accuracy of PD meters and turbines, but are relatively tolerant of dirty fluids. Vortex, magnetic and fluidic types are also relatively tolerant of dirt but sonar types may suffer from signal 'scattering'. However, scaling or corrosive fluids may necessitate the use of 'purges' on *both* low and high pressure connections to any form of differential pressure measuring system. All these types are to some degree affected by upstream conditions, except the turbine meter and also the magnetic flow meter which cannot be used on petroleum fluids

Many of the more recent types of meter rely on electrical/electronic detection techniques (i.e. sonar, fluidic, some vortex, etc.) and it is essential to ensure not only that they *can* satisfy relevant electrical requirements and standards, but also that they are so installed that they *do* in fact satisfy them.

Flow meters need to be maintained and to have their calibration checked from time to time; it is necessary to ensure, therefore, that the position in which they are installed is such that they are readily accessible.

There are only two ways in which a flow meter can be calibrated, in line or out of line. Calibration out of the process line is almost invariably impracticable on plant, and necessitates sending the meter back to the manufacturer or another calibration authority. For most applications this is not practicable and this is one of the main advantages of the differential pressure measurement systems. Provided an orifice plate is not physically damaged by some large particle carried with the flow, accuracy of measurement depends only on the differential pressure measurement device which can readily be removed for calibration. Positive displacement meters depend for accuracy on their seals, and if adequately protected by filters will not need calibration unless severely damaged; for this reason they are sometimes used as substandard meters by providing a 'spool piece' in the process line which can be temporarily replaced by a PD meter in order that it can be used to calibrate the meter permanently installed. For highly accurate measurement purposes PD or turbine meters are usually installed with in-line proving equipment; however, for custody transfer applications on large gas pipelines, nozzles or even orifice plates are sometimes used with three differential pressure measuring devices. With very careful installation much better than the usual $\pm 1\%$ accuracy can be obtained, whilst computers can be used to linearise the signal. This is because of the enormous cost of PD and turbine meters in large sizes. The calibration of most other types of meter cannot be checked in-line and is usually accepted as remaining for very long periods within the manufacturer's specification, which is usually conservative. It can be seen from the meters described in this section that the principles of operation are always such that there is little possibility of the calibration changing unless the meter is damaged. If this were not true the meter would not normally find acceptance for industrial use.

4.20 NON-FULL-FLOW MEASUREMENT

It has so far been assumed that the size and shape of the pipe or duct is such that a 'full flow' meter can be installed, i.e. a meter that measures the total flow through the pipe or duct. However, this is not always the case; for instance, where the flow of fluid will not permit any obstruction (e.g. the overheads on a distillation column) or where the pipe or duct is simply too large (e.g. heating or ventilating ducts or large steam mains).

If an obstruction can be tolerated, shunt metering may provide an answer (see Fig. 4.36). If no obstruction can be tolerated, the *velocity* of flow can be measured using a pitot tube (Fig. 4.37) and the velocity profile

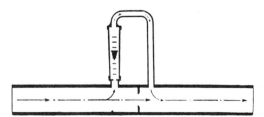

Fig. 4.36. By-pass variable aperture meter.

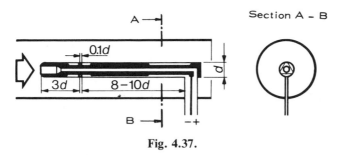

Fig. 4.37.

either assumed (for an approximate measurement) or determined by a search technique involving moving the position of the pitot in the duct or pipe cross-section. The pitot tube converts the energy of motion to pressure head at the tip and at the same time measures the 'static' pressure in the pipe or duct. The difference in these two readings is proportional to the square of the fluid velocity at the point of measurement.

CHAPTER 5

Measurement of Quantity

5.1 GENERAL

The quantity of material (volume or mass) produced, or transferred into or out of storage, is a very important function of measurement technology. It involves the measurement of the level in storage tankage, the measurement of the weight of vessels or containers with their contents, and the measurement of *total* flow quantities as opposed to flow *rate*. This chapter is concerned with the way that the techniques of measurement of flow rate, level and weight, which have been developed in earlier chapters, are adapted to the purposes of quantity measurement.

Measurements of quantity are required for batch processing, custody transfer, and to satisfy customs and excise requirements. In the last two cases the accuracy required is often an order higher than is usual in normal process operations ($\pm 0 \cdot 1 \%$ of actual measured value).

5.2 THE PRINCIPLES OF MEASURING TOTAL FLOW

The total flow through a line is the sum of all the fluid which passes through the flow meter over a given period of time. If the flow meter measures the *rate* of flow at any instant, and if the rate does not vary over the given period, the total flow is given by the product of flow rate and time:

$$\text{total flow} = \text{flow rate} \times \text{time period}$$

If, however, the rate varies significantly over the period, this relationship no longer applies. Nor can it be assumed that the correct answer will be obtained if the average flow rate is multiplied by the time period, as can be seen from Fig. 5.1.

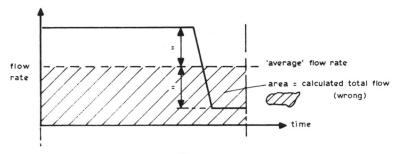

Fig. 5.1.

The true answer is given by the 'weighted average' or mean flow rate (over the period) multiplied by the time period (Fig. 5.2(a)). It is difficult to find the 'mean' flow rate over a period if the flow rate varies randomly (Fig. 5.2(b)). In any case the calculation of total flow by this method involves recording the flow rate over the whole period of measurement and calculating the total flow later, which is neither convenient nor practical.

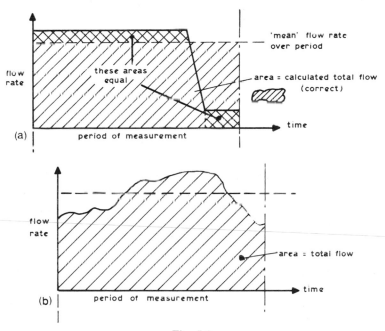

Fig. 5.2.

What is required is a method which automatically 'updates' the total flow from the time that measurement began to the present.

This is achieved in practice by assuming the flow rate is constant over a very short period of time; the 'totalising' mechanism multiplies the flow rate measured by the period and adds this quantity to the previous total (Fig. 5.3). It can be seen that the period must be small enough for the flow rate not to change significantly over the period, if the error, which will be the sum of the errors in each period, is not to be considerable. If the period is very short indeed, it appears that this process of *integration* is continuous, and under these conditions the errors are very small.

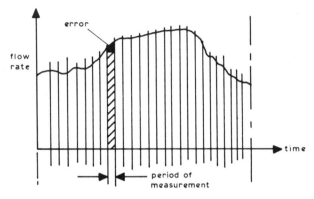

Fig. 5.3.

All 'inferential' flow meters measure rate of flow, and a mechanism must be added to them which 'integrates' this rate, in order that total flow can be measured. On the other hand, direct or non-inferential meters (i.e. the positive displacement type of meter) do in fact measure true total flow—*not* flow rate. A positive displacement meter functions by transferring a known volume of fluid (determined by the volume of the measuring chamber of the meter) from the inlet to the outlet. Providing that the seals in the meter do not leak, there is no error: the period of measurement is the time taken for the measuring chamber to travel between inlet and outlet (usually the time of one revolution of the meter signal output shaft). A graphical representation of the flow rate would look like that shown in Fig. 5.4: the volume flowing in one measurement period is known *exactly* and there is *no* error at all in the integration process.

A positive displacement meter is, therefore, the ideal meter for total flow

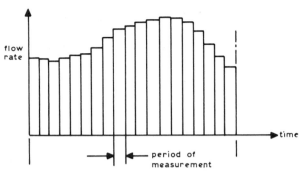

Fig. 5.4.

measurement, since it is only necessary to count the revolutions of the output shaft to obtain *exact* integration of the flow rate. All other flow meters are inferential and therefore measure flow rate: an integrating mechanism must be added to make them into a total flow meter, and often this mechanism adds to the errors of measurement.

5.3 THE PRINCIPLES OF MEASURING TOTAL VOLUME

Measurement of the total volume of fluid resident in a tank or vessel is just as important as measurement of total flow in or out for purposes of process operation and inventory, and for customs requirements. The volume can be calculated, in the case of a vessel with constant cross-sectional area, as the product of the level (measured relative to the bottom of the vessel as datum) and cross-sectional area (Fig. 5.5).

However, if the cross-sectional area varies, as for instance in the case of a TEL storage sphere, the total volume in the vessel depends not only on the

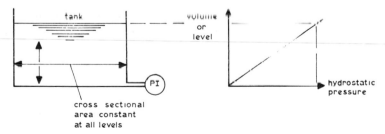

Fig. 5.5.

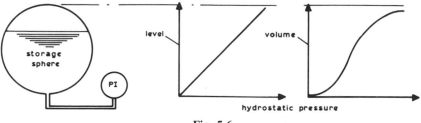

Fig. 5.6.

level, but also on the cross-sectional area; it is in fact the integral of the product of the cross-sectional area at every level and the level, just as the total flow is the integral of the flow rate at different times and the time (Fig. 5.6).

The larger the cross-sectional area of the vessel or tank, the greater the error will be owing to variation of the cross-sectional area, and accurate measurement of the volume contained, in large petroleum storage tanks for instance, demands not only accurate measurement of level but also accurate calibration based on measurements of the cross-sectional area at different levels. These measurements are not easy to make when the tank is full of product: however, the stress developed in the wall of such large diameter tanks by the weight of fluid is such that it is forced into a truly circular form at all levels (as the circular form maximises the volume) and, since the ratio of cross-sectional area to circumference of a circle is always the same, the measurement can be made by measuring the circumference of the tank at different levels, which is known as 'strapping'.

5.4 THE PRINCIPLES OF MASS MEASUREMENT

The quantity of material for sales purposes can be defined as a volume, or as a mass. In the past it has been found to be too difficult to measure in terms of mass and it has become traditional to sell by volume measure: petroleum is sold by volume even though this is illogical as its energy value is related to mass. Measurements of total flow or total volume can be converted into mass by correcting for density variation, but for accurate measurement the added source of error (in addition to level measurement errors and cross-sectional area errors) makes the final measurement too unreliable. The same problems apply to total flow measurement, since there are no positive displacement mass flow meters and the only inferential types which can measure mass flow rate are either very complex and expensive or make use of the principle of correction for density variation.

The development of the load cell makes it possible to weigh a vessel accurately, but there are considerable engineering problems involved in suspending large tanks for weighing. The weight of the tank itself in relation to its contents is often so great that the errors made in weighing tank and contents are large when compared with the weight of the contents alone. In the case of large petroleum storage tanks, the application of very accurate measurement of hydrostatic head combined with corrections for 'strapping' to provide direct measurement of mass is a possibility.

5.5 MEASUREMENT OF TOTAL FLOW USING INFERENTIAL FLOW RATE MEASUREMENT

Linear flow meters
Provided the impulse (signal) produced by the meter is proportional to the flow rate of the fluid (as in the case of variable area meters, turbine meters, fluidic, ultrasonic and magnetic flow meters), it is relatively easy to design a mechanism which will continuously multiply the impulse by time and thus give a signal output proportional to total flow. In the case of the turbine meter this is done by counting the pulses generated when the magnet embedded in the rotor passes the pick-up coil, instead of measuring the rate of pulse generation (which is proportional to flow rate).

Non-linear flow meters
Measurement of total flow using meters which produce a differential pressure across a restriction device is not so easy. The impulse signal is proportional to the square of flow rate, and multiplying this by the time will not give a signal proportional to total flow. The impulse signal must first be 'processed' to produce a signal which is proportional to flow. This processing is sometimes carried out by the pressure measuring device shown in Fig. 5.7; the manometer has one 'leg' specially shaped, so that the volume of measuring fluid displaced into the other leg, which contains a float to drive the indicator mechanism, varies. More fluid is displaced and the movement of the indicator is greater when the differential pressure is smaller; the chamber is so shaped that this exactly compensates for the smaller change in differential pressure per unit change in flow rate at low flows.

If a ring balance gauge is used to measure differential pressure across the

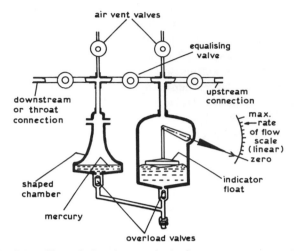

Fig. 5.7.   Shaped chamber method of square root extraction.

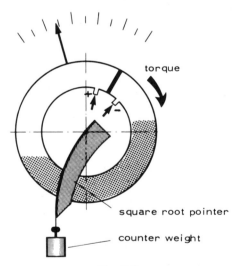

Fig. 5.8.

restricting device, the arm on which the counterweight is hung is shaped so that the moment of the weight about the pivot increases more slowly at first (low differential pressure) than it does later (high differential pressure), thus making the rotation of the ring proportional to the flow rate, rather than the differential pressure (Fig. 5.8).

It is not always practicable to modify the differential pressure measuring device in order to 'process' the impulse signal. In such cases the differential pressure measurement must be 'linearised' and integrated to obtain total flow.

5.6 MEASUREMENT RANGE AND ACCURACY

It is very important with total flow measurement to take into account the effect on the accuracy of the flow *rate*. It is obvious when measuring flow rate that accuracy will suffer if a meter, whose accuracy is a function of *maximum* flow rate (see Chapter 4) is used to measure a flow rate at the bottom end of the meter range. It is not so obvious when measuring total flow that the accuracy still depends on flow rate and not on total flow at all. This is even more difficult to accept since the flow rate may not be measured at all, and may vary with time. For this reason in particular, positive displacement and turbine meters, and other types, the accuracy of which is a function of *actual* rather than maximum flow rate, are best suited to measurement of total flow.

The most unsuitable methods of flow measurement to use for total flow measurement are those which employ measurement of differential pressure across a restriction device. Nevertheless, since large turbine meters and, even more so, large positive displacement meters are very expensive, it is necessary, particularly when measuring the total flow of gases and vapours, to employ these methods. Not only is accuracy a function of the maximum measurement, but it is a function of the maximum differential pressure measurement not the maximum flow rate. Thus an error of 0·1 % of maximum flow rate which, using a positive displacement meter, would become perhaps 0·2 % of actual flow rate at 0·1 of maximum flow rate, would become 1 % using a linear flow meter (such as a variable area meter), the error for which is a function of maximum flow rate, and would become 10 % using a differential pressure system because of the square law relationship between pressure and flow rate. Nor must it be thought that processing the impulse or transmission signal to 'linearise' the flow/signal relationship, in order to make it possible to integrate it, in any way changes this problem of accuracy; errors in measurement cannot be reduced by signal processing. Obviously, differential pressure measurement across a restricting device cannot be used for total flow measurement unless either the range of flow rates to be encountered are very small, or the accuracy is of little importance, both unlikely conditions to be satisfied.

To overcome this difficulty three different range differential pressure measuring devices are sometimes used over the 10:1 range in the example given above. Change of measuring device at a little under $\frac{1}{2}$ and $\frac{1}{4}$ of full flow rate, gives an approximately 5:1 range of differential pressure; 0·1 % of full scale becomes 0·5 % of actual measured flow rate at the lowest flow rate measured by each device, and thus the greatest error over the 10:1 range is 0·5 %.

Another way in which differential pressure measurement can be used for total flow measurement in large diameter pipes is the double venturi system shown in Fig. 5.9. The inlet to the small venturi is located in the low

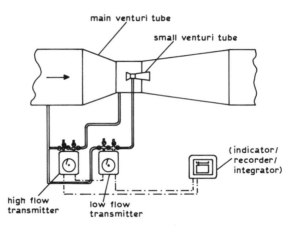

Fig. 5.9.   Double venturi installation.

pressure zone of the large venturi, and so the differential pressure of the 'low flow' transmitter is greater than that of the 'high flow' transmitter. In fact, if the two venturis are dimensionally similar, the low flow pressure difference will be the square of the high flow pressure difference. The low flow transmitter would have to be protected against overpressure, and special provision made to change over the integrator to the other range at the high flow limit of the low flow transmitter.

The error band and useful range of measurement of both positive displacement and turbine meters depends on the selection of the best size of meter. The wear rate of both types increases rapidly as the flow *rate* increases, but if maximum flow rate will not be sustained a meter can be selected which is smaller and therefore gives accurate measurement over a wider range; if the flow rate will be sustained at near maximum on the other hand, the range is less important. It is usually possible to obtain a range of 10:1 if this is borne in mind.

5.7 CALIBRATION OF TOTAL FLOW METERS

When used for accurate measurement, total flow meters often require in-line 'proving' in order to retain calibration accuracy at all times. This can be achieved, as described in Chapter 4, when the total measurement takes a long time and the 'start up' and 'shut down' periods are very short in comparison. However, when the measurement is to be made over a short time period (as for instance in filling a road or rail tanker) these 'transient' periods can cause considerable error. A batch prover tank is then used (Fig. 5.10) to calibrate total meter delivery and take into account these transient errors.

The total volume of the prover tank includes part of the 'swan neck' which, being narrow, provides a well spaced scale of volume by which to establish any error in total volume. The prover is only suitable, of course, to calibrate a meter for measuring one particular volume.

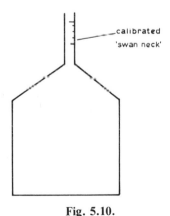

calibrated
'swan neck'

Fig. 5.10.

5.8 ACCURATE MEASUREMENT OF VOLUME STORED

It is normal to measure total flow and quantity stored in tanks by volume because, as has already been said, it is very much more difficult to measure mass or weight. Nevertheless, since the value of the product is related to weight rather than volume, it is essential to know at what temperature the volumetric measurements have been made. Product stored in tanks may change its temperature by a considerable amount owing to ambient conditions, and for the purposes of inventory control and customs and excise this can create large errors in its value. To overcome this problem, the *average* temperature of the contents of large storage tanks must be accurately measured. There are two ways in which this is commonly done:

1.   A 'stack' of thermocouples, each of different length is used to average the temperature over the total depth of fluid in the tank (Fig. 5.11). The averaging is readily achieved by connecting all the thermocouples in series (see Section 6.13). As the level changes in the tank some of them must be disconnected because they are no longer measuring fluid temperature. Thus, the level measurement is used to determine which set of thermocouples are to be connected into the measurement system, and the averaging must take account of the number of thermocouples which are connected at any time.

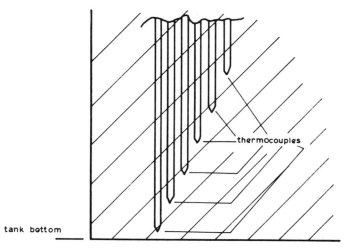

Fig. 5.11.

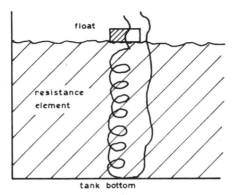

Fig. 5.12.

2: A special flexible resistance element is used in some systems (Fig. 5.12). This is attached to a float at the upper end and contracts and expands as necessary to adjust the length of the element to the level in the tank. No switching circuits are required as the resistance element remains unchanged at any level and truly averages the temperature.

5.9 TEMPERATURE CORRECTION OF TOTAL LIQUID FLOW

If the product is to be loaded at the point of sale or tax, by measurement of total flow rather than volume loaded into a container (as for instance delivery into the hold of a ship), it is necessary to correct the total *volumetric* flow measurement for variations in the temperature of the product. A continuous weighing system such as that of Fig. 5.13 is often used for this purpose. The product is made to flow through a length of pipe which is suspended from a weighing mechanism and which has flexible connections at inlet and outlet. If the temperature of the fluid changes, the weight of the column resident in the suspended pipe length at any instant will vary accordingly: the signal generated by this mechanism can be used to continuously vary the calibration of the volume flow meter in such a way that it always generates a signal proportional to the volume that would be flowing if the fluid were at some predetermined temperature. If this signal is integrated it will represent total volume corrected to the given temperature.

Correction of liquid flow rate for density variations resulting from temperature changes is not normally possible where accurate measurement

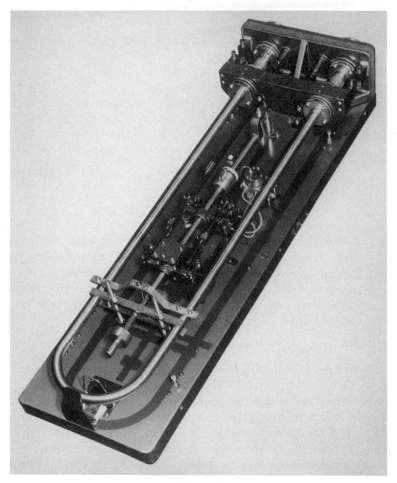

Fig. 5.13.

is required by measuring the temperature of the flowing liquid, because temperature measurement suffers from delays due to heat transfer whilst flow rate measurement is instantaneous.

5.10 PRESSURE CORRECTION FOR TOTAL FLOW OF GASES

Gases suffer change of density not only when temperature varies, but also when pressure varies. Because of this it is not possible to measure total corrected flow to the same degree of accuracy as is possible in the case of liquids; however, since the energy per unit volume of a gas is of a different order to that of a liquid, it is not necessary either. However, the change of density due to change of pressure is often so great that correction is necessary if the volume flow measurement is to be any practical use at all. Measurements of volumetric flow rate, static pressure and sometimes temperature are fed into a suitable computing device and the corrected volume flow rate integrated to provide reasonably accurate measurement of total volume corrected to 'standard temperature and pressure'.

CHAPTER 6

Measurement of Temperature

6.1 BI-METALLIC THERMOMETERS

Gases, liquids and solids all change in volume (expand) when their temperature increases: one of the simplest temperature measuring devices consists of two strips of different solid material (usually metals, for strength) joined together along their length. Different materials expand by different amounts for the same change in temperature, and since the two strips of metal are joined together they tend to take up a circular form, with the metal which expands most on the outside in order to accommodate its greater length (Fig. 6.1). The greater the difference of temperature from that at which the bi-metallic strip is straight, the more deflection increases. If one end of the strip is fixed, the 'free' end moves further as the radius of curvature decreases, i.e. the movement of the 'free' end increases as temperature increases.

To provide sufficient movement to operate an indicator mechanism, a long narrow strip of 'bi-metal' is coiled into a helix as shown in Fig. 6.2. In practice several helices are formed, each of smaller diameter than the last, from a single length of bi-metal strip. These are mounted concentrically and arranged in such a way that the longitudinal movement which takes place as the strip 'expands' is in opposite directions in alternate helices, and thus self-cancelling. In this way an indicating instrument can be built which has a relatively small 'sensitive volume' and low heat capacity. The former is necessary so that the instrument can be inserted into process pipes, the latter so that it will respond to temperature changes relatively quickly.

Such indicators are much more robust than liquid in glass thermometers, and can be read more easily. They are widely used for local indication, just as the common Bourdon tube pressure gauge is used for local pressure indication; they are relatively cheap and provide linear indication to an accuracy of $\pm 1 \%$ of maximum indication.

90

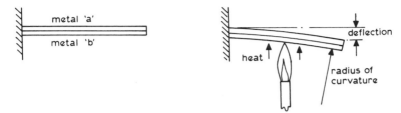

Fig. 6.1.

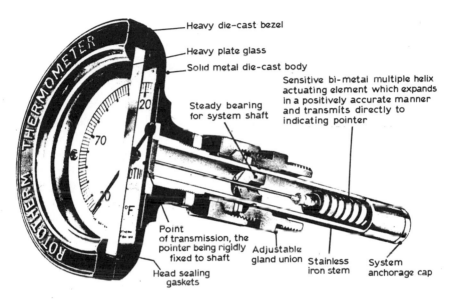

Fig. 6.2.

6.2 LIQUID IN METAL THERMOMETERS

Liquids expand very much more than solids as their temperature rises; thus, if a liquid is contained in a metal sheath, a considerable pressure will build up. If this pressure is applied to a pressure measuring element such as a Bourdon tube, the pressure becomes an inferential measure of the temperature. Such a mechanism is shown in Fig. 6.3.

As in the case of the liquid in glass thermometer, errors arise unless the whole of the 'fill' liquid is immersed in the process medium; however, this is

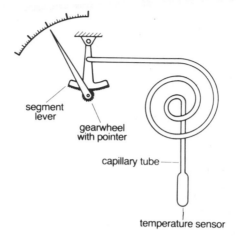

segment
lever

gearwheel
with pointer

capillary tube —

temperature sensor

Fig. 6.3.

not possible and normally only the sensor bulb is immersed. Thus, the remainder of the 'fill' liquid as well as the capillary and the pressure measuring element are 'immersed' in the surrounding air and are sensitive to changes in the ambient temperature rather than the process temperature. Such errors can be compensated for by adding temperature sensitive elements to the system, which oppose the effects of ambient temperature changes on the main measurement system. A simple example of such compensation is

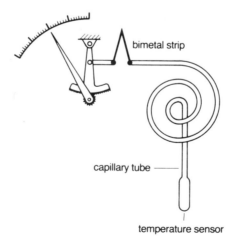

bimetal strip

capillary tube ——

temperature sensor

Fig. 6.4.

given in Fig. 6.4; a bi-metallic element tends to move the pointer in the direction opposite to that in which it would otherwise move owing to a change of ambient temperature. Since the bi-metal is not immersed in the process material it does not affect normal operation.

This is known as 'case compensation' as the compensating element responds to the ambient temperature of the instrument case. When the range of temperature to be measured is wide, this will usually be adequate, but for narrow range measurement when the capillary may be subject to a different ambient temperature (close to the plant) from that within the instrument case, this will not be adequate, and a duplicate of the pressure measuring element and capillary (which is installed alongside the 'real' capillary) are used in opposition to give 'full' compensation (Fig. 6.5). In other words the system is duplicated except for the sensor bulb; and any change of ambient conditions which might affect the accuracy of measurement of the process temperature is eliminated.

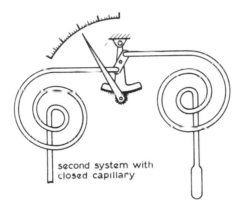

second system with
closed capillary

Fig. 6.5.

The need for compensation is reduced if the volume of the sensor bulb is large compared to the volume of the capillary and pressure measuring element. This, however, is not always possible as the bulb must fit into a small diameter pipe or vessel.

Different liquids are used as 'fill' according to the temperature range and precision required; a stainless steel capillary is required for mercury fill but cheaper metals are used for other liquids. The whole of the measuring element, bulb, capillary and pressure element must be filled with liquid at the zero temperature and sealed perfectly; therefore the length of capillary

Table 6.1

Liquid	Temperature range in °F	°C Approximate equivalent
Mercury	$-38°$ to $+1\,200°$	$-39°$ to $+650°$
Xylene	$-40°$ to $+750$	$-40°$ to $+400°$
Alcohol	$-50°$ to $+300°$	$-46°$ to $+150°$
Ether	$+70°$ to $+195°$	$+20°$ to $+90°$
Other organic liquids	$-125°$ to $+500°$	$-87°$ to $+260°$

must be decided before manufacture. For the same reason the capillary is often protected by a spirally wound steel sheath. Table 6.1 shows the liquids most commonly used.

6.3 GAS-FILLED SYSTEMS

The measuring system (bulb, capillary and pressure element) can be filled with gas instead of liquid. Because it is compressible, gas does not generate as great a pressure as liquid for the same temperature change. Response is more rapid for a bulb of the same volume, but the bulb usually has to be much larger in order that its volume is much greater than that of the capillary and pressure element: this is necessary because 'full' compensation is not practicable. The only way errors due to the effect of ambient temperature changes on the capillary and pressure element can be compensated is by duplicating the entire system including the sensor bulb (which would remain outside the process). Thus, although gas-filled systems are cheaper to make, they are less accurate and less convenient to use.

6.4 VAPOUR-FILLED SYSTEMS (CHANGE OF STATE THERMOMETER)

The 'vapour pressure' of a volatile fluid (i.e. a fluid which can co-exist in the form of both vapour and liquid) is dependent on its temperature. A sensor bulb containing a volatile liquid and its vapour, and also a more dense and non-volatile transmission fluid (liquid), will develop a pressure which can be measured by a remote pressure element at the end of a capillary as shown in Fig. 6.6.

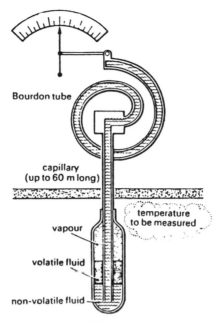

Fig. 6.6.

Expansion of the transmission fluid caused by changes of ambient temperature has absolutely no effect on the pressure of the vapour, which depends *only* on temperature: any change of volume is taken up by a little of the vapour condensing or a little more liquid vaporising. Thus, there is no need for compensation of any sort, and a very small bulb can be used (unlike a gas-filled system). The relation of pressure change to temperature is far from linear; therefore the divisions on the indicator scale are not of constant size, but become larger as the temperature increases. Thus, discrimination at the lower end of the instrument range is poor; as a result vapour pressure systems are only used for narrow measuring ranges An additional disadvantage is that the sensor bulb must be installed in the upright position, so that the transmission fluid remains at the bottom. Lastly, since the pressure developed is much less than it is in a liquid-filled system, the hydrostatic pressure head of the transmission liquid is not insignificant if the sensor bulb and the pressure measuring element are located at different levels, and this will introduce calibration errors.

The volatile fluid must be chosen to suit the range of the measurement. This is because, by definition, for a fluid to be volatile it must be well below its critical temperature (at which liquid and vapour are the same). Despite these disadvantages, the vapour system is cheaper to make than a liquid-filled system and avoids the problems of compensation: smaller bulbs than for a gas-filled system can be used, which is often of great importance. Neither vapour- or gas-filled systems, however, are as accurate as liquid-filled systems or provide as much force to drive indicator or transmission mechanisms.

6.5 CORRECT INSTALLATION OF PRIMARY SENSING ELEMENTS

All primary temperature sensing elements have a sensitive area which must be correctly located in the process fluid so that the temperature measured is in fact that which it was intended to measure. The tapping arrangements must, therefore, be carefully designed (see Fig. 6.7).

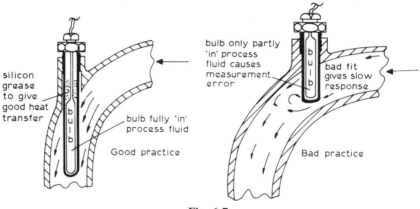

Fig. 6.7.

Thermopockets

Primary temperature sensing elements are almost always installed in thermopockets (Fig. 6.8) in order that they can be removed for service without the necessity of shutting down the process. However, heat has to be transferred from the process through the walls of the thermopocket and through any gas occupying the space between this and the sensing element. Gas is a poor conductor of heat and for this reason thermopockets, though necessary, slow up the response of most temperature measurement systems,

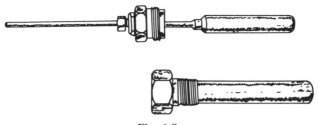

Fig. 6.8.

causing considerable difficulty where automatic control is concerned (see Chapter 8). To minimise these difficulties the sensing element is made to be a good fit in the thermowell; for this reason the latter should be manufactured and purchased with the measurement system. Silicone grease or oil should be used, provided the temperature is not too high, to fill the remaining space, as these are much better conductors of heat than gas (air).

6.6 THERMOCOUPLE TEMPERATURE MEASUREMENT

If two conductors made of different metals are connected as shown in Fig. 6.9 and one of the two junctions heated to a higher temperature than the other, thermal energy is converted directly into electrical energy causing an electric current to flow round the circuit. This is known as the Seebeck effect and can be used as an accurate method of measuring temperature since the voltage between the two junctions (which causes the current to flow) has an exact relationship with the difference of temperature between the junctions.

The two conductors are joined together by welding to form the 'measuring' junction, and usually the other ends of the two wires (of different metals) are connected to form the reference junction. A measuring instrument is connected somewhere in the circuit as shown in Fig. 6.10.

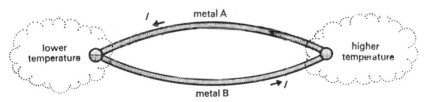

Fig. 6.9. The Seebeck effect.

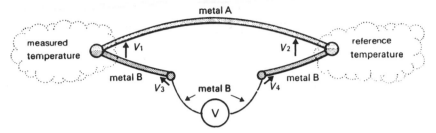

Fig. 6.10. A thermocouple circuit showing the contact potentials at the meter connections.

The temperature difference between the measuring and reference junctions is measured. It is, therefore, essential that the temperature of the reference junction should be known, in order to measure the temperature at the measuring junction; this is known as the reference temperature, and it can be established by placing the reference junction in a container of melting ice or at some other known temperature (Fig. 6.11). However, this is generally impracticable and so it is more common to use one of the methods described in the next section to compensate for changes in the temperature of the reference junction which is usually at ambient.

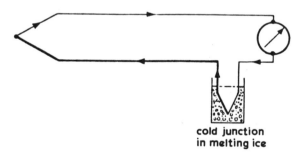

cold junction
in melting ice

Fig. 6.11.

6.7 MEASURING THERMOCOUPLE VOLTAGES

The simplest way to measure the Seebeck effect is to use a galvanometer or current measuring instrument to measure the current which flows in the circuit. However, the resistance of the leads and even the coil of the measuring instrument will vary with ambient temperature and introduce

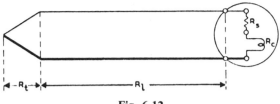

Fig. 6.12.

errors, which then have to be compensated. This is generally done by using a low resistance/high sensitivity galvanometer, and 'loading' the circuit with a 'swamp' resistor, R_s, as shown in Fig. 6.12. The swamp resistor can be made from a metal whose resistance changes little with temperature (is 'temperature stable') as a result, although the coil of the galvanometer is made from copper, the resistance of which changes considerably with temperature, the total change of resistance is greatly reduced.

Examples of cold junction compensation
In the method illustrated in Fig. 6.13 the reference junction is immersed in a bath of suitable liquid, the temperature of which is controlled at a constant value (above ambient) by a small heater and a thermostat. This too is very clumsy for plant use as the bath must be of a fairly large capacity to provide a constant reference temperature. The method shown in Fig. 6.14 is most commonly used, because it does not require baths of liquid. A 'bridge' is inserted into the circuit at the reference junction, so that it is subjected to exactly the same temperature as the junction. Three of the resistors are

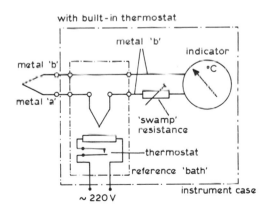

Fig. 6.13.

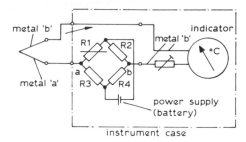

Fig. 6.14. Thermocouple circuit showing resistances involved.

made of material (manganin wire) which has a very small change of resistance with temperature, and the fourth of a material (nickel wire) which has a large resistance change with temperature. The resistances are adjusted so that the bridge is in balance at the reference temperature and no voltage difference occurs between a and b. At any other temperature a compensating voltage is generated.

In order to eliminate the errors due to resistance changes in various sections of the system a potentiometer is used for accurate measurements. The principle of the potentiometer is that the voltage generated by the thermocouple is nullified by an accurately known voltage generated inside the measuring instrument: a galvanometer is used only to detect the 'null' point. The principle is shown in Fig. 6.15, where the voltage E, generated by the thermocouple, is set off against the voltage drop along the length AC of the slide wire S. The slide wire is itself a resistance, and the position C at which the voltage drop along AC exactly equals $-E$ is established by sliding a moving contact along the line until the galvanometer indicates no nett voltage. The total voltage drop along the whole length of the slide wire AB is that supplied by the battery or constant voltage source V.

In practice the instrument is 'automated' so that the 'null' point is established by a servo mechanism operating in conjunction with the

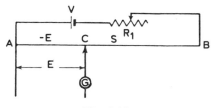

Fig. 6.15.

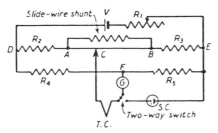

Fig. 6.16. AB, slide wire R_1, adjustable resistance; T.C., thermocouple; G, galvanometer S.C., standard cell; V, source of supply to bridge.

galvanometer. The circuit of a real instrument would be more complex, and look like that shown in Fig. 6.16. The resistors R_2, R_3, R_4, and R_5 perform the reference junction temperature correction (R_2, R_3 and R_5 being made of manganin, and R_4 of nickel), whilst at the same time R_2 and R_3 determine the measuring range of the instrument by fixing the voltages at the ends of the slide wire, A and B. The slide wire shunt resistor determines the span of the instrument. Accuracy of measurement is dependent on the value of the constant voltage from V. Periodically the galvanometer is connected to the standard reference cell SC by the two-way switch, and the resistor R_1 adjusted so that the voltage from V is equal to this reference voltage. In many instruments this is done automatically.

6.8 COMPENSATING LEADS

It is inconvenient and even impracticable to use the two metals of the thermocouple as conductors throughout the system in order that the reference junction shall be at the point of voltage measurement as shown; apart from any other consideration it would mean that much of the internal circuitry of the instrument would have to be constructed of wire of one or other of these materials, and an instrument could only be used with one type of thermocouple. In practice, therefore, connections are made to the instrument as shown in Fig. 6.17.

There are now, however, not two, but three junctions between dissimilar metals, two of them at the reference position. If these two junctions are at different temperatures, an unwanted voltage will be generated which will introduce measurement error; fortunately these two junctions are made within the instrument case and will normally be at the same temperature without any special measures being necessary.

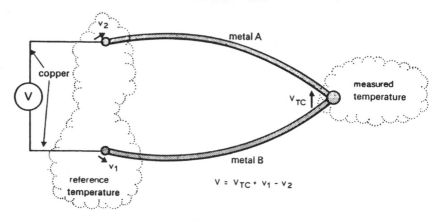

Fig. 6.17.

It will be obvious by now that for a number of reasons the reference junction(s) must be located inside the measuring instrument. In theory it (they) could be located in the plant, but in that case reference junction compensation would have to be applied in the plant, and the range of ambient temperatures would probably be greater, making compensation more difficult. In order that the reference junction(s) are at the instrument it is necessary that the conductors (leads) from the thermocouple in the plant to the measuring instrument are of the same metals as the thermocouples themselves. Thus, these connections must be made using special cables which are usually referred to as 'compensating leads'. Moreover, when connecting compensating leads, unlike normal cables, it is obviously *essential to connect the correct conductors to each terminal of the thermocouple.*

6.9 THERMOCOUPLE TRANSMITTERS

The principles of signal transmission will be covered in Chapter 7 but it is important to note here that the need to use compensating leads from the thermocouple to the measuring instrument has led to the development of a type of instrument known as a 'temperature transmitter'. This is in fact not simply a transmitter, but a measuring and transmitting instrument combined. The very small voltage generated by a thermocouple cannot be used directly to operate a transmission device, but must be amplified first.

However, amplification of a direct voltage is not easy, and such instruments are expensive and are often prone to drift problems.

6.10 CONSTRUCTION OF THERMOCOUPLES

A thermocouple is simply two wires of different metals joined together to form the measuring junction (usually by fusion or welding). The conductors must be insulated from each other, and in its simplest form a thermocouple is as shown in Fig. 6.18.

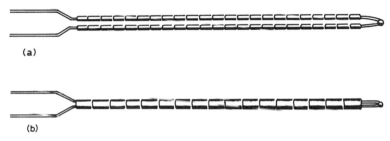

(a)

(b)

Fig. 6.18. (a) Straight-type element; wires with single-hole insulators. (b) Straight-type element; wires with double-hole insulators.

However, it must be possible to replace the thermocouple itself without shutting down the plant, and it must be protected from mechanical and other damage, for which reasons they are usually installed as shown in Fig. 6.19. The thermowell remains in the process vessel or pipe permanently, and must conform in its construction and installation to all safety and pressure standards which apply to the vessel itself. The sheath in which the 'couple' itself is fitted allows its tip to be pressed by the spring onto the bottom of the 'well' so as to ensure good heat transfer. A little silicon oil or grease should be put in the 'well' to further improve heat transfer. The compensating cables are connected to terminals in the 'head', which is waterproof, and enters through a waterproof gland. The 'well' is sometimes constructed integrally with a flange instead of the threaded mounting connection shown.

Using this type of thermocouple, a metal to metal contact is essential between the measuring junction and the bottom of the 'well' in order to provide good heat transfer from the process, through the wall of the 'well' and into

Fig. 6.19.

the thermocouple. This same metal to metal contact also ensures electrical conductance between the thermocouple and the thermowell, which is itself electrically in contact with the process vessel or pipe, which are in turn normally connected to earth potential. Earth potential can vary considerably throughout the plant: if the measuring instrument is located some distance from the thermocouple, such voltage differences can introduce serious errors into the measurement. To avoid this the instrument can be insulated from earth at the point where it is installed, and a conductor installed to connect it to earth potential at the thermocouple installation point. However, this may interfere with electrical safety (see Section 7.14), and it is preferable to insulate the thermocouple measuring junction from earth potential leaving only the measuring instrument 'earthed'. To do this a special 'sheathed mineral insulated' thermocouple is used (Fig. 6.20). This thermocouple uses powdered magnesium oxide as an insulator: the measuring junction is insulated from the sheath, so that there is no contact between sheath and thermocouple. Magnesium oxide, however, whilst being a good electrical insulator conducts heat well, so that measuring performance is good. Insulation between the thermocouple and sheath is at

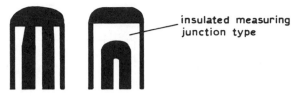

Fig. 6.20.   Mineral-insulated thermocouple probes.

least 1000 MΩ, and so this type of sensor can be used to measure the temperature of the windings of large electrical motors, etc.

6.11 MULTIPOINT POTENTIOMETRIC INSTRUMENTS

Self-balancing (servo control) potentiometric instruments are very expensive, and it is therefore common practice to use 'multipoint' forms. A number of thermocouples are connected to the same instrument and are either switched manually to the measuring circuits for indication of whichever temperature is selected by the operator, or are automatically switched in turn for recording purposes. In the recording version the instrument makes a 'dot' on the chart, of a particular colour, each time the measuring system balances in the null voltage state when connected to the appropriate thermocouple. Thus, the recording consists of a series of dots and a number of temperatures can be recorded on a single chart provided they are not too close in value. The number of temperatures which can be recorded by one instrument is also limited by the space between dots, which increases with the number of temperatures, and also by the available colours. In practice it is rarely practicable to record more than 12 points on the same chart.

Multipoint switching can be done by 'single-pole' switching, as shown in Fig. 6.21, in which case only one contact is needed for each thermocouple. One side of each thermocouple is connected by a common wire to the measuring system; this is permissible if earthed thermocouples are used, only if installed close together on the plant (so that earth potential is not likely to vary significantly). Even so the instrument will have to be insulated from earth potential at the location where it is installed.

In order to avoid these difficulties double-pole switching is used so that the earth potential for the measuring circuit is that of the particular thermocouple being measured (Fig. 6.22). If *all* thermocouples are of the insulated type, single-pole switching can be used and the measuring

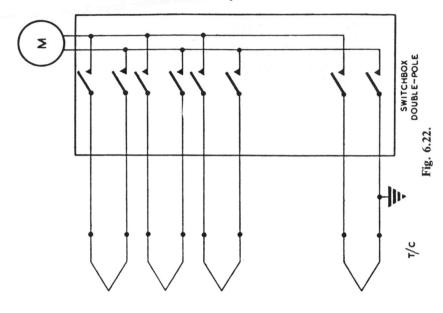

SWITCHBOX
DOUBLE-POLE

T/C

Fig. 6.22.

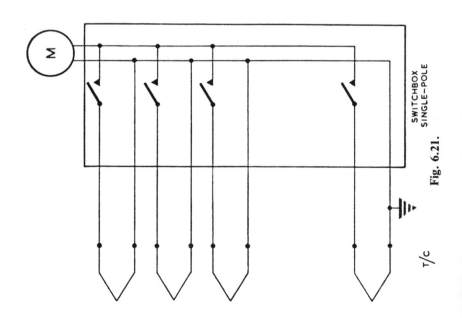

SWITCHBOX
SINGLE-POLE

T/C

Fig. 6.21.

instrument earthed at its point of installation, which is more convenient. (There are other complications connected with intrinsic electrical safety which will be discussed later in Section 7.14.)

The connections from the terminal board of the instrument to the switches and from these to the measuring circuits are made in copper wire, since an instrument may be used with thermocouples of different materials. The terminal board is therefore the location of the reference junctions, and must be maintained at constant and uniform temperature (see Fig. 6.23 where a and b are dissimilar metals of the thermocouple).

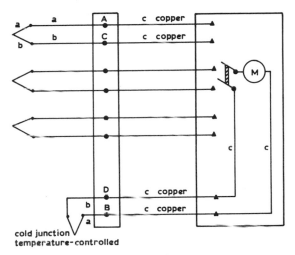

Fig. 6.23.

6.12 THERMOCOUPLE MATERIALS

The pairs of metals from which thermocouples are normally made are shown in Table 6.2; graphical plots showing the different relationships between the temperature difference (between measuring and reference junctions) and the voltage generated are given in Fig. 6.24. It can be seen that these types differ greatly in sensitivity, i.e. the voltage produced for each unit of temperature difference. They also differ greatly in their ability to withstand corrosive environments or mechanical stress, and in their precision, i.e. the reproducibility of the voltage/temperature relationship.

Table 6.2

Designated type and British Standard (BS) number	Metal or alloy for 1st wire	Metal or alloy for 2nd wire
Type S (BS 1826)	platinum	{ 90 % platinum, 10 % rhodium
Type R (BS 1826)	platinum	{ 87 % platinum 13 % rhodium
Type J (BS 1829)	iron	{ constantan (57 % copper, 43 % nickel plus small amounts of other materials)
Type T (BS 1828)	copper	constantan
Type E	Chromel (90 % nickel, 10 % chromium)	constantan
Type K (BS 1827)	Chromel	{ Alumel (94 % nickel, 3 % manganese, 2 % aluminium, 1 % silicon)

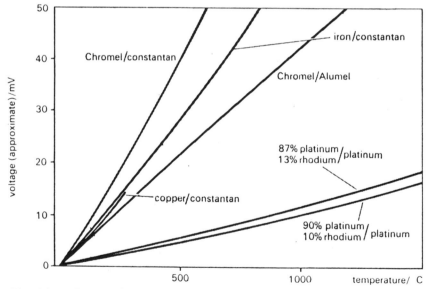

Fig. 6.24. Curves of voltage against temperature for several common thermocouple materials.

6.13 MEASURING TECHNIQUES USING THERMOCOUPLES

The voltage generated by a thermocouple depends on the *difference* in temperature of the measuring and reference junctions; if both junctions are used for measuring, then thermocouples provide an ideal method of measuring temperature difference as opposed to temperature. It is not unusual to want to measure temperature difference in process control applications; a typical circuit is shown in Fig. 6.25.

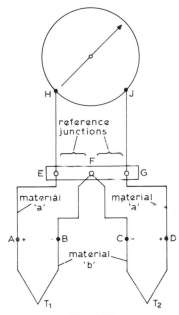

Fig. 6.25.

In the circuit shown in the figure the two reference junctions are EF and GF, and the conductors AE and DG are of the same material. This is known as 'back to back' connection; the voltages generated oppose each other, and thus represent the difference in temperature of the junctions T_1 and T_2. The terminal strip EFG can be located anywhere, provided it is at uniform temperature. Changes of temperature of this terminal strip do not matter since both reference junctions rise or fall by the same amount and the change is cancelled out. The conductors EH and GJ can be of any material for the same reason; thus, compensating leads are not necessary.

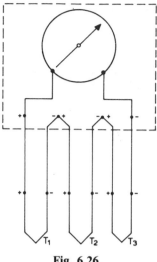

Fig. 6.26.

Average temperatures can be measured very easily using thermocouples; the voltages are simply added together as shown in Fig. 6.26. In this case all the reference junctions must be at the measuring instrument, in exactly the same way as when a single thermocouple is used. Correction must be applied in the same way, the only difference being that the voltage generated is as many times greater (than it is in a single temperature measurement) as there are thermocouples to average. (The correction voltage is similarly increased.)

Exactly the same arrangement is sometimes used to increase the voltage generated when measuring very small temperature changes—a bundle of thermocouples insulated from each other is used in place of a single 'couple'. This is known as a 'thermopile'.

An important use of thermocouples is to measure the temperature of the surface of pipes which are subject to corrosive atmosphere and heat, such as the pipes in a pyrolysis furnace. The thermocouples themselves are sometimes laid in a small groove in the surface of the pipe in order to give

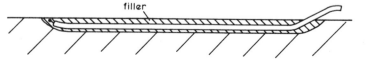

Fig. 6.27.   Thermocouple in shallow groove.

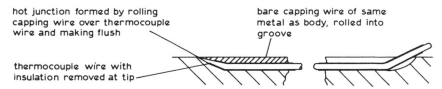

hot junction formed by rolling
capping wire over thermocouple
wire and making flush

bare capping wire of same
metal as body, rolled into
groove

thermocouple wire with
insulation removed at tip

Fig. 6.28. Thermocouple arrangement for grooves in copper and steel tubes.

them protection from direct contact with the furnace radiation (Fig. 6.27). Another method consists of inserting small mineral insulated 'couples' into holes drilled directly into the pipe wall (Fig. 6.28).

6.14 ELECTRICAL INTERFERENCE

The voltage generated by a single thermocouple is very small and in order not to introduce errors the resistances of leads are kept as low as possible. It is very easy for other voltages to be generated in these leads by unwanted 'pick-up' from electrical power equipment on the plant. Such 'pick-up' occurs by transformer effect from power supplies of alternating current, or by actual radio emission of much higher frequency. Fortunately, direct current cannot be 'picked-up' in either of these ways, and so provided precautions are taken to avoid AC pick-up, errors can normally be avoided. These precautions include built-in inductance in the measuring instrument (which will offer no resistance to direct current flow, but oppose alternating current flow) and avoiding the running of thermocouple extension leads near either electrical equipment or alongside electrical cables. Thermocouple leads can also be 'screened' from pick-up by running them in metal conduits or trays which are carefully earthed only at one end, and which, therefore, themselves pick-up the AC current and conduct it harmlessly to earth without passing through the measuring instrument (see Chapter 7).

6.15 RESISTANCE BULBS

The electrical conductivity of most metals decreases as their temperature increases (see Fig. 6.29). This property has already been seen to provide compensation for the reference junction temperature variations in a thermocouple measuring system, but is also used to measure temperature in its own right. A resistance thermometer bulb (RTB) constructed as shown in

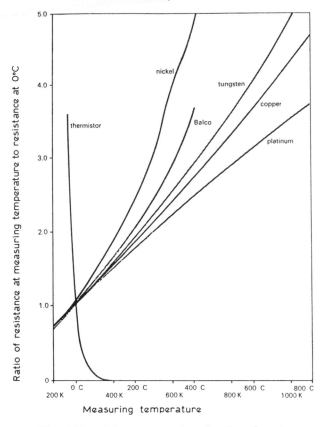

Measuring temperature

Fig. 6.29.   (Note reverse slope for thermistor.)

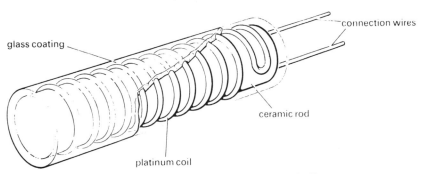

Fig. 6.30.   A resistance thermometer bulb.

Fig. 6.30, is used as one 'leg' in a Wheatstone bridge/galvanometer or cross-coil instrument in one of the ways shown in Fig. 6.31.

In Fig. 6.31(b) the lead to the RTB from one side of the 'bridge' supply is balanced by the lead from the resistance R_2 located in the instrument, so that the resistance of the leads is not added to that of the RTB, but evenly divided between the two sides of the 'bridge'. Thus, the bridge is balanced at the minimum temperature of the measuring range, regardless of the length of the connecting leads. If the leads are very long, however, the additional resistance (which it can be seen this adds to the galvanometer lead) may

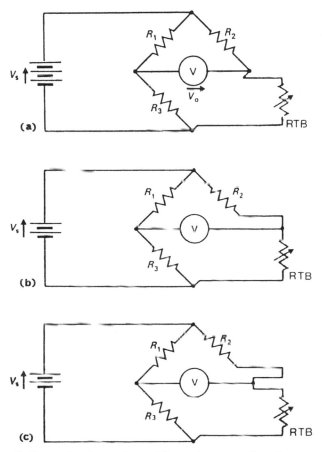

Fig. 6.31. Bridges using three-wire and four-wire connections to compensate for resistance changes in the leads.

reduce the sensitivity of the instrument: in such cases it is better to use the system shown in Fig. 6.31(c), even though this increases the cost of the leads still further, there being a total of four conductors. These systems are referred to as two-, three- and four-wire systems.

The measuring systems shown in Fig. 6.31 are known as 'unbalanced bridge' systems, because the resistance bridge is 'unbalanced', producing a voltage across the galvanometer or cross-coil measuring instrument at all except the minimum temperature of the range of measurement. For maximum accuracy a servo operated 'null balance' instrument is used, as in the case of thermocouple instruments as shown in Fig. 6.32.

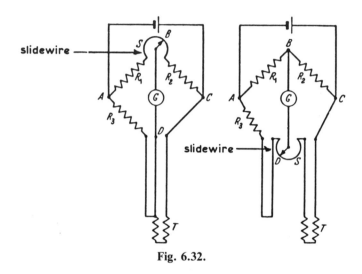

Fig. 6.32.

In this instrument the slidewire is driven to the null position by the servo control system, and the galvanometer serves only to detect this 'null point'. This system completely avoids errors due to the calibration of the galvanometer, the heating effect of current flowing through the resistors, and any variation in the supply voltage, errors which all occur in unbalanced bridge instruments. This is because the galvanometer is only used as a detector of the 'null point', there is no current flow at 'null' state, and the bridge balance depends only on the values of the resistances, not on the supply voltage. Nevertheless, in order to keep the size of the RTB small it is usually made from many turns of fine wire; this is easily heated by a very small current when the system is in the unbalanced state whilst the servo 'finds' the 'null' position on the slidewire. For this reason the

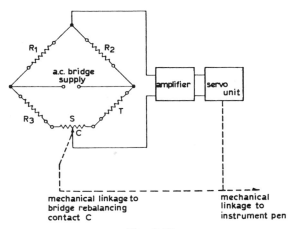

Fig. 6.33.

galvanometer (or other detector) must be as sensitive as possible so that even very small currents flowing will cause it to deflect. Very accurate instruments use an amplifier as shown in Fig. 6.33 to increase this sensitivity.

Cheaper instruments, measuring over a narrower range, often use the very much greater resistance change/temperature change ratio of a thermistor, as shown in Fig. 6.29, to increase sensitivity. Another source of error in resistance bulb measuring systems is variation in the conductivity of the resistances of the bridge circuit (other than the RTB itself). To minimise this source of error these are made of a metal which does not change much in conductivity with temperature, such as manganin; provided ambient temperature changes are not large, this reduces such errors to very small magnitude indeed.

6.16 MATERIALS AND CONSTRUCTION

Unlike the thermocouple the RTB shown in Fig. 6.30 is insulated from earth potential by the glass coating in which the resistance wire is set and there is, therefore, no problem in avoiding errors from earth 'loops'. This glass coating is applied for a different reason, however: the resistance of wire changes with strain, and the construction must be such as to avoid as far as possible any strain in the resistance wire as it is heated.

The RTB is installed in a thermowell in exactly the same way as a thermocouple, and there is exactly the same problem of heat transfer through the wall of the thermowell and sheath into the wire itself.

Compensating leads are not necessary for resistance elements, as it is the resistance which is being measured, not a small generated voltage. Nevertheless, the Seebeck effect will occur at junctions between the metal of the RTB and the leads, which will usually be of a different metal. Care must be taken that the voltages generated are not large enough to cause errors. This will determine that the bridge voltage will be several volts, which in turn determines the order of size of the resistances used, so that the currents in the unbalanced circuit will not cause self-heating problems. The standard RTB usually has a resistance of 100 Ω at 0 °C for this reason. The insulation value between the resistance element and its outer metal sheath is of the order of 10 MΩ.

Although it has the smallest ratio of resistance change to temperature increase and is, therefore, the least sensitive, platinum wire gives the most stable relationship and, therefore, provides the most accurate measurement. The other metal most commonly used is nickel, since it gives the largest resistance change. Very high repeatability is possible using platinum resistance elements with null balance instruments—in the order of $\pm 0.1 \%$ of span.

6.17 MULTIPOINT RESISTANCE ELEMENT INSTRUMENTS

Multipoint self-balancing instruments are very similar to multipoint self-balancing potentiometric types (except that the bridge circuit differs from the potentiometer circuit). Earthing problems are fewer, as already stated, but care must be taken that the resistance element, which is constructed of coiled wire, does not gain electrical energy by transformer effect from nearby inductive equipment such as electric motors, transformers, etc., as this too will cause error by self-heating.

6.18 MEASURING TECHNIQUES

Resistance thermometers can be used to measure temperature difference accurately as shown in Fig. 6.34. Two RTBs are used and are connected into opposite arms of the measuring side of the bridge. Similarly, average temperature can be measured as shown in Fig. 6.35 by connecting several RTBs in series into the measuring arm of a bridge. Alternatively, a special resistance element (in which the coil of resistance wire expands or contracts

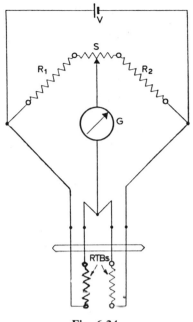

Fig. 6.34.

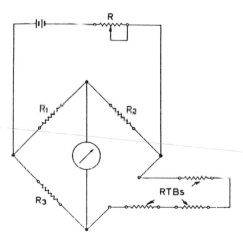

Fig. 6.35. Average temperature measurement with resistance thermometers.

between a fixed anchorage at one end and a moveable anchorage, such as a float, at the other) is sometimes used for averaging the temperature of liquid in a tank, etc. Care must be taken that the wire is not strained in any way.

6.19 NON-CONTACT TEMPERATURE MEASUREMENT

All the methods of measuring temperature described so far entail contact between the process material and the measuring element. For very high temperatures such as those found inside furnaces, this is often not practicable. Platinum/platinum–rhodium thermocouples cannot be used above 1500 °C (tungsten/tungsten–rhenium up to 2000 °C). However, any hot body radiates energy as light and heat, the difference being only the frequency of the energy emission (which is in a vibrating or oscillating form). Such energy 'emission' varies greatly (as the fourth power) as the temperature of the hot body varies (see Fig. 6.36).

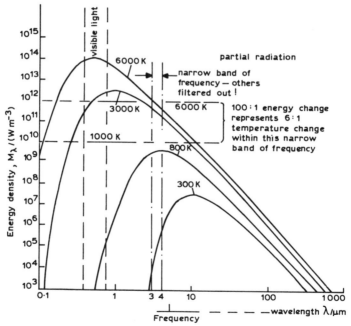

Fig. 6.36. The distribution of power radiated by a black body at different temperatures.

An instrument which allows this radiation to fall on a detecting element, such as a thermocouple or thermopile, which will heat up, can be used to measure the temperature of the hot body by inference, without contact. The amount of radiation falling on the detector is proportional to the hot body temperature. Providing the 'target' (i.e. the hot body) fills the 'cone of acceptance' of the detector, the distance from the hot body does not affect the measurement, since the target area *increases* as the square of the distance, whilst the radiation received from any given surface area of the hot body *decreases* as the square of the distance; thus, the two effects exactly cancel out (Fig. 6.37). Such instruments are called 'total radiation pyrometers'.

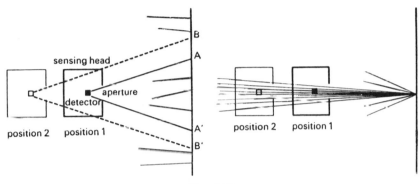

Fig. 6.37.

The sensitivity of the pyrometer depends on the aperture size and the angle of the 'cone of acceptance' (which in turn depends on the distance of the detecting element from the aperture). If a lens is introduced at the aperture to focus the radiation, sensitivity is increased and the same output can be obtained from the detecting element when the target is smaller (Fig. 6.38).

The amount of radiation falling on the detecting element does not only depend on its temperature, but also on its 'emissivity', *which must therefore be known*. In practice all materials absorb some of the radiation which falls on them (from whatever source) and also reflect some. At any given temperature the amount of energy emitted must equal exactly the amount absorbed (otherwise the body would either heat up or cool down), and it follows that a body which absorbs more than another, will, at the same temperature, emit correspondingly more; such a body is said to have a

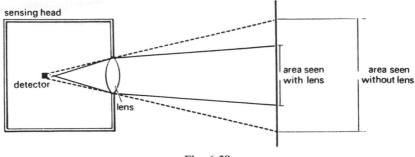

Fig. 6.38.

higher 'emissivity' than the former. A body or material which absorbs all the radiant energy which falls on it has, therefore, the highest possible emissivity—unity. Correction to the reading of the pyrometer is necessary for emissivities of less than unity. If, however, a reading is taken into a large space through a small hole, the apparent emissivity will be unity, regardless of the material of the target; this is because energy reflected from the target does not escape, but is directed back onto the target which absorbs at least part of it. Thus, little or no energy escapes from such a space and the amount falling on the detector depends only on the temperature of the target.

Total radiation pyrometers can be used, therefore, to measure the temperature inside a furnace accurately, but for most applications are only accurate if the emissivity of the material of the 'target' is known and the readings corrected to take account of it.

6.20 PARTIAL RADIATION OR OPTICAL PYROMETERS

This type of instrument, sometimes known as a 'disappearing filament pyrometer' depends on the fact that the frequency of the energy emitted changes enormously as the temperature increases or decreases, as can be seen clearly from Fig. 6.36. If only a narrow range of frequencies is allowed to fall on the detector (by using filters), then the energy falling on the detector varies greatly with temperature. A filament is heated by an electric current so that it too is emitting energy almost entirely at the same frequency as that being received from the target through the filters. The current is varied until, to the operator looking at the filament against the background of the 'target', it disappears (Fig. 6.39). The current flowing

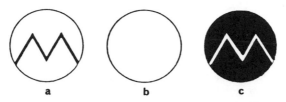

Fig. 6.39. Conditions in disappearing filament pyrometer. (a) Filament colder than 'target'; (b) filament disappears—element same temperature as 'target'; (c) filament hotter than 'target'.

through the filament is a measure of the target temperature under these conditions.

6.21 INFRA-RED 'PHOTOGRAPHY'

Heat energy is radiated in the same way as light, i.e. as vibrations. The frequency of these vibrations varies with the temperature of the radiating surface (the hot body). Most energy is radiated in the 'infra-red' part of the spectrum, to which the human eye is not sensitive, and only when a surface gets very hot indeed does it begin to 'glow' visibly. Special television/computer equipment is available which detects the frequency of the radiated heat energy from different parts of a large surface, such as a furnace tube or wall. This equipment can be used, therefore, to find 'hot spots' because it provides a heat 'picture' of the target.

6.22 CALIBRATION

Like pressure, temperature is a state and must be measured relative to either ambient or absolute zero state. Unlike pressure, however, there are no direct methods of measurement; all measurement of temperature is by inference from some effect of temperature change. This makes calibration of temperature measuring systems difficult and, in practice, all temperature measuring instruments have to be compared directly with one or more of the 'fixed points' on the International Practical Temperature Scale (Table 6.3) or calibrated against a suitable sub-standard.

For calibration checking on plant these fixed points, apart from the freezing point (triple point) and boiling point of distilled water, need apparatus that is too difficult to use and too expensive. Calibration

**Table 6.3 The International Practical Temperature Scale
(IPTS)**

Fixed point	Assigned temperature	
Freezing point of gold	1337·58 K	1064·43 °C
Freezing point of silver	1235·08 K	961·93 °C
Freezing point of zinc	692·73 K	419·58 °C
Boiling point of water	373·15 K	100 °C
Triple point of water	273·16 K	0·01 °C
Boiling point of oxygen	90·188 K	−182·962 °C
Triple point of oxygen	54·361 K	−218·789 °C
Boiling point of neon	27·102 K	−246·048 °C
Boiling point of equilibrium hydrogen	20·28 K	−252·87 °C
Equilibrium between the liquid and vapour phases of equilibrium hydrogen at 33 330·6 Pa pressure	17·042 K	−256·108 °C
Triple point of equilibrium hydrogen	13·81 K	−259·34 °C

checking is therefore usually carried out by immersing the sensors of the instrument to be checked, as well as that of a suitable sub-standard instrument, in a temperature-controlled bath, and comparing the outputs. The temperature control calibration does not affect the accuracy of this method; it is only used to maintain a steady temperature.

Such checking is necessary periodically for filled systems or bi-metal thermometers, whose calibration settings may change with time: it is not necessary for thermocouples or resistance bulbs, whose calibration is a function of the accuracy of manufacture and of the metallurgical properties of the materials from which they are made. Different error tolerances or 'deviations' are allowed under standards laid down by national bodies for manufacture, and these tolerances are also dependent on the temperatures at which the sensor is used.

CHAPTER 7

Transmission of Measured Data

7.1 INTRODUCTION

The methods of measuring plant or process variables described in the earlier chapters all produce some form of impulse which represents the measured value. This impulse may be a change of pressure in a fluid, a change of position of a float or diaphragm or other mechanism, or an electrical voltage or current. Whatever it is, the impulse is made to operate some form of indicating or recording mechanism located close to the point of measurement. There are considerable difficulties in extending the impulse lines over any significant distance in the case of fluid and electrical impulses, including expense, risk of spillage of flammable liquids and electrical safety. In the case of mechanical impulse there is no question of transmission at all. In the days when control mechanisms and measurement indication/recording were located close to the operating location on the plant, there was no problem in most cases, but with increase in size and complexity of plant and the consequent centralisation of both indication/recording and control, it became essential to devise a convenient method to transmit measurement data over much greater distances. This need led to the design of the 'transducer' or 'transmitter', in both pneumatic and electronic forms.

The transducer is a device which generates an 'analog' of the measured value in a form which is convenient for transmission. For instance, if the pressure in a pipe containing air is varied in proportion to the movement of a Bourdon tube, so that the same pressure always corresponds with a given position of the Bourdon tube, then the pressure of the air in the pipe is said to be the analog of the position of the Bourdon tube, and therefore of the pressure measured by the Bourdon tube. The pipe carrying the air can be extended over large distances in order to transmit this 'analog signal' to some remote location such as a central control room. Compressed air is relatively cheap and thus, provided that the pressures chosen to represent the measured value are not so great as to require expensive high pressure piping or so small that they are difficult to measure at the receiving end, this method of transmission is relatively cheap. In practice a pressure of 1 bar is chosen to correspond to the maximum measured value and multi-core tubes of plastic material are often used to reduce the cost over long distances as shown in Fig. 7.1. Electrical analog transmission is used with

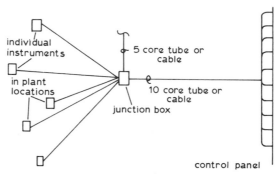

individual
instruments

5 core tube or
cable

in plant
locations

10 core tube or
cable

junction box

control panel

Fig. 7.1.

electronic instruments employing multi-core cables in the same way as multi-core tubes for pneumatic transmission. An electric current of 20 mA has now become the almost universal standard to represent maximum measured value, because this is easily measured at the receiving end and is not so large as to require heavy and expensive cables or to make unreasonable difficulties in achieving electrical safety in flammable atmospheres (this subject will be dealt with in Section 7.14).

7.2 ANALOG REPRESENTATION OF MEASURED VALUE

For a number of reasons it is not convenient to represent the minimum of the measuring range by either zero pressure or zero current in the analog form; neither is it necessary or even reasonable to do so, since the minimum of a measurement range can be any value, e.g. measurement range 50 to 150 bar pressure. Thus, any value can be chosen to represent measurement 'zero'. In the case of pneumatic analog representation it would be very difficult to 'empty' the transmission pipes of air so that the pressure was exactly zero gauge pressure. To try to measure 'zero' in this way is like trying to find out when a tank is empty using level measurement. In the same way it is not practicable to reduce the electric current in an electronic circuit to zero as transistors take current under all conditions. For these reasons a 'live' zero of 20 % of the maximum value is used, and the analog signal can therefore exceed maximum and also decrease below minimum measured values during operation, making it possible to be sure that a reading of maximum or minimum on the measuring range is genuine (Fig. 7.2).

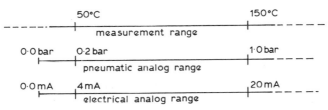

Fig. 7.2.

It is in fact possible to build an electronic transducer which generates an analog signal with a non-live zero, but only if the power supply is taken to the transducer. This has two disadvantages: first, in addition to the two conductors required to carry the signal current, two additional conductors are required to carry the power supply; secondly, it is almost impossible to make the transducer safe to use in flammable or explosive atmospheres because the electric power cannot be limited to safe levels (i.e. levels which cannot cause a spark to dissipate sufficient energy to cause ignition). Unlike pneumatic transducers, which always have a live zero, many early electronic transducers do not. However, 4–20 mA is now almost a universal standard. There is another advantage to the 4–20 mA range in that,

$$\frac{20}{4} = 5 = \frac{1}{0 \cdot 2}$$

so that conversion of an electronic analog signal to a pneumatic analog or the reverse is simple.

7.3 PRINCIPLE OF PNEUMATIC TRANSMISSION

When the need arose to transmit measured value signals to remote locations such as central control rooms, early solutions were based on

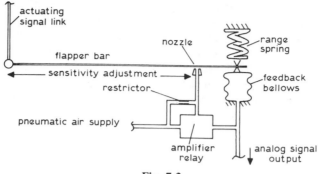

Fig. 7.3.

adapting existing local indicating or recording instruments rather than on a totally new design of instrument. Thus, since the existing instruments were designed to produce an output in the form of movement of an indicator pointer or recorder pen, the transmitting mechanism was designed to convert mechanical *motion* to a pneumatic analog signal as shown in Fig. 7.3.

This type of transducer mechanism is called 'motion balance' for the following reason. Motion of the actuating signal link brings the 'flapper' closer to or further away from the nozzle: relative movement of only 0·02 mm increases the pressure in the pipe behind the nozzle by the full range of 0·8 bar, because it obstructs the air flow through the nozzle (the nozzle is only a small hole and air flows through it at high speed). This increased pressure expands the feedback bellows, moving the flapper in the opposite direction until the higher pressure in the bellows is in balance with the spring force. The actual increase in pressure which corresponds to a given *movement* of the actuating link depends on the spring 'rate' and the position of the nozzle between the two pivots (one at the actuating link connection and the other at the range spring). This type of mechanism is called a negative feedback servo mechanism, and it provides very accurate and repeatable correspondence between the input (the position of the actuating link) and the output (the analog signal).

7.4 AMPLIFIER RELAYS

The function of the amplifier relay is to greatly increase the *flow* of air (not the pressure), so that the speed at which the feedback servo action responds is very fast. The flow rate of air through the nozzle is very small and the time it would take for a change in this flow rate to 'fill' the capacity of the bellows and the transmission pipelines would be far too long in practice. The relay (shown in Fig. 7.4) operates as described below.

In equilibrium (or steady state) the pressure behind the nozzle will be such that the flow of air through the restriction is exactly equal to that through the nozzle. If the flapper moves towards the nozzle, reducing the flow, this pressure will increase, as the air flowing out of the nozzle will then be less than that flowing in through the restriction. The increase of

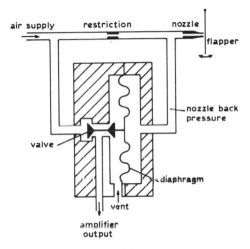

Fig. 7.4. Continuous bleed relay, direct acting.

pressure will move the thin diaphragm to the left and restrict the flow of air which is passing through the left-hand chamber to the exhaust port through the conical valve. Air flows freely to the output to 'fill' the feedback bellows and transmission pipes until the pressure in these has risen sufficiently to partially restore the thin diaphragm to its original position—negative feedback servo action. Hence, the relay itself operates by negative feedback servo action and forms part of the 'motion-balance transmitter mechanism' which also operates on the negative feedback servo principle. The diagram in Fig. 7.5 shows how the transmitter mechanism is added to an existing indicating mechanism.

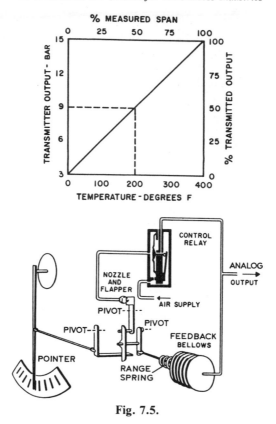

Fig. 7.5.

7.5 FORCE-BALANCE TRANSDUCERS (PNEUMATIC)

In more recent times transducers have been designed which are not indicating or recording instruments; these are known as 'blind' transmitters. Because there is no need to operate a pointer or pen over an indicator scale or recording chart, these blind transducers can be designed on a different principle known as 'force balance' (local indication can still be provided by pressure indicators or milliammeters which measure the analog signal value). Negative feedback servo action is still used to generate an analog representation of the measured value with precision and speed of response, but the impulse *force* is used, not a movement generated by this force through a mechanical mechanism, which often introduces error in the form of lost motion, friction, etc.

It can be seen by comparing Fig. 7.6 with Fig. 7.3 that a very small movement of the beam at the measurement impulse end will be required to cause an increase in pressure at the analog signal output. It can also be seen that the impulse force is opposed by the force generated in the bellows by the analog pressure—hence, the name force balance. It should also be noted that the feedback movement of the bellows does not serve to increase the movement required at the measurement impulse end as it does in the case of the motion-balance mechanism.

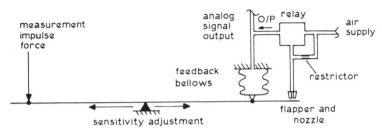

Fig. 7.6.

Probably the most commonly used force-balance transducer is the differential pressure (DP) transducer shown diagrammatically in Fig. 7.7. The force bar transfers the force developed by the capsule through the flexible seal between the process and the environment (using the seal as a fulcrum as shown in Fig. 7.7(a)) and onto the lever arm which carries the feedback bellows via the 'flexure strap'. The sensitivity adjustment shown in Fig. 7.6 takes the form of the knurled nut, which allows the span of the transducer to be altered to suit a wide variety of applications. The 'zero adjustment spring' holds this fulcrum against the frame of the instrument as well as allowing zero to be adjusted.

The instrument shown in Fig. 7.8 is a force-balance blind transducer using a liquid-filled measurement system to transmit temperature. Note that the relative positions of input force, feedback bellows and flapper/nozzle are the same as in Fig. 7.6: compare this with the relative positions on the DP cell above.

An interesting example of a force-balance transducer is to be found in the target flow rate meter shown in Fig. 7.9. This can be regarded as an orifice plate meter in which the 'hole' and the 'plate' have been interchanged. The target causes a restriction and the difference in upstream and downstream pressure acts across this to provide a force which is proportional to the

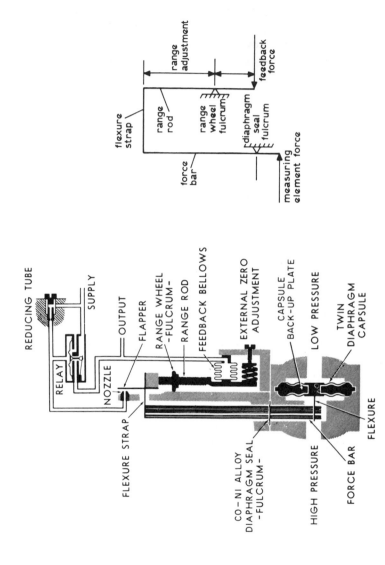

Fig. 7.7. Differential pressure transducer (DP cell).

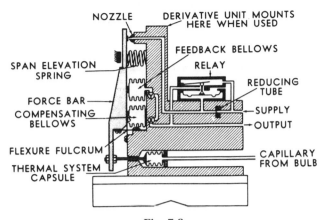

Fig. 7.8.

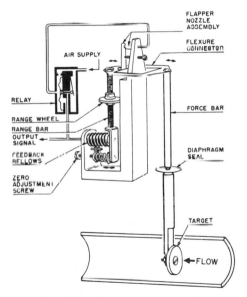

Fig. 7.9. Target flow transmitter.

square of the flow, just as the differential pressure across an orifice plate is proportional to the square of the flow rate. The force acts through a force bar in the same way as the force developed by the capsule in the DP cell; the rest of the mechanism is also virtually the same. The target flow meter is interesting as an example of a measurement device which would not be possible without the principles of force-balance negative feedback servo action.

There are many examples of force-balance pneumatic measurement systems, but they all have in common the fact that indication or recording can only be achieved by measurement of the analog pressure, i.e. the transducers are blind. This is no disadvantage when remote central control rooms are used to locate all indicators, recorders and controllers, and local indicators are often added as additional 'readouts'. In fact, one advantage of blind transmitters is that any reasonable number of indicators or recorders can be added to any transmitter.

7.6 FORCE-BALANCE TRANSDUCERS (ELECTRONIC)

Electronic transducers operate in exactly the same way as pneumatic transducers; however, the analog signal generating mechanism consists of a negative feedback electrical servo system as shown in Fig. 7.10. A power

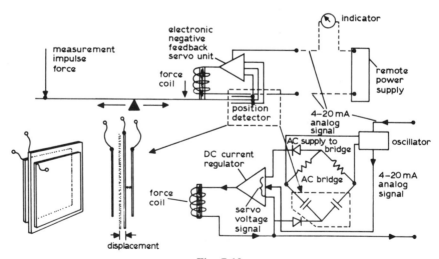

Fig. 7.10.

supply located in a remote position (usually an electrically safe area) provides a regulated voltage at one end of the two wire current analog circuit, and supplies current in the range 4–20 mA according to the impedance of the transducer. This impedance is made up of two constant elements, the inductance of the 'force coil' and that of the oscillator, together with a variable impedance, the DC current regulator unit. The AC current generated by the oscillator (from power drawn from the analog DC current circuit—hence, the need for the 'live' zero) is fed to a bridge circuit, two elements of which are the differential plate capacitance shown in the diagram. Increase in measurement impulse force causes the centre plate to move towards the upper plate and away from the lower one, unbalancing the bridge and raising the voltage fed to the DC current regulator. The impedance of the DC current regulator is reduced, increasing the current in the analog circuit and hence the force exerted by the force coil, which opposed the measurement impulse force. The position of the centre plate of the differential capacitance is thus restored almost to its original position by negative feedback servo action in exactly the same way as the flapper and nozzle are in the pneumatic transducer. The voltage generated by the bridge and therefore the change in analog current and the force exerted by the force coil for a small movement of the centre plate is much greater than that required to restore it, just as the pressure generated in the feedback bellows of the pneumatic version is much greater than is needed to restore the flapper to its original position. The feedback amplification factor (or gain) is thus very great, ensuring that the final movement of the flapper or the capacitance centre plate is extremely small.

Other devices are used by some manufacturers as position detectors, e.g. the phase sensitive detector shown in diagrammatic form in Fig. 7.11. Like the differential capacitor, it requires an AC power supply, but will produce quite a high voltage output for a very small movement.

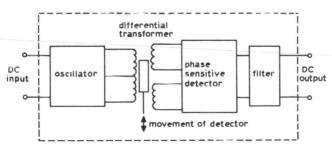

Fig. 7.11.

7.7 NON-FORCE-BALANCE TRANSDUCERS

The advantage of the force-balance principle is that the characteristics of the amplifier are not important; the current developed in the force coil or the pressure in the feedback bellows produces a force which is such as to balance the force applied by the measurement sensor at all times, by servo feedback. The relationship between the measured value and the analog signal current or pressure is not subject to drift and is repeatable within $\pm 0{\cdot}1\%$ of span. However, it is not always possible to apply the force-balance principle to the generation of analog signals, as the impulse produced by some measurement sensors is not a force. Obvious examples are thermocouple and RTB temperature sensors: it will be recalled from Chapter 6 that high measurement accuracy is obtained by the use of a potentiometer, and generation of an analog signal from such an instrument would necessitate a motion-balance mechanism. The lost motion in pivots, etc., would degrade the accuracy obtained by using a potentiometer. The variable voltage impulse generated by a thermocouple, or (together with a constant voltage supply) a resistance element, cannot be transmitted over normal cables without considerable loss of measurement accuracy, and so a transmitter is required. The voltage is amplified and can then be used to generate a 4–20 mA analog without serious error; however, unlike a force-balance mechanism the relationship between measured value and analog signal current is very dependent on the gain of the amplifier. This must not therefore change with ambient temperature or simply the age of the components.

To avoid this a 'differential' amplifier is used, the circuit of which is shown in Fig. 7.12. As the voltage on the base of the left-hand transistor increases, the current through the emitter/collector from the positive to the

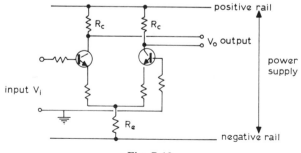

Fig. 7.12.

negative rail increases. The output is the voltage between this collector and the collector of the right-hand transistor; because the current through the left-hand transistor, and therefore its collector resistance, has increased whilst that through the right-hand transistor and resistance has not, the output voltage will increase. However, any change in either the transistors or resistors owing to ambient temperature variation or ageing will be the same provided: (1) they are matched to start with; (2) they are mounted on the same heat sink; and (3) they are of identical construction. Thus, such amplifiers are not significantly subject to drift. Several such stages of amplification may be used in one transmitter, and today such amplifiers are available in silicon chip form.

In addition to thermocouple and RTB transmitters, high stability amplification of an electrical impulse is used to generate analog signals from other sensors which do not produce a force or pressure impulse. For example, the differential pressure sensor shown in Fig. 7.13 operates on the principle of the differential capacitor which is used as the position detector in the force-balance transmitter. Increase in pressure at one end of the capsule with respect to the other causes the sensing diaphragm to move nearer to one of the fixed plates and thus further away from the other. This produces a change in voltage in the bridge circuit in exactly the same way as

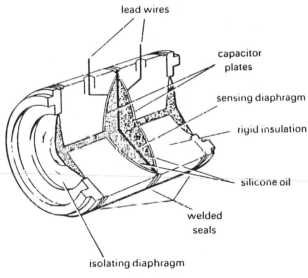

Fig. 7.13.

in the position detector; this is then amplified to generate a change in analog current. However, there is no feedback system and the amplifier must have a stable gain if the errors between the analog and the true measured value are not to be large.

7.8 DIGITAL TRANSMITTERS

The analog transmitters described so far all require an impulse input from the measurement sensor, either in the form of a mechanical force or an electrical voltage. Some important methods of measurement, such as the wire and pulley level measurement system, produce neither: nor would it be possible to translate the long movement of the wire or the many revolutions of the drum into a force or voltage with any accuracy. For such applications a digital representation of the measurement is both more appropriate (easily displayed) and much more accurate. The shaft of the drum is fitted with an 'encoder disc' (Fig. 7.14).

Fig. 7.14.

A number of light sources shine through the clear portions of the disc or are blocked by the dark portions, as shown diagrammatically in Fig. 7.15. As the disc rotates an amount equal to the distance between the outermost markings, one or more of these light sources is either blocked or uncovered. In a corresponding set of photosensors each photosensor produces a voltage or does not according to whether the light source with which they

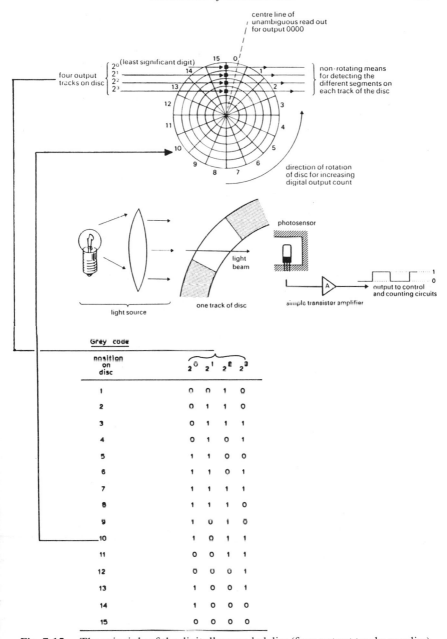

Fig. 7.15. The principle of the digitally encoded disc (four output tracks per disc).

are associated is blocked or not. Thus, for any position of the disc there is a unique set of outputs which is a coded description of the position. Measurement discrimination depends on the number of markings in the outermost band and the number of revolutions the drum makes over the measurement range. The number of markings in the outer band depends on how many bands (how many light sources) there are in the transmitter. Any code can be used, provided each position to be discriminated has a unique combination of light sources obscured or not, but in practice the code which is most common is the 'Grey' code shown for four lamps (Fig. 7.15; the disc in Fig. 7.14 is for 10 lights) which is devised so that as the disc turns only one light changes at a time. The coded outputs are decoded by electronic decoding 'logic' and drive a digital display of the measured value.

7.9   TELEMETRY

So far in this chapter measurement transmission over distances up to about half a kilometre has been considered, i.e. the distance from a plant mounted transmitter to the central control room. However, in some cases, e.g. pipelines, measurement data have to be transmitted over much longer distances—sometimes many miles. The cost of pneumatic tubing or single electrical cables would be unacceptable, as would the pressure loss or voltage drop over such distances. Other means have to be found which are cheaper, and these are generally referred to as telemetry.

If, as is often the case in process industries, it is not necessary to transmit data quickly, a simple method called pulse duration modulation is used; a tone on a telephone line, for instance, can be switched on and off during a given period of time which is made to represent the full scale value of the measurement. Thus, if the tone is switched on for the first half of this time interval and off during the second half, the measured value is one-half full scale (Fig. 7.16(a)).

Another similar method is called pulse position modulation. Again, an interval is chosen to represent full scale, but in this system a pulse of short duration is generated after an interval of time which is the same fraction of the full interval as the measured value is of full scale (Fig. 7.16(b)).

These methods require only simple converters to generate the pulse signals, but are only suitable for relatively slow data transmission over distances of a few kilometres. In the same way that processes store energy and thus cause delays (for instance, heat exchange) so also do transmission lines store electrical energy in the capacitance and inductance they

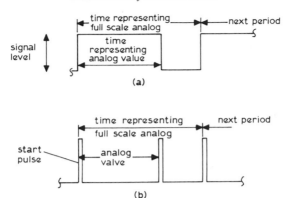

(a)

(b)

Fig. 7.16.

represent. The signal pulse is in fact a change of energy; some of this energy is stored temporarily in the transmission, rather like a bucket of water poured quickly into a bath is stored temporarily and only flows away down the waste pipe gradually. Just as the water reaches the outside drain more slowly than it is poured into the bath in the first place, so the energy of the pulse reaches the receiving end of the transmission line more slowly than it is generated at the transmitting end (Fig 7,17). It is difficult to be sure exactly when the pulse begins, and as a result errors may occur.

Fig. 7.17.

If the analog signal is converted into a digital code this rounding off of the pulse leading and trailing edges matters very much less. In fact, provided the receiving equipment can reliably detect the presence or absence of a pulse, there will be no loss of accuracy at all! Data values can be represented as a group of bits (binary digits) each of which has a value 1 or 0 to represent the binary equivalent of the value to be transmitted. Each bit is then transmitted over the 'data link' or transmission line during a fixed interval of time as shown in Fig. 7.18.

To do this the receiving equipment must be synchronised with the

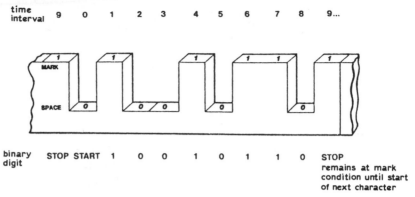

Fig. 7.18.

transmitting equipment so that it recognises the intervals of time correctly. This is achieved in one of two ways:

1. Each 'byte' or group of bits will comprise a fixed number of time intervals. At the beginning of each byte the transmitter will always send a '1' or 'mark' signal. The receiving equipment will be designed to start its timing of the intervals making up the next 'byte' as soon as it detects the end of this mark (which is not part of the data). Its own internal timer will be accurate enough to determine the end of each interval throughout the byte, at the end of which it will receive a further synchronising 'mark'. This is known as 'asynchronous' transmission (Fig. 7.19(a)).

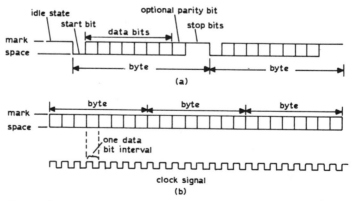

Fig. 7.19. Asynchronous (a) and synchronous (b) transmissions.

2. Clock pulses are transmitted together with the data bytes over a separate channel, so that the receiving equipment always operates in synchronism with the transmitter. This is known as synchronous transmission (Fig. 7.19(b))

7.10 ERROR DETECTION

Digitally coded signals can be transmitted over longer distances, faster with less loss of signal accuracy than pulse duration or position signals. At very fast transmission speeds it may become difficult to detect a pulse, and errors will begin to be made by the receiver. So that these errors may be detected, the whole message is sometimes repeated and compared at the receiver with a recording of the first transmission. This halves the speed of transmission, however, and is rarely done. An alternative method, known as 'parity coding', consists of adding an extra pulse to every data 'message' that contains an odd number of pulses so that every 'message' will have an even number of pulses. If then a pulse is missed by the receiver, the number of pulses will be odd and an error is detected. Error detection is actually used to find the fastest transmission speed possible over any system; the system is then usually operated a little more slowly to avoid errors.

Often, when data is to be transmitted over a long distance, only one transmission channel can be provided economically and the measurements of a number of variables must be 'multiplexed'. This is done in one of two ways. In one the data is transmitted in a fixed sequence, one variable after the other, and when all have been sent, transmission begins again with the new value of the first variable. If there are a lot of variables the response time for any one (that is the time interval between successive transmissions) is very long. This is overcome in modern systems by a technique of sampling the process signal and reconstructing it at the receiving end. This technique depends on the telemetry system being able to transmit at very high rates which are possible because of advances which have been made in the design of the communication channels themselves (telephone lines, line of sight micro-wave radio links, etc). The technique of sampling a process variable measurement and reconstructing it is based on the 'sampling theorem' which proves that a sinusoidal waveform can be *totally* defined by a sampling rate of twice the frequency of the waveform. Since *all* waveforms (without exception) can be 'decomposed' into a number of sinusoids of different frequencies and amplitudes, it follows that the sample rate has only to be at least twice the frequency of the highest frequency component of any signal, to fully describe it. In other words, provided this rule is kept, there will be *no* loss of accuracy in the use of the sample and reconstruct technique (though there may still be loss of accuracy in transmission). There is of course a snag in the practical application of this simple rule—it is not usually easy to determine what the highest frequency component sinusoid of any given signal is. Nevertheless, an estimate can usually be made and the sampling rate is chosen to give, not two, but say eight samples per cycle of this estimated component in order to ensure no loss of accuracy. This can be seen from Fig. 7.20 (if an inadequate sampling rate is used, the data in (B) can be reconstructed incorrectly to look like the data in (A)).

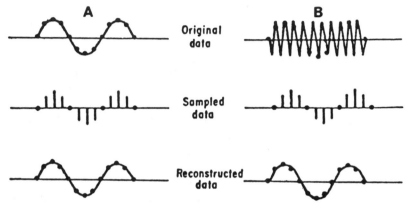

Fig. 7.20. (A) Adequate sampling (8 samples/Hz); (B) bad sampling (>2 samples/Hz).

Using this technique, a number of process variables can be sampled at intervals which, though short enough to ensure eight samples per cycle of the highest frequency component of the 'fastest' variable, are, nevertheless, long enough in comparison with the transmission rate of the communication channel to allow a number of samples of other variables to be transmitted between successive samples of the same variable. In this way the sampled data describing each process variable is 'interleaved' with that describing other variables in such a way as to utilise the very fast transmission rates possible with modern communication equipment. The number of variables to each communication channel is a function of the sample rate (dictated by how fast the fastest process variable changes) and the communication system speed. Pulse duration, pulse position or digital coding techniques are all used with this sampled data technique, though digital coding provides the fastest transmission rate.

The second way in which a single transmission channel can be used to transmit several process variables is known as frequency division multiplexing, whilst that already described is known as time division multiplexing. The principle of frequency division multiplexing is that the frequency 'bandwidth' of the communication channel is divided up between the process variables, and the transmitters and receivers for each variable are tuned to respond only over the narrow bandwidth of the channel allocated to it in the same way that a domestic radio receiver is tuned to exclude other 'stations'. Using this technique, each variable is transmitted continuously and there is no question of loss of accuracy in the data owing to sampling; accuracy can, however, be lost in transmission as in the case of time division multiplexing and, again, digital encoding is found to provide the fastest transmission rates. Perhaps surprisingly at first sight, time division multiplexing usually provides a faster transmission rate than frequency division; this is because the full 'bandwidth' is used in the former technique making faster transmission possible, without unacceptable distortion of pulse, than is possible over a narrow bandwidth channel such as is allocated in frequency division multiplexing.

In some systems there will be more than one channel for communication and some channels may be carrying less than their maximum capacity of data at any time whilst others are overloaded. 'Intelligent' time division multiplexing is a method whereby data is assigned to asynchronous communication channels on an 'activity' basis. In such a system the data gathering and communication 'channels' are separate and when over a short period of time the rate of data gathered from all sources exceeds the total capacity of the communication channels some is stored temporarily in 'buffer' storage locations.

7.11 PROTOCOL, MULTIPLEXES AND MODEMS

By now it will be realised that the transmission over telemetry systems involves a number of tasks or functions not required of the simpler analog instrument data links—data must be gathered, sampled, coded into digital form, stored and allocated to an appropriate communication channel. In addition, parity bits, stop/start bits, etc., have to be added and transmission of 'packets' of data organised in a serial manner in contrast to the parallel nature of the data gathering. At the receiving end, most of these functions have to be carried out in reverse and means must be provided to synchronise the receiving and transmitting functions. The electronic equipment required to achieve all this is generally referred to as data transmitting and communication equipment and comprises multiplexers (MUX) and modulating/demodulating units (MODEMS). The former carry out the functions of data sampling, gathering, storage and allocation, whilst the latter is responsible for organising and controlling the actual data transmission onto and off the communication link (be the latter a twisted pair of wires or a radio link).

The operation of these units demands that certain processes are synchronised in such a way that one piece of equipment is aware of what another is doing and is prepared to perform its function at the right moment. This is generally achieved by what is called 'handshaking' techniques performed by digital logic circuits. The specification of the *functions* of these logic circuits is referred to as 'protocol' which is a very good analogy to the well-defined initiatives and responses required in international diplomacy. Such 'protocol' together with physical definitions, such as voltage levels, cable capacity and inductance, etc., are embodied in the standards of such bodies as the International Telegraph and Telephone Consultative Committee (CCITT) which is part of the International Telecommunications Union (ITU) in Geneva. This body regulates data transmission standards in the western world outside the USA, whilst the Electronics Industries Association (EIA) has the equivalent function in the USA.

7.12 'NOISE' IN SIGNAL TRANSMISSION SYSTEMS

Electrical energy can readily be transferred from various sources in any process plant into cables carrying instrumentation signals by induction, capacitance or directly by reason of differences in 'ground' or 'earth' potential. Such unwanted electrical energy transfer causes errors in measurement, particularly when the energy in the signal is small, e.g. in thermocouple circuits. Such transferred energy is referred to as 'noise'.

The most obvious source of 'noise' is the capacitive or inductive coupling between any two pieces of wire, which exists when they lie beside each other (in parallel) as, for instance, when cables are laid together in a cable tray or conduit. If cables carrying power to electric motors, for example, are laid beside those carrying low energy signals, the energy transferred into the latter can be very significant when compared to the energy in the signal, and can therefore cause large errors in the measurement recorded or indicated at the receiving end. Power and signal cables should therefore never be run in parallel unless they are spaced well apart; and never in the same tray or conduit. However, even when proper precautions are taken errors will occur in signal circuits if the level of energy in the signal is low (turbine and magnetic flow meter signals, for instance). This is the reason why electrical output sensor signals are transduced into an analog signal for transmission over any significant distance (such as the distance between a plant measurement location and the central control room). This is in keeping with the original reason for developing pneumatic transducers—to make possible transmission of signals derived from sensors with mechanical outputs. Capacitive coupling can be largely eliminated or at least greatly reduced by a 'screened' cable, provided the screen is correctly grounded. The 'screen' surrounds the conductors carrying the signal, as shown in Fig. 7.21, and is grounded only at one end; the capacitive coupling existing between the power cable and the screen is much greater than that between the power cable and the signal conductors and drains away to earth any current induced in the screen, thus shielding the signal conductors. In order

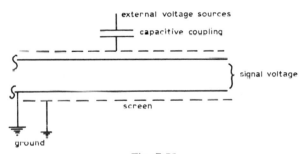

Fig. 7.21.

to reduce capacitive coupling with the signal conductors to a minimum, there should be no gaps in the screen; aluminium/milar sheath has been found to be more effective than the more traditional copper braid screen. Inductive coupling between power cables and signal conductors can be reduced greatly by twisting the pairs of signal conductors (Fig. 7.22(a)) or by a screen of electromagnetically permeable material (steel or iron) which will divert the magnetic field from the signal conductors (Fig. 7.22(b)). By twisting the signal conductors the voltage induced in adjacent sections is of

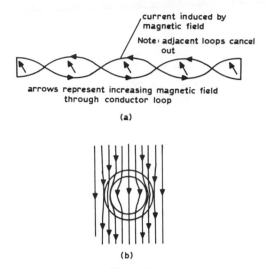

current induced by
magnetic field

Note: adjacent loops cancel
out

arrows represent increasing magnetic field
through conductor loop

(a)

(b)

Fig. 7.22.

opposite polarity and largely cancels out—hence, little or no current flow is induced.

Energy transfer into the signal conductors by capacitive or inductive coupling is only possible in the case of alternating current and any residual 'noise' in the signal transmission system when the precautions described above have been taken can be filtered out by adding capacitive/resistive delay into the signal circuit, provided that the correspondingly slower response of the measurement system is acceptable. Energy can enter a measurement signal circuit in both alternating and direct current form as a direct result of differences in ground potential between the geographical locations of the two ends of the circuit, as shown in Fig. 7.23 for a thermocouple circuit.

This type of energy transfer is best minimised by using 'differential input'

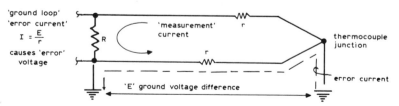

'ground loop'
'error current'

$$I = \frac{E}{r}$$

causes 'error'
voltage

'measurement'
current

r

r

thermocouple
junction

error current

'E' ground voltage difference

Fig. 7.23. (r represents the resistance of the conductors.)

receiving equipment as shown in Fig. 7.24. The resistive load of the receiving device (in the case of DC current systems) is grounded at its centre point rather than at either the negative or positive 'rail', as is usual in most electrical circuitry (e.g. car batteries). Provided the receiver circuit is designed as a 'high impedance' device, only a small error will occur (high impedance usually means about $1\,M\Omega$ at least and the current induced across $1\,M\Omega$ by $10\,V = 10^{-5}\,A$).

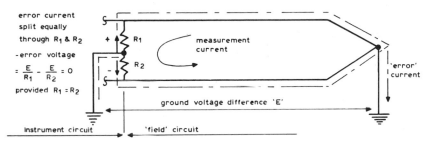

Fig. 7.24.

One other source of noise should be mentioned before leaving the subject of 'noise'—crosstalk. This is the transfer of energy between two signal conductor pairs in a multicore cable in cases where the signal is of an alternating current type (e.g. turbine meter 'pulse repetition rate' analog signals representing flow rate). The conductors are inside the capacitive coupling shield of the multicore cable and, although the energy of the signals will be very much less than that carried in a power cable, the two signal conductor pairs are very close together and of necessity parallel over the whole length of the cable. As a result, energy is transferred between the signal pairs as any telephone subscriber is aware (hence, the name crosstalk). In such cases the only solution is to use single pair screened cables or to screen each pair within a multicore cable individually. (Such cables are available but are very expensive and should only be specified if the danger of 'crosstalk' errors is real.)

In recent times powerful 'line of sight' radio transmitters have been used more and more for communication channels for telemetry and for radio communications between remote plant locations (e.g. pipeline pump stations, oil rigs, etc.). The energy in such transmitted signals can easily be transferred into any signal cable if this happens to form a suitable receiving aerial: since this is inductive coupled energy transfer the solution is the same as that outlined above; it is recognising the problem that is sometimes difficult.

7.13 POWER SUPPLY

All transducers require a power supply in order to be able to generate an analog signal. Power is always supplied to a pneumatic transducer in the field but electronic transducers can utilise the power implicit in the 'suppressed zero' (4 mA in the case of a 4–20 mA signal) to operate any electronic circuitry, thus reducing the number of conductors required between the central control room and the field-mounted transducer.

Pneumatic power is generated at a pressure of about 6 bar by a reciprocating or piston type compressor. The air *must* be entirely free of any trace of oil which would quickly stop all flapper/nozzle mechanisms from working. For this reason instrument air compressor sets usually use carbon impregnated piston rings to avoid the need for cylinder lubrication. The air must also be free of moisture in liquid droplet form *at the point of use*. The temperature of air rises as it is compressed and the air leaving the compressor is hot: hot air can 'carry' a greater weight of air in vapour form than cold air and so when the compressed air cools as it flows through pipes out on the plant in winter or at night moisture may condense out. In most cases the air is cooled and dried after leaving the compressor so that this does not happen but it is still good practice to slope all pneumatic instrument lines in the direction of flow and provide 'catch-pots' at all low points as shown in Fig. 7.25. This is in fact essential when compressor

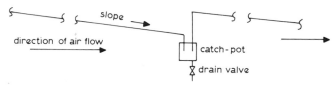

Fig. 7.25.

discharge is not cooled and dried. Close to the point of use, the compressed air is expanded to just over 1 bar (it is generated at 6 bar to minimise the size of pipe needed to distribute it around the plant), causing it to cool. Unless the air has been dried this will result in water vapour condensing and getting into the instrument. The expansion takes place in a small pressure regulator located close to the instrument (each regulator usually serves only a few instruments because it has a small capacity).

Whilst it is perfectly safe to distribute compressed air to transducers at any location around the plant, great care has to be taken when bringing electrical power into a 'hazardous area' of the plant where there is a risk of igniting flammable or explosive mixtures of air and petroleum fluids. It has in the past been the practice to enclose the instrument in a case which is constructed to be either 'flameproof' or 'explosionproof'. A flameproof enclosure is designed so that if vapour/air mixture is ignited inside the enclosure by some fault in the instrument, the flame cannot propagate to the outside and therefore cannot cause a general conflagration. An explosionproof enclosure, on the other hand, is constructed so that it can withstand the force of an explosion without rupturing (the gas space inside the enclosure is kept as small as possible to minimise the forces generated by an explosion). Neither of these methods, however, does anything to ensure that a fault in the cables connecting the transducer to the remote 'receiver' instrument (indicator, recorder, controller, etc.) does not cause either an explosion or a fire. Most electronic systems today employ the principle of 'intrinsic safety' to ensure that there can be no risk of either.

7.14 INTRINSIC SAFETY

This is a subject in its own right but it is essential that the basic requirements as they apply to 4–20 mA analog transmitters are understood. The principle of intrinsic safety is only possible in conjunction with large centralised control rooms which can be made 'safe areas'. On a refinery or other plant, where there is a risk that flammable vapours may escape, it is normal to designate areas of the plant safe, possibly dangerous or dangerous, according to the risk of such vapours existing in dangerous concentrations. A control room, regardless of where on the plant it is located, can be made safe by pressurising it to a very slight pressure; in this way it is not possible for gases or vapours to enter from outside. The supply of pressurising air *must* of course be taken from a safe area (usually at some height above the ground) and other precautions, such as high level cable and services entry (to avoid the possibility of vapour entering through cable ducts) and effective air locks at doorways, are essential.

Intrinsic safety means that the measurement and transmission (and control) system must be designed, constructed and *maintained* in such a way that it is not possible for sufficient energy to exist in that part of the system which is outside the safe area to cause ignition or explosion (on the assumption that flammable or explosive mixtures *do* exist). This in turn means that the transducers and cables must not have enough electrical inductance or capacitance to store the critical amount of energy, nor must it be possible to transfer this amount of energy into the 'hazardous area'

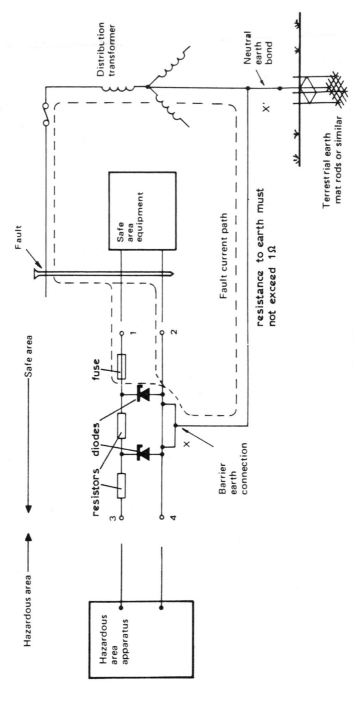

Fig. 7.26.

from the 'safe area' in an interval of time equal to that in which a spark endures. The amount of energy required to ignite a mixture of any particular gas with air is extremely small but varies with the gas or vapour. The transducers themselves must be designed to satisfy the requirements laid down by suitable national certification authorities, who have the results of considerable research into the energy of ignition to draw on. In addition 'barriers' are installed in cables leaving the 'safe area' to ensure that the energy transfer rate is limited to a safe value. These barriers which are normally of the passive type (that is, they consist only of resistors, fuses and diodes) are intended to provide a low resistance path to earth if a fault occurs in the power supply side, i.e. before the cable leaves the safe area. Figure 7.26 illustrates the principle of operation. If the current (flow of energy out of the safe area) rises, the resistances cause the voltage to rise at the diodes which conduct the energy harmlessly to earth inside the safe area. The second diode and resistor are there in case the first fail and the fuse will normally 'blow' to prevent overheating should a fault develop.

A diagram of the same circuit showing that one of the conductors in the cable to the transducer has to be connected to earth is given in Fig. 7.27. Because the receiver is connected between the earth connection at the barrier and the power supply (in order that it is located in the safe area) the

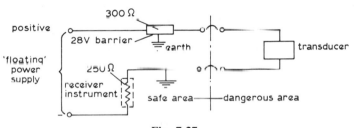

Fig. 7.27.

power supply has to be 'floating'. This means that as the current flow in the circuit (the analog signal) varies, the positive terminal of the power supply increases in voltage, whilst the negative decreases with respect to earth. This has the disadvantage that a common power supply cannot be used for a number of 'loops' which would be less expensive than a separate power supply for each.

The solution is to use two barriers as shown in Fig. 7.28. In fact the lower barrier can differ from the upper; it can have lower resistance values. Two barriers (one 28 V and one 10 V) are commonly constructed in one unit for

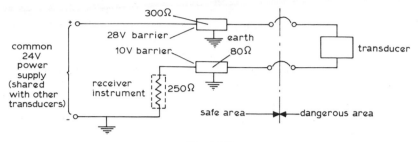

Fig. 7.28

this purpose. The disadvantage of this solution is that it limits the impedance of the transducer and some manufacturers have difficulty keeping within this constraint when designing the equipment. The reason for this is easy to see: at a maximum analog current flow of 20 mA and a supply voltage of 24 V (the 28 V barrier diodes start to conduct at about 26·5 V) the total loop resistance must not exceed

$$R = \frac{V}{I} = \frac{24}{0·02} = 1200\,\Omega$$

It can be seen from Fig. 7.28 that, excluding the transducer, the loop resistance is $250 + 80 + 300 = 630\,\Omega$, which leaves only $570\,\Omega$ for the transducer. Since the function of the transducer is to modulate (regulate) the current flow, it can be regarded simply as a variable impedance in the circuit. Thus, when a 20 mA analog current flows in the circuit, the transducer adjusts to offer an impedance of $570\,\Omega$, whilst at 4 mA current

$$\text{total } R = \frac{24}{0·004} = 6000\,\Omega$$

Hence

$$\text{transducer impedance} = 6000 - 630 = 5370\,\Omega$$

CHAPTER 8

Principles of Control

8.1 INTRODUCTION

Previous chapters have been concerned entirely with techniques of measurement of process variables and with the transmission of signals representing the measured values. Such measurement systems are essential in order that the process and the plant operations can be controlled, whether such control is carried out by the human operator or by automatic control systems. In most cases control is implemented by manipulating the position of a throttling valve in a pipeline, so as to increase or decrease a pressure, flow rate or temperature. The valve is called the 'final control element'; other final control elements can be speed control systems on pumps or prime movers, or any other device which manipulates energy or material flow. Early in the history of industrial development it was realised that it was an inefficient use of human skills for a human operator to have to set the position of the final control element to a new value every time there occurred any change in the process conditions. As a result mechanisms were developed which could regulate a flow rate, pressure or temperature at any value the human operator set (the set or desired value) even when process conditions changed (disturbances). These mechanisms used the same feedback servo control principles that were described in Chapter 7 to match the measured value to the desired value by either opening or closing the control valve as appropriate. However, this is a much more difficult control problem because the process variable cannot usually be made to change quickly, unlike the transmission signal; care has to be taken to 'tune' the control action to suit the way the process can be made to 'respond'. Initially, these mechanisms were constructed locally—they developed before signal transmission—as an extension of non-transmitting (impulse indication) instruments. Later, as signal transmission was

153

developed and process plants grew too large for the operators to control them from local scattered control rooms, the control mechanisms were transferred to a centralised control room remote from the final control elements so that the operator no longer had to go out on the plant to adjust a flow rate, temperature or pressure setting.

The term process control covers *all* aspects of the control of each process and the operation of the plant within which the processes take place. In a modern process plant, such as a refinery, this always includes many of the control mechanisms described above. It is very important to realise that the human operator still controls the process, with the help of these mechanisms, though it is also true to say that it is no longer possible to operate any modern process plant without many such mechanisms. These mechanisms *do not automate the plant*; development of automated plant is just beginning. The design, construction and operation of such mechanisms is control technology.

8.2 NATURAL REGULATION

The system shown in Fig. 8.1(a) will respond to a change in the inflow rate in a stable manner; the level will change until the hydrostatic head *h* is again just sufficient to overcome the resistance of the valve at an outflow rate exactly equal to the new inflow rate. In other words, the system will come to another state of equilibrium without the need for any control action at all. Such a system is said to have natural regulation. Only if it is necessary to maintain a constant level is any form of control necessary (Fig. 8.1(b)).

The system shown in Fig. 8.2, however, does not exhibit natural regulation. If there is any change in the inflow to the system (Fig. 8.2(a)) the tank will either empty or overflow eventually; the system is unstable

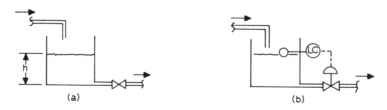

(a)   (b)

Fig. 8.1.

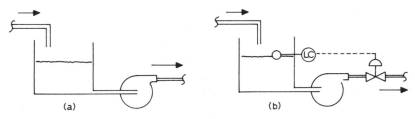

Fig. 8.2.

without control. It is obviously necessary to add a control loop as shown in Fig. 8.2(b) in order to operate the system at all. Obviously the control action is more difficult to define in the second case.

8.3 ON–OFF CONTROL ACTION

Control action must oppose the disturbance: the simplest control action is 'on–off'. In this form either the final control element is in one extreme position or the other (fully open or fully closed), according to whether the error has a positive or negative value (Fig. 8.3). However, this form of control action is always too great because it is not proportional to the size of the error, but always a maximum. Even more important, delays in the

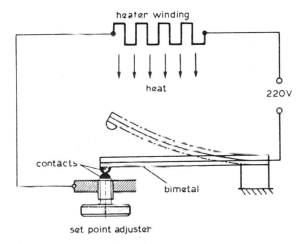

Fig. 8.3.

system will nearly always ensure that changes of control action are 'out of phase' with changes in the controlled variable. Control action will only be applied at all after an error has developed. This combination of excessive control action and poor timing makes on–off control action suitable only for the simplest and least critical applications, such as space heating, where the process exhibits very considerable self-regulation and large capacity.

8.4 PROPORTIONAL CONTROL ACTION

Nearly all industrial control is of the 'modulating' type, in which a final control element 'manipulates' the process variable (usually flow rate of a fluid) to proportion the control action to the size of the error. Control action is thus never excessive in magnitude although it may still be out of phase with the process disturbance. Two examples illustrate this principle.

Example 1: gas pressure regulator (Fig. 8.4)

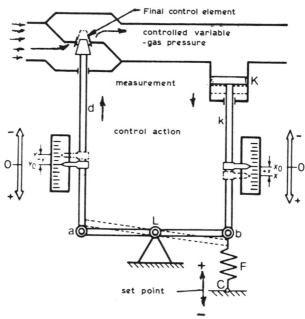

Fig. 8.4. Gas pressure regulator. Greater gas pressure causes smaller valve opening and therefore reduces flow of gas. Spring force (F) opposes the gas pressure. 'Set' pressure is increased or decreased by moving 'C' up or down to adjust spring force.

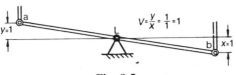

Fig. 8.5.

A unique value of the correcting variable (y) corresponds to every value of the controlled variable (x). The movement of the graduated indicator is equal on both sides when the pivot (L) of the lever is exactly in the middle of the lever (Fig. 8.5). If the pivot is moved to the right, small movements of the actuating piston result in larger movements of the final control element; hence, proportionally greater control action (Fig. 8.6). This effect is called 'amplification'.

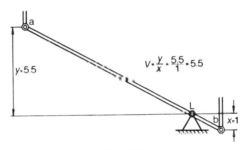

Fig. 8.6.

The amplification factor (V) is determined by the choice of the position of the fulcrum (L). As can be seen in Fig. 8.6 the factor may be greater or less than unity.

$$V = \frac{y}{x}$$

Displacing the fulcrum to the left means that large x values will yield small y values. Strictly speaking, it is not a matter of amplification here, but rather of attenuation (Fig. 8.7).

Fig. 8.7.

Example 2: level control (Fig. 8.8)

If the lever arms *a* and *b* in Fig. 8.8 are of equal length, the final control element will move 1 cm when the water level moves 1 cm. Thus, the maximum inflow of water will be obtained when the final control element is wide open, whilst flow will cease altogether when it has moved a distance equal to the inside diameter of the pipe. Hence, the control range is equal to the diameter of the pipe; in other words, control action varies from maximum to minimum when the level in the tank varies by an amount equal to the diameter of the pipe. If, however, the fulcrum point is moved to left or right so that the ratio of *a* and *b* is less than or more than unity, the range of level change corresponding to full control action will be greater or less, respectively. The ratio *a/b* is called the *proportional action factor* of the control mechanism.

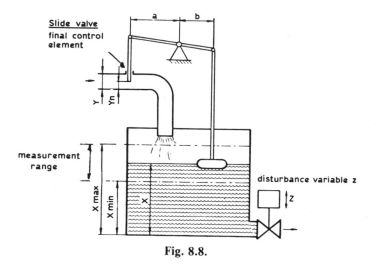

Fig. 8.8.

8.5 INTEGRAL CONTROL ACTION

Suppose that in Example 2 in the previous section the valve z is opened, increasing the outflow from the tank. If the level is to be maintained, the slide valve at the inlet (the final control element) must be opened to increase the inflow until it is equal to the outflow rate. However, in order to achieve this the float must fall sufficiently to open the slide valve enough to increase the inflow by the required amount. Therefore, when the system is restored to equilibrium, the level must of necessity be lower than before the disturbance; in other words complete regulation of the level is not possible using proportional action control. There will always be a change of controlled variable for every change in the disturbance variable, though it will be less than if there were no control mechanism (only natural regulation). The greater the proportional action factor, the less such 'offset' will be. However, if there are delays in the control loop, it may not be possible to use a high proportional action factor without causing instability and so in many systems it is necessary to define some other form of control action if offset is to be avoided.

In the system shown in Fig. 8.9 it is the voltage applied to the motor (M) which varies as the level changes in the tank; the position of the slide valve only *begins* to change when the level changes and the *rate* at which it changes is proportional to the change in voltage and therefore to the change in level. This is called 'floating' or 'integral' control action: at any

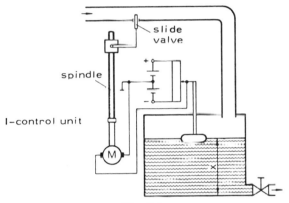

spindle

I–control unit

slide valve

Fig. 8.9.

instant the control action is the sum of the movement of the slide valve since the time when the measured value was last equal to the set point. (In mathematical terms it is the 'time integral of the errror', in exactly the same way that total flow is the time integral of the flow rate. Hence, the name 'integral action'.) Since control action continues to change whenever there is an error, it follows that, once the disturbance variable stops changing, the level will (eventually) be restored to the desired value without any offset. However, since the position of the slide valve only starts to change when the disturbance variable changes (while proportional control action is immediate), a further delay has been added to those of the process and measurement, and the danger of instability is increased.

8.6 PROPORTIONAL PLUS INTEGRAL CONTROL ACTION

It hardly needs stating that better control can be obtained by a combination of the two previous control actions. Proportional action provides an immediate correction which, provided the proportional action factor is not too large, is less likely to make the system unstable, while integral control will eventually remove the offset which cannot be avoided with proportional action alone. For this reason integral control action is often referred to as automatic reset. The two previous mechanisms are combined in the diagram given in Fig. 8.10. Control action is added at the 'summing point' but notice that the fulcrum is now at the top of the 'spindle': the proportional action factor is therefore the ratio of the lever arm from the summing point to the fulcrum over the total length of the arm a/b, and will always be less than unity for this mechanism.

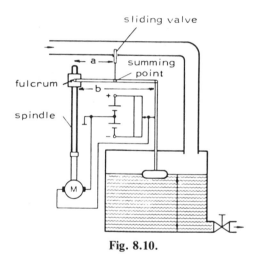

Fig. 8.10.

The rate at which the motor is driven, and therefore the rate of integration, can be varied and this is defined as the integral action factor. For convenience the integral action factor is numerically defined as the time taken for the integral control action to move the final control element the same distance that proportional action would move it for a given error, and therefore it changes with the latter. It should be appreciated that under proportional plus integral control action, when equilibrium is restored there remains no proportional action. This is because there is no longer any error.

8.7 DERIVATIVE CONTROL ACTION

Although integral control action removes the offset which is unavoidable with proportional action alone, it actually makes the possibility of instability greater, because it adds a further delay into the control loop. The possibility of instability is unavoidable in any feedback control loop because the effect of the disturbance on the measured value cannot be detected until after the delays are incurred. In order to partially overcome this problem and decrease the possibility of instability, an additional control action can be added which 'anticipates the maximum magnitude of the disturbance by increasing the proportional action factor temporarily in proportion to the rate of change of the measured value. This has the effect of increasing the control action initially, but as the error between the set point and measured value decreases the proportional action reverts to its normal magnitude. Although originally referred to as 'anticipatory control action' this is now known as 'derivative action' because the mathematical expression for the rate of change of a variable is 'the derivative'.

Derivative control action is not in fact a third independent type of action, but a way of modifying proportional action so as to reduce the disadvantage of delays around the control loop. It cannot be used independently. Derivative action, like proportional and integral action is numerically defined by the 'derivative action factor' which is the rate of change of the *process* measured value which will produce control action of the same magnitude as the normal proportional action for any given error. In order to generate derivative control action it is obviously necessary to measure not only the value of the measured value, but also its rate of change. For this reason derivative control action is not possible with the simple 'local' type of mechanism described so far; its generation will be discussed later for more complex mechanisms.

8.8 THE CLOSED LOOP

Any process control regulating mechanism or system has three essential elements:

(i)   Measurement system
(ii) Process system
(iii) Control system

Note that each of these elements is in fact a system or rather a sub-system.

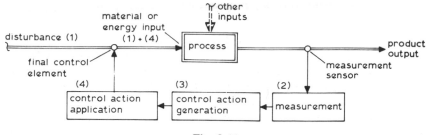

Fig. 8.11.

From the diagram of such a control system (Fig. 8.11) it can be seen that these sub-systems are arranged in a loop and the system is usually referred to as a 'control loop' for this reason. Because the system forms a loop, information about the behaviour of the process variable (pressure, flow rate, temperature, etc.) can be fed back to the control system by the measurement system and for this reason it is referred to as a 'feedback control loop'. The feedback control loop is, and probably always will be, the basic element of 'automatic process control'; it has already been stated that this is not the same thing as automated process control.

The closed loop includes the process as well as the control mechanism and measurement systems and it is essential, therefore, to consider how the process behaves before considering the behaviour of the closed loop as a whole.

Provided the process is stable, a given change in the position of the control valve (or other final control element) will, after elapse of a period referred to as the settling time, cause a change in the measured variable. The ratio of the magnitude of this change in process variable *steady state* value to the magnitude of the change in the control action which caused it is referred to as the open loop process gain. Open loop means that the controller is not operating because this is the only way in which such a ratio can be determined, since the purpose of the closed loop is to prevent change in the measured variable.

If there were no delays anywhere in the system, the settling time would be zero and, because any change in the measured variable is fed back and causes a control action which is in a direction to cancel it, there would be only a small change, dependent on the proportional action factor. The greater the product of the process gain and the proportional action factor of the control mechanism the smaller this change; in fact with zero settling time there would be no limit to this factor, the change could be reduced to very small values, and there would be no need to employ either derivative or integral control actions, since proportional control would also be instantaneous in action. Needless to say, real systems always contain delays and therefore this scenario is totally unrealistic; it is also clear that the delays in any system are *entirely* responsible for the problems of control. It is therefore essential to start by considering the nature of these delays and how they arise. For the most part the delays in the process system are beyond the control of the designer of the control system (this subject will be dealt with later), unlike the delays in the control system or mechanism, and it is therefore even more important to understand how they arise and how they affect the design of a control system.

8.9 CAUSES OF DELAY IN PROCESS SYSTEMS

Whenever material (solid, liquid or gas) or energy (heat) flows into or out of a vessel, it takes time—instantaneous transfer is contrary to the laws of physics. Thus, the level of a liquid, the pressure of a gas or the temperature of the vessel contents cannot change suddenly but are subject to delays which are dependent on the magnitude of the capacity and the resistance to the inflow of material or energy. Such delays are referred to as capacitive/resistive delays for this reason. It is a feature of such delays that the force causing transfer diminishes as equilibrium is approached, as, for instance, where the temperature of a vessel contents approaches that of the water or steam in the heating coil. For example, consider a system in which gas at a higher pressure than that inside a vessel flows into the vessel; as it does so there will be an increase of gas pressure in the vessel (Fig. 8.12). Pressure in the vessel increases until it is equal to the pressure which is forcing the gas in and at that point the pressure ceases to rise—equilibrium, or 'steady state', has been reached and no more gas will enter.

This form of response to a sudden change of flow rate, supply pressure or heating (capacitive/resistive delay) is referred to in mathematical terms as 'exponential' delay. Note that the form of the response is the same whether pressure, flow rate or temperature is the measured variable. Such delay occurs in the process whenever a vessel has to be filled with liquid or emptied, or the gas pressure increased, or the temperature of its contents raised or lowered. Similarly such delays occur in measurement when heat has to be transferred through the wall of a thermowell into a filled system or thermocouple. Exactly the same type of delay occurs when the compressed air of the pneumatic control signal is increased in pressure and flows into

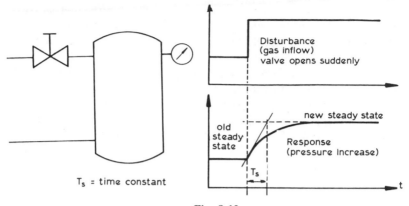

Fig. 8.12.

the large capacity of the motor of a control valve. Hence, delays of this sort are encountered in the process, measurement and in the application (rather than the generation) of control action.

Delays are also caused by the time taken for material to travel along pipes or conveyors from one place to another. This type of delay, shown in Fig. 8.13 is called 'dead time'.

All delays in either process or measurement are of one of these two types. Often, however, several delays are combined 'in series' (one after another)

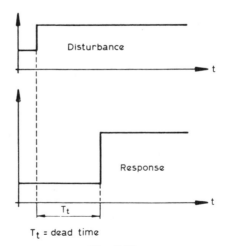

Fig. 8.13.

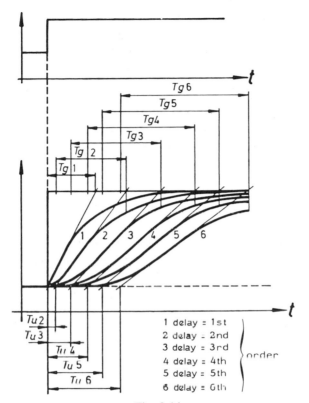

Fig. 8.14.

1 delay = 1st
2 delay = 2nd
3 delay = 3rd   } order
4 delay = 4th
5 delay = 5th
6 delay = 6th

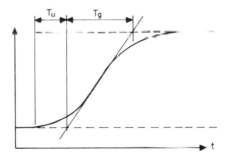

Fig. 8.15.

and when this happens it appears that there is just a single capacitive/ resistive delay combined with dead time; Fig. 8.14 shows how this happens. Because of this it is always possible to consider *any* system as a single 'lumped' capacitive/resistive delay plus dead time.

Only when the measurement variable *begins* to change in response to a change in the disturbance variable is it possible to take *any* control action. On the other hand the speed at which the control action must act on the process is proportional to the lumped time constant. It can therefore be seen that the difficulty of control is proportional to the ratio of dead time to lumped time constant, T_u/T_g (Fig. 8.15).

8.10 DYNAMIC STABILITY

As was stated in Section 8.8, delays in the system are the cause of most of the problems of designing a control system: so far the response of plant items to one type of disturbance only has been considered—a step change in measured value. In fact this form of disturbance is very rare and it is essential that the response of units to more realistic types of disturbance is considered. The diagrams in Fig. 8.16 show the typical response to three types of disturbance. In practice disturbances will be some combination of these three types in most cases.

Because the control system, process and measurement system are connected in a loop, there is always the possibility of cyclical response and it is this which determines whether the system is stable or not. All cyclical responses can be considered as a combination of several sinusoidal responses of different frequencies and amplitudes; the effect of delays on sinusoidal response is to produce a phase lag, that is to say the response at the measurement point 'lags' behind the input of the process. Once cyclical behaviour has set in it must be appreciated that the control action will also be of a cyclical nature; it should of course be in anti-phase to the disturbance so as to cancel it out, but because of delays in the process and measurement systems it will not be. If the delay is such that the control action lags the disturbance (or any given sinusoidal component of it) by half a cycle, or 180°, the control action will in fact be in phase with the disturbance instead of in anti-phase and, in respect of that particular sinusoidal component of the disturbance, the closed loop system will be unstable if the product of the open loop process gain and the control system action factor is more than unity. The higher the frequency of oscillation of any component sinusoid in the response, the more it will be attenuated in its

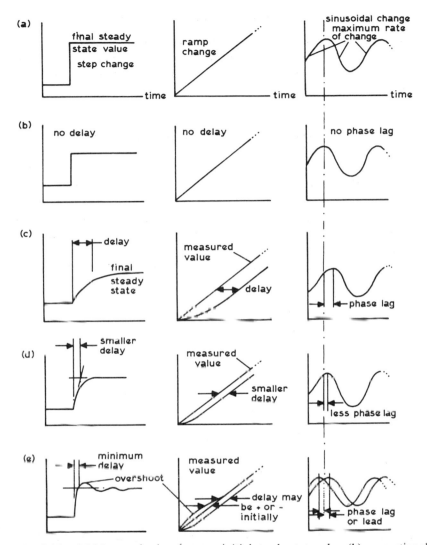

Fig. 8.16. (a) Measured value change—initial steady-state value; (b) proportional control action—can be generated without significant delays (hence it does not add to process and measurement delays); (c) integral control action—introduces delay or phase lag to any system in addition to measurement and process delays and lags; (d) proportional plus integral control action—introduces less delay or phase lag than integral action alone; overcomes 'offset' problem; (e) proportional plus integral plus derivative control action—may cause excessive control action to be generated if the measured value changes quickly, causing overshoot or phase advance. Derivative control action is difficult to use unless the *rate* of change can be reliably predicted.

passage through the process (by the natural damping of the process) and so the process will only be unstable if the frequency of the sinusoid, which will be delayed by half a cycle, is not in fact attenuated in its passage round the loop.

8.11 DESIGNING FOR DYNAMIC STABILITY

The criterion for dynamic stability of the *closed loop* system—process plus measurement plus control—is that a sinusoidal disturbance of a frequency at which the delays impose 180° phase lag must be attenuated rather than amplified in its passage through the *open loop* system—process and control (note that the latter includes the final control element). Assuming that such data are available either from design or test, then it can be plotted as a polar graph as shown in Fig. 8.17. At very low frequencies of disturbance there

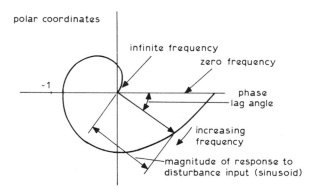

Fig. 8.17.   Phase/gain or Nyquist plot.

will be very little delay and very little attenuation; at zero frequency there will be none: hence the phase angle is zero and the magnitude of response a maximum. The magnitude will depend on the process open loop gain and the control action factor alone at very low frequencies, but at higher frequencies will depend also on the attenuation introduced by the process response.

It will be recalled that, in addition to delays due to the process and measurement, the controller itself will cause delay if integral control action is used, whilst derivative control action achieves the opposite—phase advance. There will also be delays due to the operation of the final control element.

It is easy to see how the stability of an existing system can be established by carrying out a series of tests to find the phase lag and magnitude ratio when the system is disturbed by 'forcing' it with sinusoidal variations of varying frequency through the final control element. It is not easy to see how the system may be designed so that it is stable in the face of disturbances of a given speed (frequency). It is necessary, in order to do this, to be able to calculate the effect of the process delays on the closed loop response.

Figure 8.18 shows a typical capacitive/resistive process element; in this case liquid flows into a vessel and out through a restrictor valve (the resistance). The outflow depends on the head of liquid in the vessel and the

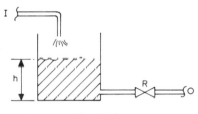

Fig. 8.18.

resistance of the valve (and other pipework). Any change in the inflow rate will cause a mismatch between the inflow and the outflow, which will not immediately change. Because of this mismatch the level in the vessel will begin to rise or fall and the head (and therefore the outflow) will start to change. As the head approaches the value which will again give equilibrium between the inflow and outflow (the new steady state), the mismatch will diminish and the rate at which the head changes will slow down, giving the type of response described earlier which is typical of any capacitive/resistive process element.

The 'dimensions' of the system are defined as the capacitance of the tank, C, and the resistance of the valve R. Capacitance is defined as the rate at which the head in the vessel (the measured value) increases or decreases for unit increase in the inflow rate; resistance is defined as the head required to support an outflow of unit dimension (any consistent set of units can be used). The rate of change of head *at any instant* is obviously proportional to the mismatch between the rate of inflow I and outflow O and also to the capacitance. It can therefore be expressed mathematically as

$$\frac{dh}{dt} = \frac{1}{C}(I - O) \qquad \text{(assuming for simplicity that flow is laminar)}$$

but

$$O = h/R$$

hence

$$\frac{dh}{dt} = \frac{1}{C}\left(I - \frac{h}{R}\right)$$

or in operator form

$$\frac{d}{dt}h = p.h = \frac{1}{C}\left(I - \frac{h}{R}\right)$$

hence

$$p.h = \frac{I}{C} - \frac{h}{CR} \quad \text{or} \quad h\left(p + \frac{1}{CR}\right) = \frac{I}{C} \quad \text{or} \quad \frac{h}{I} = \frac{1/C}{\left(p + \dfrac{1}{CR}\right)}$$

The operator p is used to represent purely transient behaviour, and in order that the expression above shall represent both transient and steady state behaviour p is replaced by s the Laplace operator.

Now the dimensions of C are

$$\frac{\text{length}^3}{\text{length}} = \text{length}^2$$

whilst the dimensions of R are

$$\frac{\text{length}}{\text{length}^3/\text{time}} = \frac{\text{time}}{\text{length}^2}$$

Hence the dimensions of CR are time (T) and CR is in fact the time constant of the process unit. Thus, the relationship between the measured value h and the disturbing variable I is given by:

$$\frac{h}{I} = \frac{1/C}{\left(s + \dfrac{1}{T}\right)}$$

which is known as the transfer function of the process plant unit, and is usually denoted $G_{(s)}$.

A process element with two capacitive/resistive delays will have a transfer function (i.e. an expression in Laplace operator form defining the steady state and transient relationships between the measured variable and the disturbing variable) of the following form

$$G_{(s)} = \frac{1/C_1 C_2}{\left(s + \dfrac{1}{T_1}\right)\left(s + \dfrac{1}{T_2}\right)} \quad \text{or} \quad \frac{T_1 T_2 / C_1 C_2}{(sT_1 + 1)(sT_2 + 1)}$$

and so on for process units containing more than two such delays.

From the theory of complex numbers it can readily be shown that for a sinusoidal disturbance of frequency f cycles/unit time the phase lag due to a single such delay is given by $\tan^{-1}(T.f)$ whilst the attenuation caused by the process unit to a disturbance of this frequency is given by $1/((Tf)^2 + 1)^{1/2}$. (The mathematical development of these expressions can be found in any standard text on the Nyquist diagram; what is presented here is only what is required to carry out a design calculation to determine stability.)

Dead time can be added, making the transfer function of a second order system with dead time

$$\frac{k \exp(-Ls)}{(sT_2 + 1)(sT_2 + 1)}$$

where $k = T_1 T_2 / C_1 C_2$. The additional phase lag is given by $L \times f \times 360°$ where L is measured in appropriate units of time. There is of course no attenuation associated with dead time, which is why it is so troublesome.

If a level controller were added to the vessel shown in Fig. 8.18 the 'motor' of the control valve would constitute a capacitive/resistive delay and there might well be significant dead time between the vessel and the control valve (Fig. 8.19). The transfer function through the process,

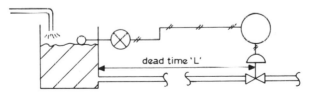

dead time 'L'

Fig. 8.19.

measurement and control system might then approximate to

$$\frac{k \exp(-Ls)}{(sT_1 + 1)(sT_2 + 1)} = G_{(s)}H_{(s)}$$

The maximum phase lag which can result from any one capacitive/resistive delay is 90°, and so the Nyquist diagram for a system such as the open loop (without control) system above will be of the form given in Fig. 8.20(a). Two such delays give a maximum of 180° phase lag and the Nyquist diagram will be of the form given in Fig. 8.20(b).

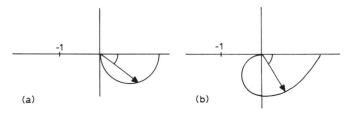

(a)   (b)

Fig. 8.20.

It can be seen that even with two such delays the magnitude of response will always be less than unity (i.e. it will be attenuated) however large the control action factor, and therefore the system can never be unstable though it may well oscillate. However, the addition of dead time increases the phase lag without any further attenuation and instability becomes possible. The Nyquist diagram will then be as given in Fig. 8.21; if the -1 point is 'encircled' meaning that the response is actually amplified rather than attenuated for a sinusoidal disturbance of such a frequency that the phase lag is 180°, the system is unstable in closed loop.

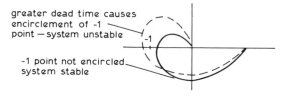

greater dead time causes
encirclement of -1
point — system unstable

-1 point not encircled
system stable

Fig. 8.21.

8.12 THE SISO PROCESS CONTROLLER

The examples taken in earlier sections to illustrate the principles of control action have been of simple 'self-acting' mechanisms, such as were devised to make possible the regulation of process parameters *at local level*. Modern plant demands much more sophisticated mechanisms; in most cases these accept transmitted signals representing measured value and transmit a control signal over quite large distances to a final control element. The modern SISO (single input/single output) process controller generates control action which is a combination of proportional, integral and derivative actions, but it is much more flexible and can be combined with the other controllers in several ways, as will be seen, to enable complete control systems to be designed for the largest plant.

SISO controllers require a power supply (the motive force for a self-acting controller can be derived from the process pressures), which can be pneumatic, hydraulic or electrical. In diagram form the control loop using a SISO controller can be depicted as shown in Fig. 8.22. From this diagram

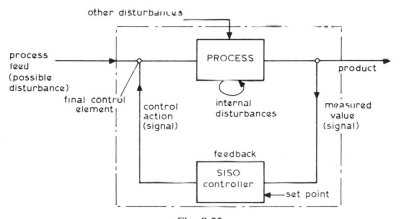

Fig. 8.22.

it can be seen that the process and the control and measurement systems can be regarded as a system. Material and/or energy enters this system in two places and leaves as product. This type of system is called an 'open' system because energy and material enter and leave it (a closed system is one where nothing enters or leaves).

A practical example of the above system is given in Fig. 8.23, which shows a heat exchanger in which heat is extracted from waste steam to raise

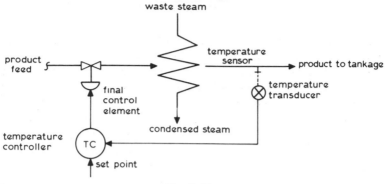

Fig. 8.23.

the temperature of the process material before it enters some other
processing stage. Disturbances can occur in the flow rate of the 'product
feed' which will cause the temperature of the 'product to tankage' to
change. Other disturbances can arise owing to change of pressure or flow
rate of the waste steam. If the condensed steam is not immediately removed
from the heat exchanger coils it may 'back up' and reduce the heat transfer
causing internal disturbances.

8.13 CONTROL SYSTEM DESIGN

The objective of control is to suppress any disturbance as early as possible:
variations in the flow rate of the product feed in the system shown in
Fig. 8.23 will disturb the measured value, i.e. product temperature, but only
after delays due to heat transfer in the heat exchanger. It has been seen that
these delays make feedback control very difficult. If the variations in flow
rate are themselves controlled, there will be no disturbance in product
temperature due to this cause. Another SISO controller can be added to the
system to control the flow rate (Fig. 8.24). However, temperature will still
be disturbed by other causes and so the temperature controller must cause
the (controlled) flow rate to vary in order to compensate for these other
disturbances. This use of one controller to 'reset' another is called 'cascade
control'.

   The delays in measurement of flow rate and in the flow itself (process) are
very small compared to those of heat transfer, and very fast control of flow
is possible (large proportional action factor). Quite fast disturbances of

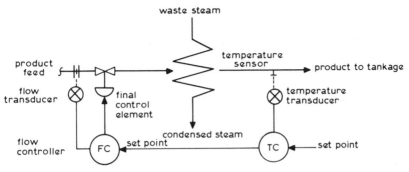

Fig. 8.24.

temperature, which could not be controlled by a single controller, can be controlled by a cascade system.

If the pressure of the waste steam rises or falls, the rate of heat transfer will rise or fall with it, especially if the temperature difference between the steam and the process material is small. Thus, changes in steam pressure will also disturb the product temperature and, since it is waste steam, it may not be possible to control this pressure. If, however, the steam pressure is measured (relative to a datum equal to the pressure at which the steam temperature equals the set point of the product temperature controller— suppressed zero) and the product flow rate reset in 'ratio' to it, little disturbance to the product temperature will be caused by changes in steam pressure. By adding feedback control action generated by the temperature controller, the process will suffer minimum disturbance from either change of product flow rate or steam pressure (Fig. 8.25). There is no way that the effect of disturbances arising internally in the process, such as condensed steam back up, can be reduced by control—this is a matter for better plant

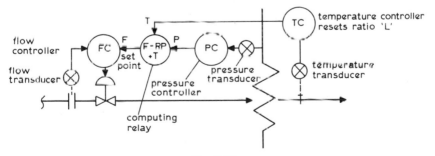

Fig. 8.25.

design. The above description of a system design illustrates the way that more than one SISO controller can be used to form a complete control system. There are, however, difficulties associated with these techniques which will be discussed in Section 8.16.

8.14 PROPORTIONAL BANDWIDTH

The proportional action factor—the ratio of the control action taken to the actuating or measuring movement—is not applicable to a SISO controller that receives an analog signal which may represent any measuring range, and that generates a control *signal* which, when applied to the final control element, may produce any control action (depending on the size of the final control element and the process characteristics). The term used to express the ratio of the control action *signal* generated by proportional action to the measurement error *signal* is 'proportional bandwidth'. Proportional control action is generated in a controller by amplifying the error (set point—measured value). The amplification factor is known as the 'gain' and the proportional bandwidth is the inverse of the gain expressed as a percentage. In other words:

$$\text{control action signal} = \text{error} \times \text{gain} \times -1$$

$$= \text{error} \times \frac{100}{\text{proportional bandwidth}} \times -1$$

Thus, with the controller 'tuned' to a proportional bandwidth of 100%, the maximum control signal will be generated when the error equals the full measurement range. That is to say that the maximum control action will not be applied to the process until the measured value has departed from the set point by an amount equal to the maximum which can be measured. For smaller errors the proportional control action will be less than the maximum possible. Of course, where derivative control action is added, the maximum control action may be applied for an error of much less than this but only whilst the measured value is actually changing. When integral control is added the steady-state value of the control action can eventually reach any value within the analog range, however large the proportional bandwidth (however small the gain).

It can be seen from Sections 8.6 and 8.7 that the integral action factor and the derivative action factor both vary in proportion to the proportional action factor, and are defined as times: they are often referred to as the integral time and the derivative time. Tuning a SISO controller therefore consists of setting the proportional bandwidth, the integral time and the derivative time, so that the total control action best suits the behaviour of the process.

8.15 SELECTING THE CONTROL ACTION TO SUIT THE CONTROL SYSTEM

It was shown in Section 8.7 that the addition of integral control action makes it more likely that the controlled system will be unstable. However, without integral action there will always be a steady-state offset because an error is required in order to generate any control signal at all. Since the control signal generated by proportional action depends also on the gain, the offset will be greater for lower gains, i.e. for greater proportional bandwidth. How much gain can be used depends on the effect of the process and measurement delays and, therefore, it may not be possible in controlling some processes with proportional control action alone to avoid large offset. Taking the example of the heat exchanger system in Section 8.13, it would not be possible to avoid large offset in the case of the simple single temperature controller system because of the heat transfer and measurement delays. However, the flow controller in the second cascaded system is not subject to either measurement or process delay of any size and could easily be tuned to a small proportional bandwidth, giving little offset. Moreover, the integral action of the temperature controller will reset the set point of the flow controller to a value which will make the measured value of temperature exactly equal to the set point. The control system is intended to control product temperature and so the offset in the flow controller is really unimportant. The temperature controller is called the master or primary controller, the flow controller the slave or secondary controller of the cascade system.

There is one circumstance when it might be necessary to use integral control action on a slave controller; that is if a small gain (large proportional bandwidth) has to be used. If the proportional bandwidth were greater than 100%, it would be impossible to generate maximum control action (the error would have to be greater than the measurement range to do so) using only proportional action and the slave controller would therefore not be able to respond to all the demands of the master controller unless it (the slave) had integral action. Fortunately, such conditions are rarely met, as slave controllers are usually capable of fast response (small proportional bandwidth).

8.16 FEEDFORWARD CONTROL

The system described in Section 8.13 (Fig. 8.25) uses three SISO controllers, two of them in a feedback cascade (Fig. 8.26). The third acts in a 'feedforward' fashion, and is not part of the feedback loop at all. Feedforward control is open loop control, i.e. measurement, control and process elements do not form a loop at all, as can be seen from the diagram.

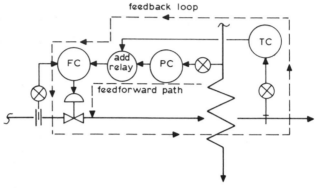

Fig. 8.26.

This form of control cannot be used on its own, as there is no feedback of information to enable the steady-state value of the measured value to be compared with the set value. The aim of feedforward control action is to reduce the effect of disturbances on the measured value, by reducing the size of the disturbance itself before it enters the process. Feedback control is then applied to control the effect of the residual disturbance; it can never be 100% effective in this because control action cannot be generated until the measured value has started to change in response to the disturbance.

The proportional action bandwidth of the pressure controller is adjusted so that the flow of process fluid is regulated in proportion to the rate of heat exchange, as this varies with steam pressure. Disturbance of the product temperature which would otherwise result from such steam pressure fluctuations will be greatly reduced; however, the effect of the changes of flow rate of the process fluid will not be fed back to the pressure controller and it can be seen, therefore, that this control action is feedforward.

Whereas delays are introduced into the feedback control loop by the process and measurement as described above, feedforward control action is likely to act too early. For instance, in the example of the heat exchanger system it will be some time after the steam pressure changes that the process fluid passing through the heat exchanger will start to vary in temperature; this is because heat is stored in the metal walls of the heat exchanger itself. Often suitable delays are introduced into the feedforward path in order to match these process delays and ensure, as far as possible, that the feedforward control action takes effect at the right time (something that cannot be achieved with feedback action). A 'first order' delay can be achieved quite simply as shown in Fig. 8.27 for both pneumatic and electronic systems. The components required are a capacity and a resistor (or needle valve in the case of pneumatics). The resistance is adjusted to provide the right time constant. Second or higher order delays can be used, enabling a process with small dead time to be matched, but dead time itself is almost impossible to achieve (see Section 8.9).

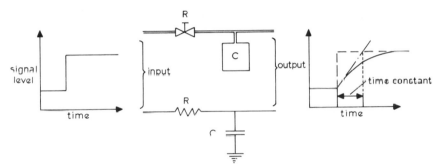

Fig. 8.27. First order delay.

8.17 INTEGRAL SATURATION

Proportional control action, and therefore the position of the final control element, changes with the error between measured and set values. Integral action, however, continues to either increase or decrease as long as there is an error and, unless the error is removed, it will eventually drive the final control element to the physical limit of its travel. In controllers which add the two control actions, proportional and integral, together, either action alone must be capable of driving the final control element over its full range; hence, once integral control action has driven the control valve (final control element) to its wide open or closed position, it is not possible for the proportional control action to cause it to even start to move in the other direction as the measured value responds to full control action and the error begins to reduce. In fact, when, as a result of applying maximum control action, the measured value changes so that the error decreases to zero, as it must in due time, proportional action will be zero and the valve will still be firmly at its limit. Only when the error has changed sign and increased sufficiently and for a sufficient time will the combined proportional and integral control actions *begin* to move the valve away from its limit position. This state of affairs is made much worse by the fact that control action can in practical controllers exceed the analog limits (0·2 bar, 4 mA; or 1·0 bar, 20 mA), which results in the integral control action taking even longer to desaturate or 'unwind'.

The problem of integral saturation can occur with processes which have considerable dead time or very long 'lumped' time constants. It is an almost invariable problem with 'batch' or discontinuous processes because during periods when the process is not operating the measured value cannot equal the set point and it is inevitable that integral control action will saturate, unless precautions are taken to limit integral action to less than the full analog range.

8.18 DISCRETE CONTROL ACTIONS

It has been assumed so far that the control actions generated are continuous, and position the final control element smoothly in a continuous manner. This does not necessarily have to be the case; in a type of control action known as 'boundless' the final control element is positioned in a series of steps at fixed intervals of time. Proportional and derivative control actions are generated in the same way as for the controllers so far described, i.e. from the error and rate of change signals. However, at the interval time the final control element is made to move an amount proportional to the combined control action signal in the appropriate direction. At the next interval time the control action will be different because the error will have changed, and the rate of change of the measured variable may be different. Again, the final control element will be made to change an amount proportional to the control action. Each change will be *in addition* to the last and so the final control element is made to sum or integrate the control action. Since proportional action is proportional to error at all times, control action generated in this way is the same as for conventional control (apart from its 'jerky' application) but not if derivative action is added, since then the derivative component as well as the proportional component is 'integrated'. Such a controller will desaturate very quickly, both because the final control element (which is the integrator) cannot exceed the operating limits and also because the integration rate is increased by derivative control action, unlike the more conventional control action which simply adds the three 'terms', integral, proportional and derivative.

Some processes have such large 'lumped time constants' that control action can only cause the measured value to change extremely slowly (e.g. space heating). In these cases a very simple type of controller is possible which generates 'proportional time control action'. A suitable time interval is selected and within this time the final control element is set to maximum for a period and then to minimum for the rest of the interval. The ratio of the time which the final control element (which is often a simple switch) spends in the 'maximum' position to the time it spends in the minimum position is proportioned to the error. Thus, over a relatively long period of time the average control action is proportional to the error. Integral and control action terms can be generated in the same way as for other controllers, the ratio of times at maximum and minimum being equivalent to the position of a 'modulating' final control element.

8.19 DIRECT DIGITAL CONTROL

Direct digital control (DDC) is a term which has come to be used to describe control action generated by digital rather than analog computation, as, for instance, by a digital computer. The control action is exactly the same as has been described in the previous sections but it can be convenient to transmit it to the final control element in digital form to drive a stepper motor, for instance. Generally digital computation is more accurate than analog and it is possible to switch integral action out in a digital controller, which effectively solves the saturation problem. There are other advantages and disadvantages of DDC, but these will not be discussed here.

CHAPTER 9

Control Mechanisms

9.1 INTRODUCTION

In Chapter 8 principles of control were introduced; it is now necessary to understand the mechanisms which are used to apply these principles in the plant. The three mechanisms shown in Fig. 9.1 all do the same job but with different degrees of flexibility and precision.

In all three mechanisms the level in a vessel is measured by a float. In the first mechanism the buoyancy of the float moves the final control element (the valve), through a system of mechanical levers, to a position at which the inflow to the vessel equals the outflow, and the level is constant. However, the buoyancy of the float must also balance the forces generated by out-of-balance pressures in the valve; this affects the accuracy of measurement, as the float position is not then an accurate measure of level. The second mechanism uses pneumatic pressure to operate the valve and thus avoids this problem and is more accurate. In both these mechanisms the proportional action factor can be adjusted to suit the process, but neither is capable of any other form of control action. The third mechanism only uses the float as a measuring device and employs a separate mechanism to generate control action; not only is measurement not affected by the control valve out-of-balance forces, but the controller can generate any combination of control actions. In addition, the controller can be sited at any reasonable distance from the plant.

9.2 LOCAL CONTROL MECHANISMS

For many control purposes a simple local 'self-acting' (i.e. not requiring any electrical, pneumatic or hydraulic power supply) mechanism, such as

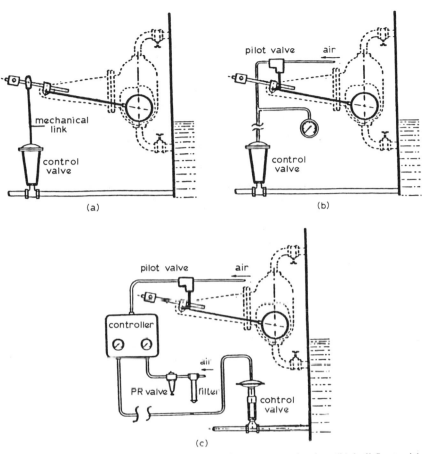

Fig. 9.1. (a) Ball float with direct connection to control valve; (b) ball float with pilot valve; (c) ball float with controller.

the first of those above, is adequate. Some, like the simple pressure regulator shown in Fig. 9.2, combine measurement, generation of control action, and application of control action (final control element) in one mechanism. In this mechanism the pressure in the pipeline acts on the diaphragm, and is opposed by the range spring. The movement of the final control element is *proportional* to the compression or extension of the spring. The set point can be adjusted by 'loading' the spring, and the proportional action factor can be changed by replacing the spring with a stronger or weaker one. However, this type of mechanism is very crude,

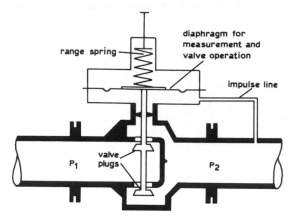

Fig. 9.2.   Self-acting controller.

inaccurate and inflexible, and is only used where this is acceptable. Such a self-acting mechanism does have one advantage, however—it is very fast acting.

Sometimes the fast response of a local control mechanism is essential, such as when controlling the speed of a gas turbine set. Then a hydraulically powered controller (not self-acting), such as that shown diagrammatically in Fig. 9.3, is often used. Hydraulic power has the advantage over pneumatic power, that it is faster acting (hydraulic fluid being a liquid, is incompressible, and the delays which occur in 'filling' the large space of a

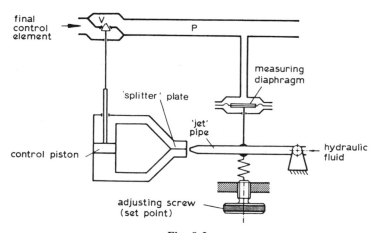

Fig. 9.3.

pneumatic valve 'motor' are avoided) and can develop much greater forces for a given size of valve motor.

In a hydraulically powered controller any change in pressure in the process pipeline acts on the measuring diaphragm to move the 'jet' pipe (Fig. 9.3). Hydraulic fluid is pumped at very high pressure and velocity from the jet pipe onto a 'splitter' plate, which converts the velocity energy into pressure again. As the jet pipe moves to one side or the other, the pressure at one side of the control piston increases whilst the pressure at the other side decreases. The force generated by any difference in pressure across the control piston balances the out-of-balance forces in the final control element, so that when the jet pipe moves, the piston moves the final control element to a new position.

It will be appreciated that the control action thus generated is integral action (see Chapter 8). The force generated by even a very small change of position of the jet pipe is very large and will cause the valve to *continue* to move as long as the jet pipe remains in the displaced position. Thus, control action continues until the pressure in the pipeline is restored to the set value and the jet pipe returns to its equilibrium position. In theory, therefore, no offset is possible with this type of control, though in practice, to the extent that the out-of-balance forces in the control valve (final control element) vary under different process conditions, some offset does in fact occur. Since control action is integral, saturation (or wind-up) will occur, and the control valve will always go to the fully open or fully closed position whenever the set value cannot be attained—such as when there is a

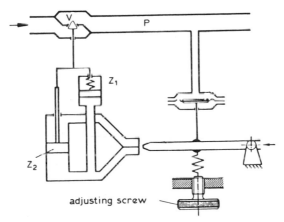

Fig. 9.4. Control mechanism. Z_1, proportional control cylinder; Z_2 integral action control cylinder.

blockage in the process line or when the plant is shut down. This is not usually a serious disadvantage (and may actually be an advantage sometimes) because the control action is very fast; but, obviously, it would be a mistake to use this type of controller to regulate a slowly changing process variable.

A variation of this type of control mechanism is shown in Fig. 9.4; here proportional control action has been added to the basic integral action. The pressure in the second cylinder Z_1 increases when the jet pipe moves downward (in the diagram) moving the piston upward against the spring. The spring force will be such that there is no proportional action when the jet pipe is in the central position, i.e. when there is no error between measured and set values. Under these conditions the position of the final control element is determined solely by the integral piston Z_2.

9.3 REMOTE CONTROLLERS—MOTION BALANCE

Modern control systems can be divided into two categories—local and remote. Local systems or mechanisms are most often used to regulate a variable (such as steam pressure or turbine speed), the set point of which does not need to be changed frequently; they also have the advantage of a faster response to disturbances than 'remote' systems. However, the majority of control systems today have the controller sited in a central control room where the process operators can vary the set points as necessary to operate the plant. Such controllers cannot operate directly from the measurement impulse signal but receive analog signals from pneumatic or electronic transducers and generate an analog control output to operate the final control element. Since the full scale input and output is always the same (0·2–1·0 bar or 4–20 mA), such controllers can be absolutely standard in this respect for every application. The design of these controllers is based on the force balance principle described in Chapter 7; however, as in the case of transmitters, early examples of pneumatic controllers were motion balance mechanisms added to (usually large) impulse driven indicating or recording instruments. A typical example, the model 40 Foxboro controller is shown diagrammatically in Fig. 9.5.

It can be seen that, as in the case of a motion balance transmitter, the *motion* of the recorder pen is opposed by the feedback bellows (called the proportioning bellows). The only difference in fact between this controller and a transmitting instrument is that the ratio of the output to the

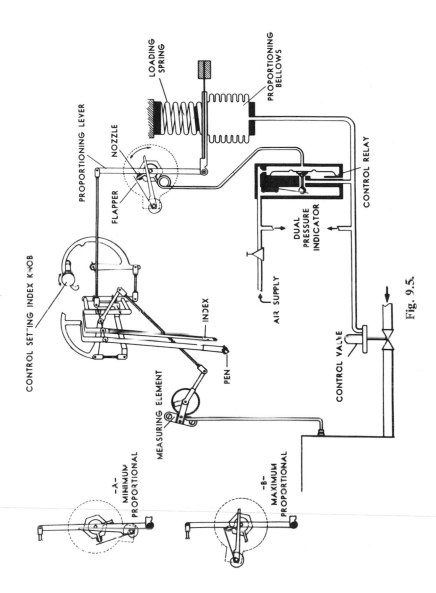

Fig. 9.5.

measured value signal input of the pneumatic mechanism—the proportional action factor—can be varied.

Integral and derivative control actions can be added to this type of controller as shown in Fig. 9.6. The loading spring is replaced by the integral bellows which act as a spring of variable stiffness, the stiffness being a function of the pressure in the bellows. Whilst an error persists, air continues to flow into or out of the integral bellows through the variable integral restriction which serves to slow up the rate of flow. An error will cause the flapper to

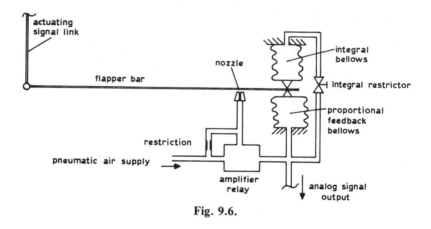

Fig. 9.6.

move closer to or further away from the nozzle. The integral bellows will continue to expand (in the case of a positive error), causing the flapper to continue to move closer to the nozzle. Thus, whilst the proportional-action-only controller will develop an output pressure proportional to the error, the proportional-plus-integral-action controller will continue to increase or decrease the output pressure at a *rate* proportional to the error. Eventually, the control action will result in the error being eliminated and at this point the flapper and nozzle will be in exactly the same position as they were in originally and the pressure in the integral and proportional bellows will again be equal, though different from the original value.

It should be appreciated that the generation of integral action is achieved by building into the control mechanism first order resistive/capacitive delay of exactly the same kind that is found in the process itself. Such delays are constructed, in terms of pneumatic equipment, by connecting fixed or adjustable restrictors in series with capacity chambers which may be bellows in some cases (Fig. 9.7).

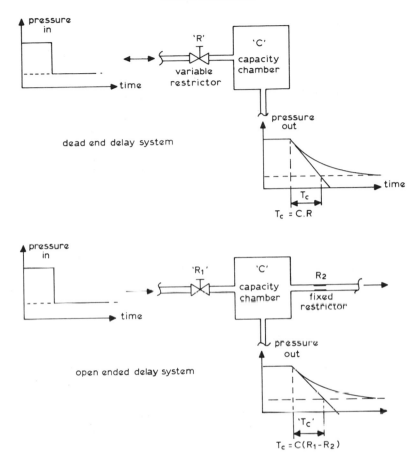

Fig. 9.7.

The diagrams in Fig. 9.7 illustrate two types of delay systems used in pneumatic controllers to generate control actions. Capacity is measured in units of pressure rise per unit of mass flow of air into the chamber. The resistance of the restrictors is measured in units of mass flow of air per unit of pressure difference across the restrictor. In most cases it is not possible to easily change the capacity, so the time constant of the delay is altered by varying the setting of the variable restrictor.

The diagram in Fig. 9.8 shows how derivative control action is added to a motion balance controller. The derivative restriction delays the air flow into the proportional bellows when an error causes the flapper to move

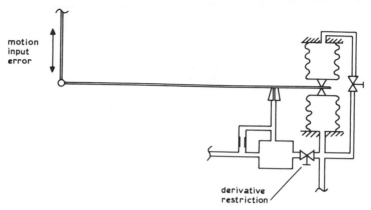

Fig. 9.8.

closer to the nozzle, thus causing the pressure to increase behind the nozzle. Thus, the feedback bellows is slow to expand and move the nozzle in the opposite direction (negative feedback), reducing the pressure rise behind the nozzle. In this way the proportional action factor is increased temporarily, which is why derivative control action was originally called 'delayed proportional' action.

Ideally, the control actions should be generated separately and then added together as shown diagrammatically in Fig. 9.9. However, it will be obvious that, generated in the way described above, the control actions are not really independent. For instance, the derivative restriction, in delaying air flow into the proportional bellows, also delays the transfer of air from the proportional bellows to the integral bellows, and thus changes the integral action factor.

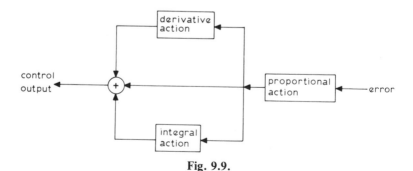

Fig. 9.9.

9.4 FORCE-BALANCE PNEUMATIC CONTROLLERS

The force-balance pneumatic controller was developed to be used with analog transmitted signals in a remote location (usually a central control room), in contrast to the motion balance controller which is suitable for mounting in an indicating or recording instrument only, and is usually mounted local to the process. The force-balance controller has the same advantages of precision as the force-balance transmitter and for this reason, when local mounted controllers are required today, the force-balance types are often chosen and transmitters used. The principle is shown in Fig. 9.10.

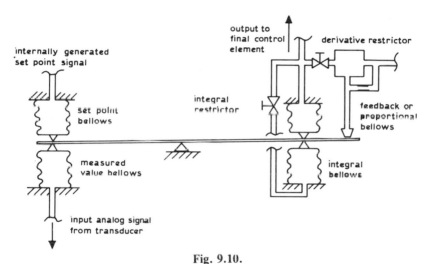

Fig. 9.10.

Instead of the input force generated by the transducer, the input force is the error between the measured value analog pressure and the set value pressure generated by a mechanism within the controller. Integral and derivative actions can be added in exactly the same way as in motion-balance controllers as shown in the figure (the integral bellows is replaced by a spring in the proportional-action-only version).

Flexible diaphragms can be used instead of bellows as in the proportional-action-only 'stack' controller shown in Fig. 9.11. Air flows through the fixed restrictor (i) to the flapper/nozzle and through the adjustable proportional restrictor to chamber b. The pressure in chamber b acts on the diaphragm to produce a force on the centre post. The difference

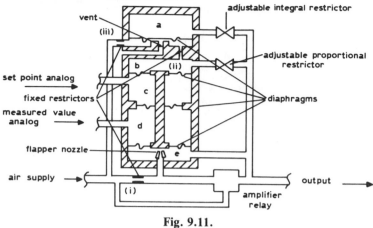

Fig. 9.11.

in the measured value and set value pressures—the error—also produces a force which acts on the centre post (chambers c and d), and the flapper/nozzle adjusts its position to produce a pressure in chamber e which applied through the lowest diaphragm provides the negative feedback. Thus the 'error force' is balanced by the force generated in the proportional and feedback chambers b and e, in the same way as the beam balance/bellows type. The pressure in chamber b depends on the pressure drops through the adjustable proportional restrictor and the fixed restrictor (ii) as well as on the output pressure. Integral action is generated when the adjustable integral restrictor is opened to allow air to flow into chamber a, forcing the top diaphragm down so as to restrict the flow out through the vent and increasing the pressure in chamber b.

Derivative control action is generated in a separate unit as shown in Fig. 9.12 and this avoids the interaction between integral and derivative restrictors mentioned in connection with the beam balance/bellows type of controller. The output of the proportional and integral controller becomes the input of the derivative unit. Increasing pressure in chamber f, acting on the upper diaphragm, forces the flapper closer to the nozzle, causing the output pressure to rise. The increase in output pressure causes air to flow into chamber g slowly through the derivative restrictor, which increases the pressure in chamber g and tends to oppose the increase in chamber f. If the input pressure (output from proportional and integral controller) is increasing, the pressure in chamber g will always be less however, owing to the delay caused by the restrictor valve; this difference will be proportional

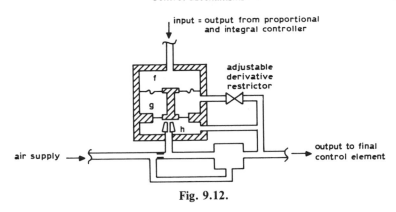

Fig. 9.12.

to the *rate* at which the input is increasing. The output of the derivative unit will therefore be higher than the input by an amount which is proportional to the rate of increase of the input. Thus, in effect, the proportional action is increased by an amount proportional to the rate of change of the error, i.e. derivative control action

9.5 ELECTRONIC CONTROLLERS

Like force-balance pneumatic controllers, electronic controllers have been developed for use with analog transmitted signals, normally being located in a remote position. The electrical current analog signal is converted to electrical pressure (voltage) and the same elements can be seen in electronic controllers as in pneumatic. For instance, compare the electrical 'delay' system shown in Fig. 9.13 with the dead-ended pneumatic system described in Section 9.3.

Electronic DC amplifiers are used instead of pneumatic amplifier relays and flapper nozzles to provide the sensitivity and precision required through negative feedback action. Thus, a basic circuit for a proportional-action-only controller will be as shown in Fig. 9.14; it can be seen that the negative feedback resistor performs the same function in conjunction with the amplifier that the flapper/nozzle does in conjunction with the pneumatic amplifier relay. The set point and measured value voltages are subtracted to give the error voltage in the same way that the set point and measured value pressures are opposed in the pneumatic force-balance controller. The output voltage V_o will normally be converted to a 4–20 mA analog signal for transmission to the final control element, where, in most systems, it will

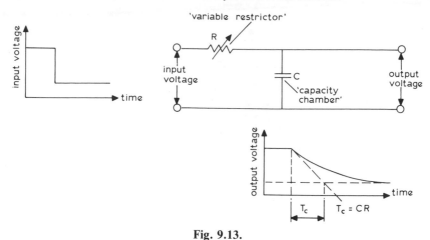

Fig. 9.13.

be converted to a pneumatic analog signal to drive the final control element, the control valve.

Integral control action can be added to this controller as shown in Fig. 9.15 by adding the equivalent of an open-ended pneumatic delay; this acts in exactly the same way as the integral restrictor and bellows of the pneumatic controller, in that whilst an error persists current flows into or out of the integral capacitor, increasing the proportional output voltage.

Derivative action is also generated in the same way as it is in pneumatic controllers, i.e. by delaying the amplifier feedback, and thus temporarily increasing the proportional action factor whilst the measured value is changing, in proportion to the rate of change (Fig. 9.16).

The amplifier with negative feedback in the circuits of Figs 9.14–9.16

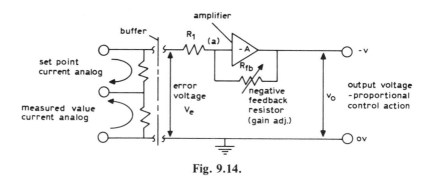

Fig. 9.14.

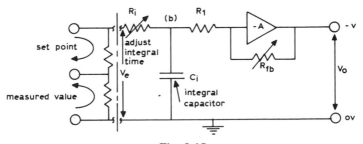

Fig. 9.15.

operates as follows. Current flowing through the load resistor R_1 into point (a) must equal the current flowing out of point (a) by Kirchhoff's law. The amplifier can be assumed to draw no current, and so if the voltage at the amplifier outlet is less than at the circuit input, the same current must flow through the load and feedback resistors. Hence,

$$I = \frac{V_e - V_a}{R_1} = \frac{V_a - V_o}{R_{fb}}$$

and therefore

$$\frac{(V_e - V_a)}{(V_a - V_o)} = \frac{R_1}{R_{fb}}$$

Thus, the gain and therefore the proportional action factor depend on the ratio of the load resistor value to that of the feedback resistor.

In Fig. 9.14, if there is no error voltage, no current flows in the amplifier circuit and the output voltage is zero. If an error develops however, voltage is higher at the input, and current must flow through R_1 and R_{fb} to the output circuit, causing V_0 to fall. This is the proportional action.

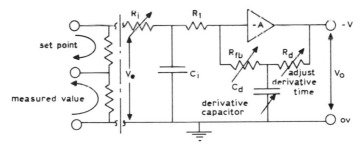

Fig. 9.16.

When an error voltage appears at the input to the circuit shown in Fig. 9.15 current flows through R_i, R_1, and R_{fb} producing proportional action in the same way. In addition current flows through R_i into the capacitor C_i, charging it and raising the voltage at point (b). As the voltage at point (b) rises, the current flowing through R_1 and R_{fb} increases so that the control action (output V_0) is increased. This is integral action. Eventually, because of the effect of control action on the process, the error will be reduced to nothing and current will cease to flow into C_i. However, current will continue to flow in the amplifier circuit because the voltage at point (b) is higher than that at the output, V_0. This current is drawn from C_i and therefore the voltage at (b) will gradually fall, which would allow an error to develop again, which in turn will cause the capacitor to be charged up. Because of this, there will in fact be a slight residual error, but this can be made insignificant if the value of C_i is large, the value of R_i small, and the values of R_1 and R_{fb} are much greater than R_i.

In the circuit shown in Fig. 9.16, when an error voltage V_e first develops, the current flowing through R_1 and R_{fb} must charge C_d, thus increasing the current flowing through R_{fb} and R_1 initially, and reducing V_0 (i.e. increasing control action) temporarily. This is derivative action.

The current flowing in the amplifier circuit must not be allowed to disturb the error measuring circuit, and some form of 'buffer' circuit is used to overcome this problem (a differential amplifier or bridge circuit). The output voltage is used to regulate a current analog control signal.

9.6 MANUAL CONTROL AND 'BUMPLESS TRANSFER'

Under certain operating conditions or circumstances (for instance, start-up, or for maintenance) automatic control action is stopped and the set point generating mechanism is used simply to position the final control element without reference to the measured value at all. This is 'open loop control' and is usually referred to as 'manual mode'. When the controller is being used in this way it is very difficult to stop the generation of control actions even though the process no longer responds to them. In any case it is important to arrange that the output of the controller, which is the sum of the control actions, does not change suddenly when it is switched back into 'automatic mode'. When there is no error, the output of any controller is only the integral control action term, since there is no proportional action without an error and no derivative action if the error is not changing. Therefore, to ensure 'bumpless transfer' from manual mode operation to automatic mode, two things are necessary: (i) the set point must equal the measured value, and (ii) the integral action must be equal to the controller output.

In order to achieve these two things, the measured value signal is connected to the set point system inside the controller (to the set point bellows in the case of a pneumatic controller) and the output of the controller (generated by the set point mechanism in manual mode) is connected to the integral action generating mechanism (to the integral bellows in the case of a pneumatic controller). Thus, when the controller is switched from manual mode operation to automatic mode, the set point is equal to the measured value, whatever the latter may be. There is, therefore, no error and the integral action is equal to the output of the controller which does not therefore change. After transfer the set point mechanism can be set by the operator to any value he requires and the controller will vary the output to the final control element smoothly until this measured value is attained.

9.7 INTEGRAL TRACKING

The principle of bumpless transfer; from manual mode operation to automatic mode, can be extended to the transfer of control from one controller to another alternative or standby controller. This is not an uncommon need in process control: only one of two (or more) controllers is connected to the final control element at any time and the other controller/s must 'track' the output of the operational controller so that transfer can take place bumplessly. Such an arrangement is often required where a computer is used to carry out the functions of a number of controllers simultaneously (so-called direct digital control—DDC) and analog controllers, provided as back-up, must operate in 'standby' mode. The diagram in Fig. 9.17 shows how this is done using a 'stack' type pneumatic controller.

The external selector switch is positioned to select the required controller—both will be in automatic mode as selected by the position of the 'auto-man' switch. In the case of the standby controller pneumatic pressure will operate the switch associated with the set point generating unit, putting it into the 'tracking' mode. Its output will then be equal to its input (the measured value) and hence, as far as the stack controller is concerned, the setpoint and measured value inputs are exactly the same and there is no error. Supply air pressure is also applied via the auto-man switch

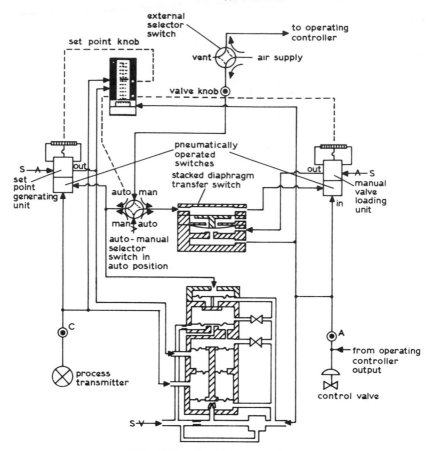

Fig. 9.17.   Stand-by controller.

to the pneumatically operated switch associated with the manual valve loading unit, putting this too into 'tracking' mode. The output of this unit is thus connected via the stacked diaphragm transfer switch to the output of the controller and into the common connection of both controllers with the control valve. At the same time supply air pressure is applied to a switch at the top of the controller, which causes the integral restrictor to be bypassed. Thus, since the output to the manual valve loading unit follows the input and is connected in an unrestricted loop with it, the pressure in this part of the system would 'float' if it were not connected into the output of the operating controller. The output of the standby controller therefore 'follows' that of the operating controller; when the standby controller is selected its set point equals its measured value and its output equals its integral action term and is also equal to the output of the other controller. As a result, the process is not disturbed by the transfer operation and the 'new' controller controls the process so as to maintain *its* measured value (whether this is the same or different from the measured value of the other controller) at the value it was at at the moment of transfer. The operator can then change the set point to some new value if he wishes, in the normal way. When the selector switch is operated in order to select the other controller, the set point generating unit of the selected controller (which up to that time had been the standby) resumes its normal function and the integral restrictor is no longer by-passed. The controller therefore generates both integral and proportional control actions. The manual valve loading units of both controllers remain in 'track' however, since both controllers are in 'auto' mode, and both follow the output of the operating controller.

Integral tracking is very important, not only for standby arrangements but also for systems where control is exercised on a different basis at different stages of the process operation, particularly in batch control. Note that in Fig. 9.17 only the control valve, not the measurement transducer, is shown connected to both controllers. Each controller can have its own measurement which does not have to be the same variable. In principle, several controllers, each with a different measured value, can be connected in such a way that any one of them can be selected as the operating controller at any time.

Not all controllers operate in the same way and it may be found that a particular design will not allow bumpless transfer from one to another as described above. Obviously a good understanding of the principles of operation of the controller mechanisms is essential when choosing the correct equipment for a particular application.

9.8 EXTERNAL RESET

It should be remembered that the purpose of integral control action is to remove the offset which is otherwise inevitable with proportional control. It is helpful in this context to consider that rate or derivative control action is achieved by increasing or decreasing the proportional gain temporarily, so that rate action cannot in fact be dissociated from proportional control whereas integral control action is entirely separate and can be used alone.

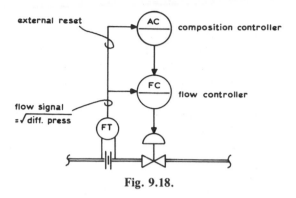

Fig. 9.18.

In a cascade loop the output of the master controller is the desired value (set point) of the slave controller; hence, if the measured value of the slave is fed back to the master and used as the reset signal, it will be seen that the desired value of the master controller will be satisfied *without error* when the process is operating in steady state. In steady state there is no proportional control action or rate action term and the output of the master controller, i.e. the set point of the slave controller, is equal to the integral control action term, in this case the measured value of the slave controller. Only when an error develops in the master-controlled variable will a proportional action term develop in the master controller and the set point of the slave controller be different from the measured value. Then the slave controller will act to change the slave-controlled variable, continuing to do so until the error in the master controller is removed, when the set point of the slave will again be equal to the measured value. The system can be appreciated from the diagram in Fig. 9.18 which shows a typical cascade system, comprising a composition controller as master with a measured value derived from an on-stream analyser and a flow controller as slave. Generation of integral control action in the normal way inside the master controller would serve the same end but would be prone to integral 'windup' (see Section 8.17) which is avoided by this method.

9.9 MICROPROCESSOR-BASED CONTROLLERS

Recently, electronic controllers have become available that, although they receive analog measured value signals and generate analog control action, nevertheless, operate internally on an entirely different principle to the analog controllers so far described. These new controllers incorporate a microprocessor—in reality a miniature *digital* computer.

Inside the controller the measured value signal is sampled on a regular basis, say once every tenth of a second; proportional and integral control actions are then computed digitally in a series of programmed steps as shown by the 'flow chart' in Fig. 9.19(a). The analog control signal to the final element is then updated and remains at its new value until the next sample has been made and a new value computed. Generation of derivative control action is more difficult, as the rate of change of the process variable has to be measured; however, this too can be done as a separate 'time shared' task by the microprocessor. Other tasks can also be time shared, such as calculating the square root of a differential pressure measurement to obtain the flow rate signal, and any of the functions of analog computing relays (see Chapter 11). A separate program called an 'executive' or 'operating' program regulates the operation of the microprocessor in carrying out these different 'tasks' (Fig. 9.19(b)).

The number of 'tasks' that can be included in a microprocessor controller will depend on the frequency of repetition required and the speed of the microprocessor. More frequent operation of one task than another can readily be incorporated into the executive program but there will obviously be a limit in both the number of tasks and the size of any one task which can be accommodated. Since most microprocessor-based controllers will inevitably be standard products, the tasks included will be a matter of judgement for the manufacturer. An alternative use of the microprocessor is to provide the user with a system which is already programmed to carry out the standard tasks of signal input/output and signal processing, and the means to program his own 'tasks'. This approach is being taken by a number of manufacturers and will find acceptance undoubtedly amongst research establishments or other organisations which wish to develop unusual control strategies.

Some of the most useful extra tasks, over and above the actual control action generation, integral desaturation, tracking, etc., are signal processing and calculation of algebraic functions involving more than one signal (for ratio control, etc.). Some manufacturers have also included 'adaptive' control, but this subject will be dealt with later.

In Chapter 11 the advantages of simple multivariable control are explained. One of the great advantages of the microprocessor-based controller over its analog equivalent is the ability, based on digital computation, to carry out matrix algebraic calculations. This ability makes

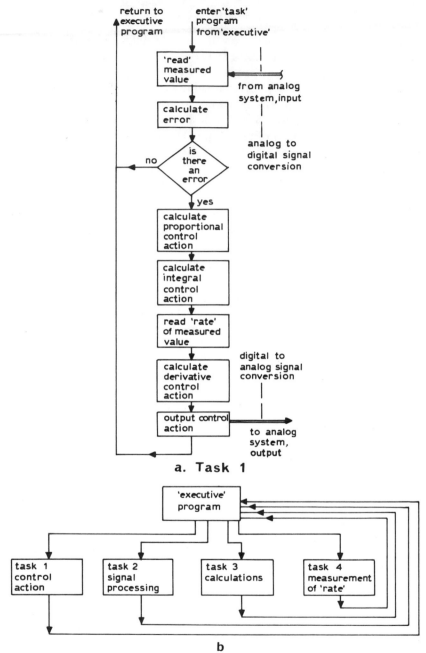

a. Task 1

b

Fig. 9.19.

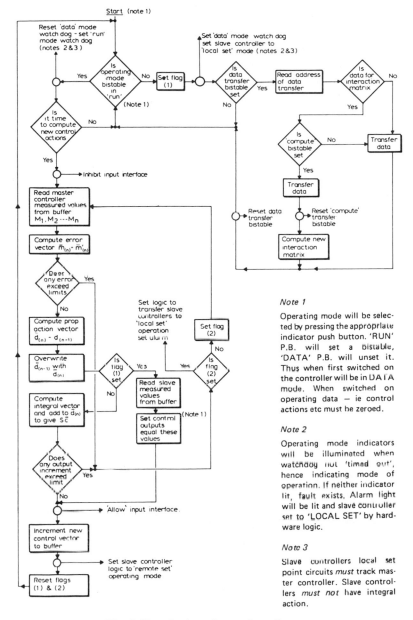

Fig. 9.20. Basic software flow diagram.

Note 1

Operating mode will be selected by pressing the appropriate indicator push button. 'RUN' P.B. will set a bistable, 'DATA' P.B. will unset it. Thus when first switched on the controller will be in DATA mode. When switched on operating data — ie control actions etc must be zeroed.

Note 2

Operating mode indicators will be illuminated when watchdog not 'timed out', hence indicating mode of operation. If neither indicator lit, fault exists, Alarm light will be lit and slave controller set to 'LOCAL SET' by hardware logic.

Note 3

Slave controllers local set point circuits *must* track master controller. Slave controllers *must not* have integral action.

the microprocessor-based controller peculiarly suitable for applying such multivariable control algorithms. Strangely, in the author's opinion, this particular capability has not yet been exploited by manufacturers, perhaps because they do not recognise a demand for such a controller. Figures 9.20–9.22 show a flow chart, block diagram and suggested front panel layout for a microprocessor controller capable of applying the techniques of control outlined at the end of Chapter 11. Such a controller could only be used as a 'master' in cascade with several 'slave' controllers.

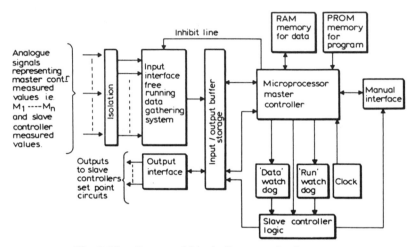

Fig. 9.21.   Suggested block diagram of sub-systems.

Controller operation (Figs 9.20–9.22)

When first switched on the master controller will operate in the 'DATA' mode (see Fig. 9.20). Fixed logic will be set to put the slave controllers into 'LOCAL SET' operating mode. The slave controllers must therefore be capable of being switched from LOCAL SET to REMOTE SET remotely and must also 'track' the remote set point signal when in LOCAL SET operating mode. Control will be transferred bumplessly to the master cascade–REMOTE SET mode by pressing the 'RUN' push button which will set a bistable (see Fig. 9.20). At this point the master controller outputs will be set equal to the *measured values* of the *slave* controller *variables*. Thereafter the *set points* of the slave controllers will be driven by the master controller outputs to the new values dictated by the master controller under the influence of integral control. (The slave controllers must not have integral terms.)

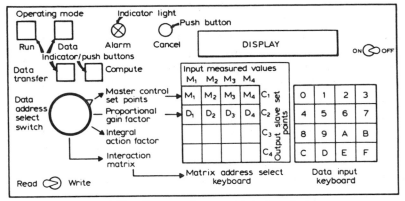

Fig. 9.22. Suggested manual interface design.

In the 'DATA' mode control action by the master controller is therefore frozen while regulatory and interaction control data are entered or changed. The set points for the master controller measured values (as distinct from the slave controller measured values) can be entered by setting up the data address using the DATA ADDRESS and MATRIX ADDRESS, SELECT switches, entering the value on the DATA INPUT KEYBOARD and pressing the DATA TRANSFER pushbutton. The proportional action factors and the integral action factor can be entered in a similar fashion. To set up a new interaction matrix the necessary new data can be entered in the same way; however in addition the 'COMPUTE' pushbutton must be pressed *before* entry of the last datum.

In the 'RUN' mode control action computation, measured value inputting and control action outputting routines will iterate at an appropriate frequency (say 1/10 s). Checks are included (see Fig. 9.20) to ensure that corrupted data are first ignored: then on the second successive iteration will automatically go to the LOCAL SET mode of operation and alarm. A similar check is applied to the computed outputs. In addition an independent 'watchdog' timer is set at each iteration to ensure that software 'hangups' if they occur lead to similar back up action. A separate watchdog timer will monitor operation in the 'DATA' mode (see Figs 9.20 and 9.21).

9.10 ADAPTIVE CONTROLLERS AND ON-LINE IDENTIFICATION

Microprocessor-based controllers are available, that can adapt their control actions to provide near optimal loop response over a wide range of process operating conditions, even when the process response is highly non-linear (see Section 11.7) and also non-stationary (a stationary process is one the response of which does not vary with time; however, plant gets dirty, or less efficient with age, and stationary process response is rare in fact).

In order to adapt its own control actions a controller must obviously be supplied with a plant measurement which tells it how the process condition, which dictates the response required, is changing. This is sometimes the measured value it is controlling, as in the case of level measurement in vessels of non-constant cross-section (see Section 5.3) when level is the measured value in a control loop regulating filling or emptying of the vessel. In other cases a separate measurement may be required (see Section 11.7). By observing the closed loop response under several different process conditions the adaptive algorithm in the controller can be characterised so that, as one of its internal tasks, it changes the gain to suit process conditions. It is normally only necessary to change gain, as integral and derivative actions are defined in terms of gain. This type of controller is adequate to compensate for a stationary cause of non-linearity but it cannot cope with non-stationary effects. Even if loop response is linear over the operating range of process conditions, it may change considerably with time as heat exchangers foul, etc. Thus, there is a need for a controller which recognises the change in response of the plant and tunes control actions accordingly. One manufacturer does provide such a controller, based on microprocessor circuitry, which recognises the process response by sampling and storing values of the appropriate plant measurement and analysing these (using statistical methods) to determine the dead time and lumped time constant values, *which is a non-stationary process change with time*. Three facts make such a controller possible:

1. The response of *all* single input, single output (SISO) control loops can be defined in terms of dead time plus a single lumped time constant.
2. Digital computation is very accurate and enables statistical regression techniques to be used to 'identify' the dead time and time constant.
3. Digital parameters can be stored, allowing 'historical' records to be analysed and the recent loop response identified.

Obviously a controller which, in addition to its normal 'tasks', identifies the process response and calculates its own optimal control actions is very much more complex than a conventional controller, and will only be used in a small number of cases. The *modus operandi* of such an equipment system is beyond the scope of this book but the principles involved should be clear to the reader at this stage.

The principles which make it possible today to automatically identify and thus optimise control of a simple SISO system can be applied to much more complex multivariable (interactive) systems—i.e. whole plants—to optimise operation. This is obviously infinitely more complex in execution and design, but multivariable system identification is already perfectly possible and such systems will emerge in time.

9.11 THE FINAL CONTROL ELEMENT

So far we have been concerned with the *generation* of control action, not its application to the process. There are in fact two problems which arise from the application of control action to the process through the action of the final control element. First, the final control element (usually a control valve) may add further delay into the system. Secondly, the design of the control valve (or other final control element) will almost certainly modify the proportional action factor. Moreover, it will probably be such that the proportional action factor and therefore control action will change according to how far open or closed the valve is. The reason can be seen from the diagram in Fig. 9.23.

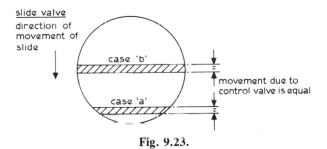

Fig. 9.23.

The diagram represents a slide valve such as that shown in Figs 8.8–8.10. Control action will cause the slide to move up or down, thus increasing or decreasing the flow of liquid through the opening. For the same amount of control action the slide valve will move the same distance whether the valve is nearly closed (position 'a') or half-open (position 'b'). However, it is clear that the amount by which the area of opening of the valve increases or

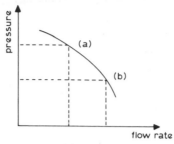

Fig. 9.24.

decreases is not the same (being greater in case 'b'). Expressing the control action proportional action factor as the change in opening which results for a given change in measured value, it can be seen that it is not constant but varies according to whether, before control action takes place, the valve is approximately half-open or nearly closed. The system is said to be 'non-linear' and will have to be retuned each time the steady state or equilibrium operating state changes significantly because of the change in proportional action factor.

The non-linearity-variable proportional action factor also arises in another way, i.e. from the characteristic of the plant. The flow of fluid through the valve opening depends not only on the size of the opening but also on the pressure upstream of the valve, and this may change with the operating conditions. The upstream pressure is often provided by a centrifugal pump, and the pressure delivered changes with flow rate as shown in Fig. 9.24. Therefore, if the flow through the pump increases, moving the 'operating point' from (a) to (b), pressure at the control valve will fall. Under these new conditions a given control action (movement of the valve) will not cause as much change in flow rate as it would if the operating point of the pump had remained at (a). The change in flow rate through the pump may be caused by an operating change which has

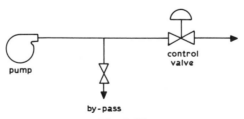

Fig. 9.25.

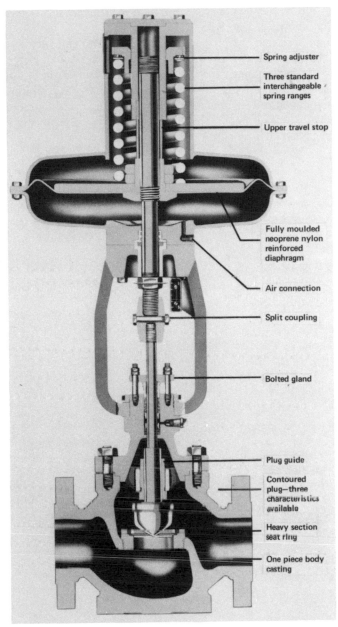

Fig. 9.26. Typical single seat globe type control valve.

nothing to do with the control loop, as, for instance, if a bypass valve is opened as shown in Fig. 9.25.

It can be seen that the proportional action factor can vary owing to the characteristic of the control valve (or other final control element) or to plant operational changes. It is possible to 'characterise' the relationship of the controller action to the valve movement so as to partly compensate for these factors and restore 'linearity'; this will be dealt with in more detail in Chapter 10. Some of these factors, such as the bypass problem in Fig. 9.25 can only be avoided by careful design.

CHAPTER 10

Final Control Elements

10.1 INTRODUCTION

The final control element applies the control action, generated in the controller mechanism, to the process; if it does not perform its function adequately there will have been little point in measuring or in generating control action. Hence, the final control element is in some ways the most important part of the control system. Certainly it is often given too little attention, with the result that the control system performs very badly.

Processing is usually controlled by regulating the flow of gases, vapours, liquids or fluidised powders through pipelines. For this reason, the final control element is almost always a throttling valve; however, it may be a thyristor control element for regulating the flow of electrical energy to an electrical machine, a damper in a ventilation or forced draught duct, or any regulating mechanism. Whatever it is, it will have a characteristic relationship between its input (the control action signal generated by the controller) and its output (the effect it has on the process), which will not usually be one of simple proportionality. In addition, its response is unlikely to be instantaneous—there will be delays as there are in both the process and the measurement. It should be appreciated therefore that the final control element will inevitably modify the control action generated in such a way that control will be different under different processing conditions. As in the case of the process and the controller, it is necessary to understand how the input/output relationship of a control valve affects the closed loop.

In order that a fluid can flow through a given piping system there must be a pressure difference between the input and the output of the system: in order that the flow rate can be adjusted, that pressure difference must be manipulated—reduced to reduce flow rate, increased to increase flow rate.

211

Less power is required to drive the lower flow rate, and the function of the throttling control valve is to waste the additional power available in the system from a pump or other driving force provided to cater for the maximum flow rate required. It is in fact much less energy-wasteful to manipulate a speed control system on the pump as the final control element than to throttle, but the capital investment is much higher. In the case of a gas or vapour, it would always be less energy-wasteful to manipulate the pressure of generation (a steam boiler for instance), but this is not usually practicable. In the majority of systems, therefore (with the exception of those which use a very large amount of power, such as long distance pipelines), unneeded power is simply wasted by throttling flow through a valve. *A control valve, therefore, is a device for wasting energy so that the required measured value can be maintained.* In doing so it must convert the analog signal, which is the output of the controller, into a corresponding change in the process variable.

10.2 THE CONTROL VALVE

The control valve is simply a variable restrictor in the process pipeline; it can take many forms, as shown in Figs 10.1–10.3. Whatever form it takes however, it must have certain essential elements:

(i)   a means of varying the opening through the valve;
(ii)   a mechanical linkage to (iii);
(iii)   an operator or motor, which translates the analog control signal into motion.

In the case of the globe valve (Fig. 10.1), (i) takes the form of a plug and seat, or for the 'double-beat' valve two plugs and two seats. (ii) is a stem and (iii) is a diaphragm 'motor'. In the case of the ball valve (Fig. 10.2) (i) takes the form of a ball with a large hole drilled through it, which seats against a seal ring. The butterfly valve (Fig. 10.3) uses a disc, pivoted about an axis as shown, so that in one position it presents its narrowest profile to the flow, whilst pivoted through 90° it completely blocks the pipe. Both the ball and butterfly valves are operated by an arm and spindle, which rotates in bearings, and the operator may also be a diaphragm motor or other pneumatically, electrically or hydraulically powered motor. All valves also have a gland at the point of exit of the mechanical linkage.

The operator or motor shown on the globe valve in Fig. 10.1 positions the stem: the pneumatic analog control signal is connected into the

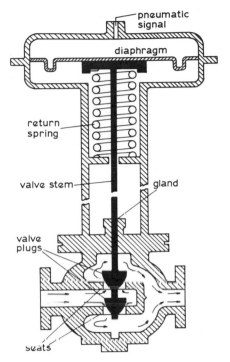

Fig. 10.1. Double-beat globe valve.

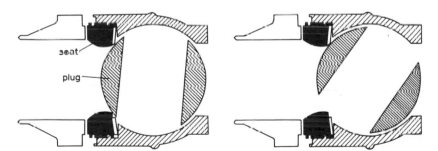

Fig. 10.2. Ball valve.

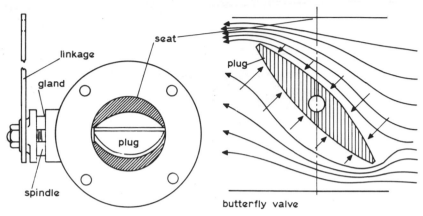

Fig. 10.3. Butterfly valve.

diaphragm chamber, and the pressure acting across the area of the diaphragm provides a force which is opposed by the spring and by whatever forces are produced by the process pressures acting on the valve plugs. As the analog signal pressure increases, the spring is compressed and the stem moves downwards closing the valve and 'throttling' the flow of process fluid through it. Since the spring force is proportional to the distance through which it is compressed, the movement of the valve stem is proportional to the change in the analog signal pressure. Two causes of error in this relationship are:

(i)   the forces acting on the plug of the valve, which vary with the process conditions and with the position of the valve (these are called the out-of-balance forces); and

(ii)   'stiction' between the stem and the gland, which is inevitable.

The 'double-beat' valve shown is really two valves mechanically linked. This is done to reduce the out-of-balance forces as much as possible. Flow is upwards through the top plug and downwards through the lower plug. Because there is a pressure loss through the valve (that is its function), the pressure acting upwards over the cross-sectional area of the plug produces a different force from that acting downwards. The resultant out-of-balance force is, however, upwards in one case and downwards in the other, and provided the cross-sectional areas are carefully balanced, the resultant out-of-balance force on the stem of the valve, which will produce error, is very small. Provided the spring force and the force produced by the diaphragm are much greater than this out-of-balance force, the error in positioning of the valve stem will be small. Some smaller globe-type control valves are 'single-beat', i.e. they have only one plug and seat. The out-of-balance forces in a single-beat valve will obviously be much greater than in a double-beat valve, and to ensure that this does not result in large errors of positioning, a larger motor and stronger spring are used. Nevertheless, single-beat valves cannot be used where there are large pressure drops through the valve, unless a positioner (see Section 10.3) is used to overcome these errors of positioning. Single-beat valves do have the advantage that they can control accurately at much smaller openings, because any inaccuracy of manufacture, damage, or differential thermal expansion in a double-beat valve is likely to result in one plug 'seating' before the other.

The problem of out-of-balance forces is much worse in the case of the butterfly valve as can be seen from the graph in Fig. 10.4(a) which shows a plot of torque (rotary force) against the angle of opening of the valve. This shows clearly that the force required from the operator merely to hold the valve plug in position varies from almost nothing when the valve is slightly open to a very large maximum value when it is 80° open. A very considerable decrease in the out-of-balance torque can be achieved by using a 'fishtail' plug as shown in Fig. 10.4(b); the 'tail' breaks up the air flow in the same way as a 'spoiler' on a car and thus reduces the pressure acting on the face of the plug.

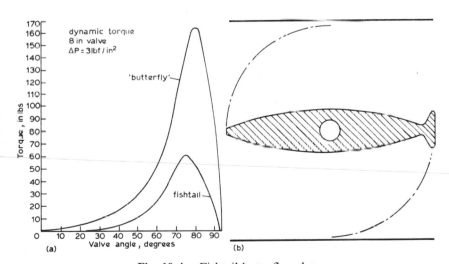

Fig. 10.4. Fishtail butterfly valve.

The ball valve too has very variable out-of-balance torque characteristics which cannot be overcome.

10.3 POSITIONERS

The effect of out-of-balance forces (or torques), together with the static friction (or stiction) of the gland, introduce hysteresis and repeatability errors into the relationship between input signal and plug position. Where these errors would be unacceptable, the size of the operator can be increased so that its force and that of the spring are much greater than the error-producing forces. However, except in the case of the double-beat globe pattern valve, this may require an unacceptably large operator; in such cases a valve positioner can be fitted. The valve positioner is really a controller which has as its measured value the position of the stem of the valve, transmitted to it by mechanical linkage; it is mounted on the frame or 'yoke' of the valve itself. The control action is usually proportional only, so the errors are reduced but not eliminated altogether. The linkage can be 'characterised' (usually by using a cam) to change the relationship of the stem movement of the valve to the opening between plug and seat (the advantage of this will be seen later).

The positioner is in fact a 'slave' controller to the process controller, and the two are in cascade, as described in Section 8.13. In order that any tendency to oscillatory behaviour in the slave loop of a cascade system should not be transferred to the master controller (in this case from the positioner to the process controller) or vice versa, it is essential to observe the rule that the speed of response in the minor or slave 'loop' shall be at least four times faster than that in the major or master loop. (The 'interference' which would otherwise occur is similar to that which occurs between radio stations operating on 'frequencies' which are too close together.) It is rarely possible to keep this rule in the case of flow control, which is why positioners are not normally used on flow control valves.

10.4 CONTROL VALVE CHARACTERISTICS

It will be recalled from Chapter 9 that the relationship between the movement of the stem of the valve, or other linkage, and the increase or decrease in the opening between the plug and seat, is not constant but varies with the valve position. The valve characteristic is the name given to that relationship. The characteristic of an ordinary butterfly valve is shown in Fig. 10.5.

It can be seen that when the valve is nearly wide open or closed a given movement of the spindle causes the opening to change in area less than the same spindle movement does when the valve is near the middle of its movement. If the characteristic plot were a straight line, it can be seen that the change in valve opening for a given movement of the spindle would be constant, no matter what position the valve was in at the time. Such a

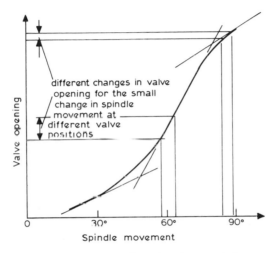

Fig. 10.5. Butterfly valve characteristics.

characteristic is called 'linear'; it might be thought that this is the ideal characteristic, since valve opening will be proportional to input (the control signal) throughout the valve movement. However, two other characteristics are common and have considerable advantages in certain situations. These are 'quick opening' and 'equal percentage' characteristics (see Fig. 10.6).

The 'quick opening' character is self-explanatory. The 'equal percentage' character is such that at any point in the valve movement a given stem or spindle movement results in an equal fractional increase in the opening. Thus, when the valve is only a little open, the change in opening for the given stem or spindle movement is small, but when nearly wide open the change in opening for the same movement of the stem or spindle is much greater. One of the main advantages of this characteristic is that the valve

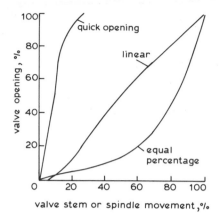

valve stem or spindle movement, %

Fig. 10.6.

positioning becomes progressively less critical as it nears the closed position, which effectively extends the range of opening over which the valve can operate adequately. The butterfly valve characteristic is a mixture of these three characteristics and is therefore not likely to be very suitable for any application. The main advantage of the globe type of valve is that the plug shape can be made so as to give any characteristic (see Fig. 10.7).

The flow rate through the control valve depends on the valve opening and the pressure difference between the inlet and the outlet—the pressure drop across the valve. It will also depend on such factors as the 'flow profile': for instance, the capacity of a right-angle-bodied valve will not be as large as that of a straight through valve because the flow has to change direction in passing through the valve. On the other hand, a valve with a 'flared' exit will

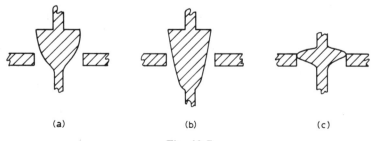

Fig. 10.7.

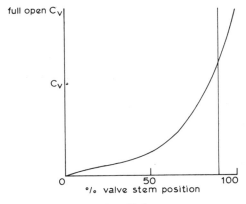

Fig. 10.8.

have a larger capacity. All valves have a capacity coefficient for any particular opening:

$$C_v = f\sqrt{\frac{SG}{dP}}$$

where f is the volumetric flow rate of the process liquid through the valve with a pressure drop of dP across it, and SG is the specific gravity of the liquid.

Any given valve can best be described therefore by its characteristic plot of C_v against stem or spindle movement (Fig. 10.8).

10.5 INSTALLED CHARACTERISTICS

Because the flow rate through the valve depends on the pressure drop across it, it is not necessarily true that a linear characteristic is ideal. Ideally the change in the *process variable* resulting from a given change in valve stem or spindle position should always be the same, because only then will the control valve not modify the control action generated by the controller. However, in most systems the pressure drop across the valve changes with flow through the valve, and it is therefore not sufficient to ensure that the valve opening varies linearly with stem movement; the valve characteristic must be chosen so that it compensates for changes in pressure drop. This can be understood by reference to Figs 10.9 and 10.10.

In Fig. 10.9 the process system is such that the pressure drop across the

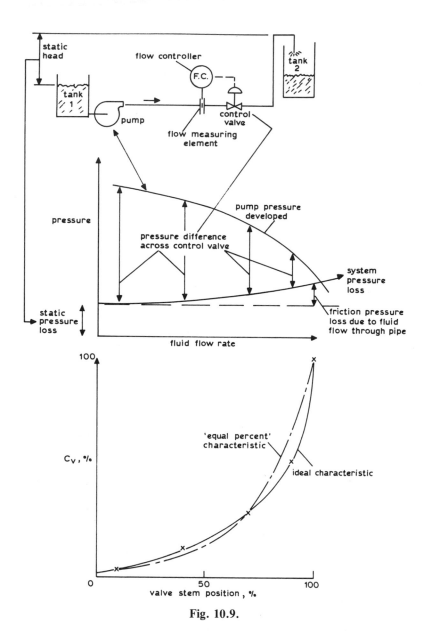

Fig. 10.9.

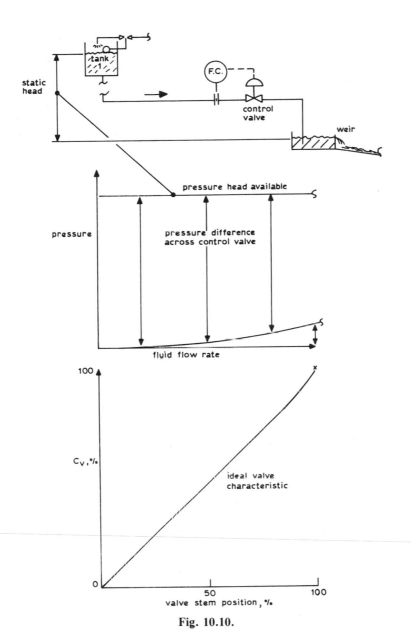

Fig. 10.10.

valve reduces as the flow rate increases, until, when the valve is almost fully open, it is very small indeed. It is obvious therefore that the valve should open slowly when it is nearly closed, whilst it must increase its opening by a large amount for each unit movement of the stem as it nears the fully open position. By calculating the *required* C_v for different flow rates and plotting these in such a way that each increment in flow rate is proportional to the corresponding increment in valve stem movement (and hence to the control signal) as shown, the 'ideal' valve characteristic can be found. In this case it can be seen that it is very similar to the equal percentage characteristic. If a linear characteristic valve were used in this case, the proportional action factor would be very much smaller at high flow rates than it would be at low flows, and the system could not be tuned for the best response at both high and low flow rates.

In Fig. 10.10 the pressure across the valve is provided by static head rather than a pump, and although the pressure lost by friction in the pipe increases as flow increases, the pressure drop across the valve changes little between maximum and low flow rates. In this case, therefore, the flow rate will be approximately proportional to the valve opening, and the ideal characteristic can readily be seen to be close to the linear form. It would be just as wrong to install an equal percentage valve in this system as it would be to install a linear valve in the first system.

The correct choice of valve characteristic will differ with *every* system and depends, as is seen from the examples in Figs 10.9 and 10.10, on the process characteristic as well as the valve characteristic. The ideal *installed* characteristic is that which makes the (steady state) change in the *process variable* proportional to the valve stem movement.

Often the ideal installed characteristic lies between equal percentage and linear, and on other occasions it is more important to obtain the maximum rangeability, which favours the equal percentage characteristic. This is why equal percentage characteristic valves are chosen more often than linear, but *it must be remembered that if the characteristic does not suit the process, it will only be possible to tune the system for correct response under one set of operating conditions.* Often a compromise solution is acceptable, but in cases where both maximum rangeability *and* correct tuning are essential— as when the process system must operate over a wide range of operating conditions—the valve positioner offers a partial solution. As mentioned in Section 10.3 the linkage transmitting the valve stem position to the positioner can be characterised in such a way as to compensate for mismatch between process and valve characteristics. This is, however, a very difficult design problem and is only resorted to in exceptional cases.

10.6 VALVE SIZING

A control valve which is too large or too small cannot properly apply the control action generated by the controller from measurement of the process variable. The capacity of the valve at any opening is given by its C_v, and the values of this coefficient must be matched to the design normal, maximum and minimum requirements. The smallest flow rate which can be effectively controlled will obviously be related to the leak rate across the plug and seat of a fully closed valve. All valves leak, and the rate depends on the 'shut-off' pressure drop; the type of valve will also have a considerable influence on the leak rate. It was mentioned in Section 10.2 that differential thermal expansion may cause one of the plugs of a double-beat globe valve to seat before the other, which will obviously increase the leak rate considerably. In the butterfly valve the seating is very poor because of the difficulty of accurate guiding, and high leak rates are inevitable. On the other hand, a ball valve in good condition has a very low leak rate. Obviously the condition of the valve and the severity of service also, in practice, affect the leak rate and limit the lower end of the valve range. Taking all these factors into consideration, it is probably reasonable, and therefore good practice, to limit the operating range at the lower end to 10% of the full-open capacity in the case of double-beat globe valves and butterfly types, and 5% in the case of single beat globe valves and ball valves. Even then it has to be remembered that, in order to control the process in the face of disturbances to the steady-state 'design' conditions, a control valve must be capable of increasing or decreasing the flow rate about a mean steady state *at all operating conditions*. Thus, in matching the valve capacity to the process, these limits become 20% and 10%; for the same reason the upper limit is usually taken as no more than 80% of the full-open value. Thus, the rangeability—the ratio of the maximum usable C_v to the minimum usable C_v—lies between 5:1 and 10:1, depending on the type and condition of the valve. As was seen from the previous section, when the pressure drop across the valve rises as the flow rate falls, this range is reduced still further, and it is not uncommon to find that the *effective* rangeability is no more than 3:1 in practice.

One way in which errors of sizing can be corrected after commissioning of the plant is finished (and it can be seen whether the valve is *in fact* too large or too small) is to install a valve body with a 'reduced' size 'trim'. Most globe pattern valves can be obtained with a seat and plug one size smaller than that which the body of the valve would normally contain; thus, in effect, a smaller valve is installed with the option of increasing it later (it is much cheaper and easier to replace 'trim' than to remove the whole valve from the pipe once the plant has started up). However, this option is only possible in the case of globe-type valves (single- or double-beat), as can be appreciated from the construction of other types, this is one reason why this type of valve, though expensive, is still the most widely used. The other reasons are more precise positioning and greater flexibility of characterisation.

10.7 MAINTENANCE OF CONTROL VALVES

From the foregoing it must be obvious that the stem or spindles and the glands of control valves must be maintained in good condition at all times. Failure to do so will result in poor control usually long before it results in breakdown. Care should be taken to ensure that valves are installed in the pipeline in such a location (having due regard to control requirements, especially response) that access for maintenance is good. Often, in designing the pipework, it will be overlooked that sufficient clearance must be provided, not only to get at the valve but to withdraw its internal parts (trim, for instance) for inspection and repair without removing the body from the pipeline (which can usually only be done at a shut-down). This often prevents adequate maintenance, with disastrous results.

10.8 DYNAMIC RESPONSE

It was mentioned earlier in this chapter that, in addition to modifying the steady-state relationship between control action signal and process variable, the control valve introduces delays because of the time it takes for instrument supply air to 'fill' or 'empty' the large capacity of the operator or motor. This is likely to be a problem with 'fast' process loops, such as flow and some pressure controls, particularly where the controller is located in a central control room a long distance from the control valve (which is common today). A solution is often found by fitting an amplifier relay like that used in the controller (and usually referred to as a 'booster' relay) at the valve itself. This isolates the controller output signal from the valve motor, so that air from the controller, travelling through the considerable restriction of the signal line from the remote control room, has only to fill the very small capacity of the relay chamber, with the result that hardly any delay is generated in that part of the system. Air to fill the motor chamber is supplied at high pressure (5–7 bar) close to the valve and is subject to much less restriction; thus, the delay in filling the motor chamber is greatly reduced. If the delay is still too great, high pressure motors can be obtained, with the advantage that the same force can be generated with a smaller capacity, using air at a higher pressure.

10.9 CONTROL VALVES AS PLANT EQUIPMENT

The control valve is the only part of the control loop which is also an integral part of the plant itself (measurement sensors, which are also installed into the plant, do not take any part in operation). It is to be expected, therefore, that the proper specification of a control valve is as much concerned with process and mechanical considerations as with control.

A control valve must *never* be used as an isolating valve; it is not designed for this purpose, and its seats and plugs will probably be damaged to such an extent that control will be badly affected if it is used as a shut-off device. Where the plant operation requires them, isolating valves *must be installed in addition to control valves.*

The direction of flow through the valve is of great importance, except possibly in the case of a simple butterfly valve. The seal on a ball valve must face the flow; the tail of a fishtail butterfly must be downstream when the valve opens. In the case of a globe valve, both the operator and the capacity of the valve will be affected if the flow direction is changed. This is illustrated in Fig. 10.11, which represents a type of single-beat globe control valve. If flow is downward through the plug and seat, the upstream pressure, which must always be the higher, acts on the smaller cross-sectional area because pressure on the valve stem does not act downwards. Because of this the out-of-balance forces can be reduced; in fact, it may be possible, if the stem is of a large enough diameter, to virtually eliminate them. Thus, the actuator can be smaller than would be required if the same valve were installed so that flow is upwards, in which case the highest pressure acts on the largest area, and it is not possible to reduce the out-of-balance forces.

Other considerations may dictate that flow must be in the direction which would maximise the out-of-balance forces on a single-beat valve, and this may be a reason for selecting a double-beat valve despite its greater cost and leak potential. Because the flow in a double-beat valve splits between the two 'plugs' there need be no out-of-balance forces, providing the valve is

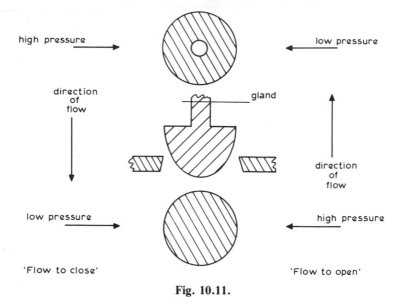

Fig. 10.11.

designed with the correct cross-sectional areas as shown in Fig. 10.12. For instance, it may be vital that if the pneumatic air supply fails the valve should open.

The capacity of a control valve may vary considerably according to the direction of flow through it, especially if the body has been designed to give a high 'recovery' on the downstream side by shaping it like a measuring nozzle or venturi (see Chapter 4).

In considering the mode of failure of the valve it should be remembered that the plug is only driven in one direction by pneumatic force; the spring provides the force to drive it in the other direction. Apart from the direction

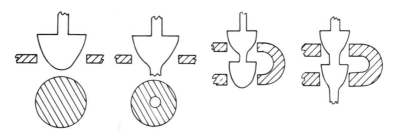

Fig. 10.12.

of flow through the valve, there is another option—whether spring or pneumatic pressure is employed to open or close the valve if there is a failure of the pneumatic supply pressure. Finally, it may be important to consider what will happen if the control signal should fail but not the pneumatic air supply (if electronic control and transmission is used or if either a positioner or 'booster' relay is used at the valve). The answers to all these questions will decide the size of actuator required.

The process conditions under which the valve has to operate will decide the type of construction appropriate for the internals of the valve. For instance, the stem may be top guided only or may be supported top and bottom if turbulence or 'flashing' (sudden change from liquid to vapour as the pressure drops through the valve) is expected. The effect of these options on out-of-balance forces and capacity, can be appreciated from the diagrams shown in Fig. 10.12.

Materials of construction of the body, and particularly of the seat and plug, are of considerable importance. One reason why it is not desirable for the valve to be oversized is that it would then be operating with a small clearance between the plug and seat for much of its life; this will inevitably accelerate wear by erosion, particularly where the process fluid contains solid matter (dirt) or where flashing may occur, and this in turn will adversely affect control.

10.10 SPLIT-RANGE OPERATION

It was explained in Section 10.6 that the useful range of operation of any control valve is often quite small. Fortunately, most process plant tends to be operated close to design conditions; it is not uncommon, however, to find that the rangeability available, when all the constraints have been allowed for in the design and selection of equipment, is not adequate. In such cases it is possible to install two control valves in parallel, one normally being larger than the other, to greatly extend the operating range. Each valve must have a positioner, which can be adjusted so that it operates over its full range of opening in response to only a part of the control signal range (Fig. 10.13). The operating ranges of the two valves overlap to ensure that there cannot be a part of the total operating range where no increase in capacity occurs for an increase in control signal; however, selection of the most appropriate valve characteristic can pose a considerable problem. In very special cases it would be possible to characterise both valve positioners so that the combined character of the two valves would be close to ideal.

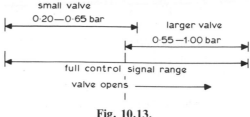

Fig. 10.13.

This is so difficult in practice that it is rarely if ever done, and increasing rangeability is normally achieved at the expense of installed characteristic and, therefore, poor tuning over the operating range.

10.11 MOTOR SPEED CONTROL

While it is true that the great majority of final control elements in process systems are throttling valves, there is increasing use of variable speed control of drive motors for pumps, fans compressors, etc., as an alternative to throttling away unwanted energy. In terms of the other parameters of the pump or compressor—flow and pressure—there is a different operating characteristic for each value of speed. Thus, the operating characteristic of the pump, fan or compressor can be altered so that the combined plant operating characteristic suits the process requirements without the addition of a throttling valve to the system. For instance, as shown in Fig. 10.14, if fluid flow rate is to be reduced, the operating point can be moved to the left in the system diagram by reducing the speed until the pressure

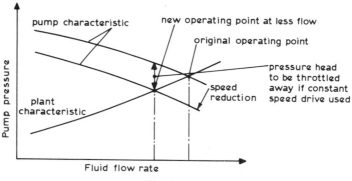

Fig. 10.14.

produced by the pump exactly equals that dissipated in the system pipework, etc., at the lower flow rate.

Variable speed drives have, in the past, consisted of DC motors: speed is varied in simple cases by means of a variable resistor in the armature circuit, manipulation of which varies the armature voltage and thus the motor speed. However, this is in effect a form of throttling, as energy is dissipated in heat to waste in the resistor which has to carry the full armature current. For large drives the Ward–Leonard system has been used; in this a separate motor/generator set is used to supply the armature current, but this is very expensive in capital terms and hard to justify economically for any but the largest energy users. In any case DC electric power is very expensive to distribute and would normally have to be generated on site or obtained by inefficient rectification of AC power, which again increases the capital investment required—all in all not a very cost-effective alternative to throttling.

The development of the thyristor—the solid-state equivalent of the thyratron thermionic valve—has made speed regulation of AC motors of all sizes economically feasible. The 'squirrel cage' induction motor, the armature of which is constructed of bars rather than mere wires, and which looks a bit like a cage, has a very low armature impedance and consequently loses little power in wasteful heating. However, the torque/speed relationship is as shown in Fig. 10.15(a), from which it can be seen to be effectively a one-speed machine. By increasing the armature resistance a little as shown in Fig. 10.15(b) a near ideal torque/speed relationship can be obtained, and, although the additional armature resistance implies some increase in wasted energy (lower motor efficiency) and a slight derating to allow dissipation of the additional waste heat (a slightly larger motor may

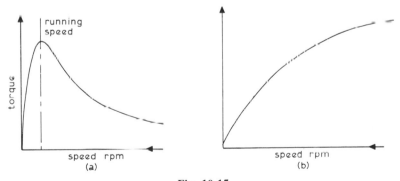

Fig. 10.15.

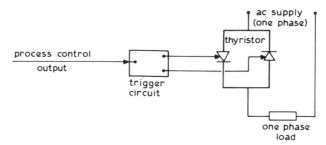

Fig. 10.16.

be required for a particular duty), these are small penalties compared to the enormous waste of energy implied by the inclusion of throttling devices in the process/plant system.

The 'final control element' in a variable speed drive system is termed a 'power controller', and consists of a trigger circuit, which is set by the process controller output, and a pair of thyristors per phase in the AC supply to the motor itself (Fig. 10.16).

There are three ways in which the power entering the motor is modulated by the power controller. The first is phase angle control under which the thyristors are triggered to 'fire' (i.e. conduct) during only part of each cycle of the alternating current supply. That part can be increased and decreased so that the *mean effective power* input over a number of cycles is modulated in proportion with the control signal from the process controller (Fig. 10.17).

The use of this method of power modulation produces considerable 'harmonics' in the AC system owing to the irregular 'chopped up' nature of the output from the power controller thyristors, and these harmonics may cause signal interference. For large equipment, such as very large compressors, the expense of more complex solid state power controllers may be justified: these convert the AC power supply to DC, smooth it using

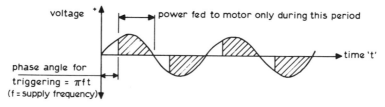

Fig. 10.17.

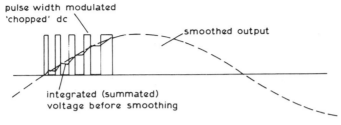

pulse width modulated
'chopped' dc

smoothed output

integrated (summated)
voltage before smoothing

Fig. 10.18.

capacitors, and then 'chop' it up using pulse width modulating inverters to provide an AC supply to the motor at variable frequency (Fig. 10.18). Such controllers are very expensive and complex, and contain control loops of their own, but they can drive standard squirrel cage motors at speeds which relate to the alternating frequency output of the controller (whereas with the simpler type of controller the motor speed is not related to the frequency of the supply, which is constant).

A simple form of power controller is sometimes used in which the supply is switched on and off, not during each cycle, but every few cycles (Fig. 10.19). The on/off ratio is varied within a fixed total period so that at one extreme no power at all is fed to the motor, whilst at the other the normal power supply is continuously connected. In between these two extremes the motor, of course, receives 'bursts' of power. This is a form of proportional time control and it is only suitable for systems in which there is a large inertia or flywheel effect to smooth the irregularities in power supply.

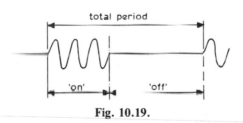

total period

'on'   'off'

Fig. 10.19.

The design of motor drive controls is beyond the scope of this book; however, it has been mentioned here as in many cases there is no longer any excuse for the use of energy wasteful throttling valves as final control elements. Pumps, fans compressors and other motor-driven equipment can be controlled at least as well, and often better, by regulation of the drive motor speed.

CHAPTER 11

Process Control and System Design

11.1 INTRODUCTION

Processes are developed in the laboratory in the first place and later in small-scale pilot plant. After this stage full-scale plant is designed to carry out the process, not by instrumentation and control engineers, but by chemical process engineers. Automatic control systems are designed to assist with the operation of the plant in much the same way as human operators would do: often their function is merely to maintain a given steady state which is different from the natural steady state of the plant (level control on a vessel, for instance). Nevertheless, the way such regulating controls will react to disturbances, and indeed react with each other, has to be considered at the design stage. This behaviour will depend as much on the design of the plant and the plant equipment items as on the design of the control system themselves. The technician must learn how to diagnose unsatisfactory behaviour which will often be wrongly blamed on 'the instruments', as well as to diagnose faults in the instrumentation itself. The designer must learn how decisions taken by other design engineers or equipment manufacturers can seriously influence his ability to design a good control system, and must then apply this knowledge *early in the design process*, to ensure that the best compromises (all design is compromise) are made from his point of view. All this must come largely from experience; in this chapter it is only possible to introduce the concepts which will guide a well-educated engineer or technician who has wide knowledge, not only of instrumentation and control principles, but also of the functions of other designers. In short the good instrument technician or control engineer must be a jack-of-all-trades as well as master of his own.

This chapter will start by outlining the purposes of the various engineering drawings which the technician, as well as the engineer, must know how to use. It will go on to show how lack of consideration at the design stage can lead to operating problems, and later to show how system design should be approached. The later parts of the chapter will describe the design of typical systems.

11.2 PROCESS FLOW DIAGRAMS

The process flow diagram is a drawing which is intended to show the quantities and flow rates of material and energy in the plant. Usually values are shown at three different operating rates: minimum, design, and maximum. The information is needed in the first place by design engineers, to enable the ranges of instruments, such as flow meters, pressure sensors and temperature sensors, to be fixed and to 'size' final control elements. This drawing will also show where flows start from and go to in the plant, and where control loops are required or measurements have to be made in order that the operator can do his job. Perhaps most important of all it will

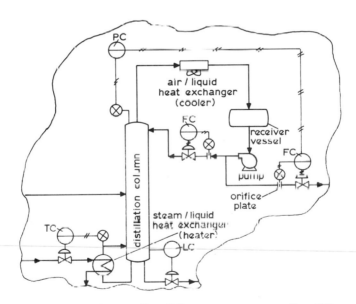

Fig. 11.1 Key: LC, level controller; TC, temperature controller; PC, pressure controller; FC, flow controller; ○, local controller; ⊖, panel-mounted controller; ⊗ transducer; ——, process pipe;' ⧣⧣, pneumatic signal connection; ——, impulse connection.

show the relative positions of plant equipment in piping systems; e.g. whether the control valve is upstream of the flow measuring device or downstream.

The process flow diagram will *not* normally show elevations, i.e. the heights above a datum (usually the ground) at which items of equipment are mounted. For this information the structural drawings will be required. Such information is often of vital importance in establishing the cause of faults, especially soon after start-up of new plant, because the design engineer may have overlooked some change in piping made late in the design. This may affect the working of a level, pressure or temperature measurement system (see Chapters 2, 3 and 6 for a fuller discussion), or it may mean that a control valve is now too large or too small.

The portion of a typical process flow diagram, shown in Fig. 11.1 (without process data), shows that the instruments and controls required are given only in enough detail to illustrate how the control systems operate. In the flow sheet shown in Fig. 11.2, for the same plant, a more complicated control system is shown; this has a level/flow cascade control for the receiver, and a cascade system with temperature controller as master and a flow ratio control system as slave to control temperature in the column itself.

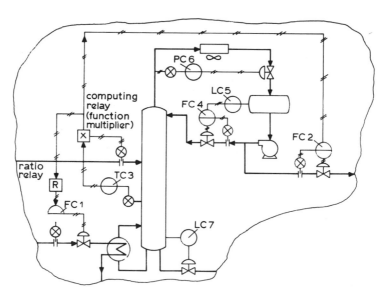

Fig. 11.2.

11.3 INSTRUMENT DIAGRAMS

The way in which the process is to be controlled is shown on the process flow diagram, but not the way in which the control system will achieve this. The instrument engineer or technician needs to know exactly what connections must be made between the different component items which make up the control system(s), where each item is located, where power supplies are to be connected, and details, such as earth or cable screen connections, which do not concern the process operation. The existence of such items as valve positioners or booster relays, which are important for the operation of the control system, will not always be shown on a process flow diagram.

Once the process flow diagram has defined the way the process is to be controlled, a drawing called the 'instrument diagram' is produced to show how the instruments and controls will do this. There are a number of ways in which this can be done, the most usual being 'loop schematics'. It can be seen from the flow diagram in Fig. 11.1, that the control system for the process unit (distillation column) really comprises four separate and independent control systems or loops. This is not an uncommon situation, but in contrast the flow diagram in Fig. 11.2 includes one system, the temperature/flow ratio system, which contains three controllers, two

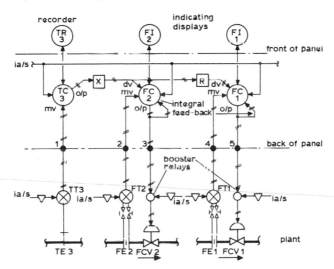

Fig. 11.3. Pneumatic loop schematic. Key: mv, measured value; dv, desired value; ia/s, instrument air supply; o/p, output (control action); FCV, control valve (flow); TT, temperature transducer; TE, temperature sensor element; TC, temperature controller.

computing relays, three transducers and three control valves. A typical 'loop schematic' of this is shown in Fig. 11.3 for a pneumatic system: an electronic system loop schematic (Fig. 11.4) would not be very different, but might be more complex if intrinsic safety barriers have to be used to overcome the explosion and fire hazard.

It should be noted that in both the loop schematic (Fig. 11.3) and the process flow diagram (Fig. 11.2) (and in the specification) each item of

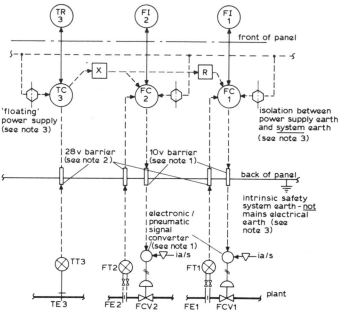

Fig. 11.4 Equivalent electronic loop schematic. (Integral feedback not shown— would normally be an internal connection.)

Note 1: Electronic/pneumatic converters are devices which operate on the force-balance beam principle to produce a pneumatic analog of the electronic (analog) signal. The type of barrier used will depend on the impedance of the force-balance coil in this device.

Note 2: The dotted lines represent *two* core connections: one core is in each case connected to *system* earth (not the same thing as power supply earth). Thus, transducers, electronic/pneumatic signal converters and controller input and output circuits are all connected to system earth through the intrinsic safety barriers.

Note 3: The floating power supplies isolate the instrument system from the power supply earth. This satisfies the requirements of intrinsic safety and also prevents electrical 'noise' from entering the analog signals through 'earth return loops'. Care should be exercised to ensure that the analog circuits are not connected to the control panel, and hence to power supply earth (the panel will almost certainly be earthed in this way).

equipment is given an identification number which identifies it with the measurement and the loop.

Figures 11.3 and 11.4 are divided into three areas: plant, back of panel and front of panel. The panel is usually built by a specialist contractor, and the loop schematics are usually all the contractor needs, together with a front of panel layout (to show where the indicating and recording instruments should be mounted) and the equipment specifications. For this reason, connecting terminals for connections to the plant are shown and numbered. The construction engineer will use the loop schematic, together with the equipment specifications and detailed engineering drawings, to show how each item should be mounted or installed in the plant.

Once the plant is built and commissioned the process flow diagrams and loop schematics should be corrected to take account of any changes made during construction and commissioning, as should the equipment specifications (the 'trim' of a control valve may have been changed, for instance, because it was found, during commissioning, to be too large). All these documents become the record of the plant and are used by the maintenance staff; if they are not corrected and then kept up to date it will be difficult to know what is actually installed, and therefore to maintain the plant properly.

11.4 OTHER DRAWING RECORDS

In addition to the process flow diagrams and loop schematics (or other form of instrument *diagrams*) several other types of drawing have to be produced at the design stage. Of these the signal piping interconnection drawing or schedule informs the construction and commissioning engineers of the route to be followed by each pipe or cable from the central control panel to the plant-mounted items (transducers, control valves, etc.). Each connection may pass through several junction boxes and be made through one core of a multicore cable or pipe over part of the distance. Drawings are also needed to show how sensors are to be mounted in vessels or pipes, etc. (to ensure that the temperature sensor is inserted into the pipe the correct depth, for instance). These drawings too, if kept up to date, are of great help to maintenance staff and others after start-up of the plant.

Finally, at the design stage the installation of such items as sensors, control valves and impulse connections have to be detailed on the piping drawings as they become part of the plant itself. *The instrumentation engineer should always ensure that installation is such that the equipment will operate as intended.* Ensuring that the pipework upstream of a flow measuring sensor will provide suitable flow conditions is a case in point; i.e.

ensuring that control valves are installed *downstream* of flow measuring sensors, or that sensors and final control elements are not so far apart that appreciable dead time is introduced into the control loop because of the time taken for process material to travel between the two (see below). All these drawings should be available, and may help maintenance staff to find the cause of faults which are not simply caused by failure of instrument equipment.

(Note that in the system shown in Fig. 11.4 integral control action has to be used on the two flow controllers even though they are 'slaves' to the master temperature controller. This is because they are also part of a ratio control system and therefore the flow rates in both cases must be controlled at the desired value (i.e. there must be no offset). Feedback of the controller output signal may have to be connected externally so that some form of integral action limiting can be applied. Details of the actual controllers and other items must be obtained from the manufacturers before the loop schematics can be completed.)

11.5 PLANT DESIGN FOR CONTROLLABILITY—STEADY STATE

As was pointed out in an earlier chapter, the plant itself is part of any control system. It has already been shown (in Chapter 10) that the 'installed' characteristic of a final control element depends on the plant performance characteristic as well as on the performance characteristic of the valve itself. The purpose of a control system is to 'manipulate' some variable of the process and it must not be overlooked that there will be finite limits beyond which this manipulation will be *impossible*. As a simple and not unusual example consider the diagram of a heating coil in a vessel shown in Fig. 11.5.

The rate of heat input to the process fluid depends on the temperature difference between the steam condensed in the coil and the process fluid. Steam at 2 bar (gauge) pressure is at a temperature of 134 °C. Regardless of the size of the control valve no more steam can enter the coil than can be condensed at a temperature difference of: temperature of process fluid -134 °C.

At the other end of the range, no matter how wide open the control valve may be, no steam at all can condense (in steady state) unless the condensed steam can be discharged. In the system in Fig. 11.5(a) condensed steam will cease to be discharged when the pressure in the coil is less than 0·5 bar, at which pressure steam temperature is 112 °C. Thus, if the temperature of the

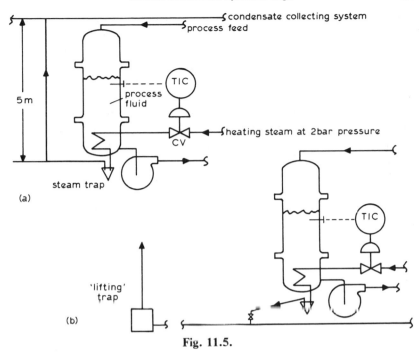

Fig. 11.5.

process fluid is 100 °C the range of the heat input and therefore the process
feed flow rate, can be no more than·

$$\frac{134 - 100}{112 - 100} = 2{\cdot}83{:}1$$

and this has absolutely nothing to do with the sizing of the control valve. In
fact, the heating coil will have been oversized by the utilities engineer for
duty at design process flow rate, to allow a margin of safety in his
calculations and for fouling (reduction of heat transfer owing to deposits
on the steam coil surface—inside or outside). Thus, it is quite possible that
the range of operation will be considerably less.

When during operation, the process feed flow rate is reduced below the
minimum rate thus established, the temperature control will start to behave
in a most unsatisfactory manner. Once control action has caused the
control valve to close to the position at which the differential temperature is
12 °C and the pressure in the coil 0·5 bar (gauge), condensate will cease to
flow out through the steam trap and will accumulate in the coil. After a time
(depending on the volumes in the coil and in the process vessel) this

condensate will cool to 100 °C and the *effective* heat transfer surface of the coil will be reduced to the extent that it is full of condensate at the same temperature as the process fluid. Eventually, after further delay, the whole coil would be full of condensate, and no heat would be transferred to the process fluid. However, before this extreme position can be reached, the temperature of the process fluid will have fallen and the controller will have reacted by opening the control valve, with the result that pressure will have risen in the coil and *all* the condensate will have been expelled. Depending on the rate of steam condensation required to maintain the temperature of the process fluid at the desired value (which will in turn depend on the temperature and flow rate of the process feed) and the volume of the steam coil, the controlled temperature will be seen to cycle in such a way that it will probably be said that the temperature control is not working properly. It should be realised, however, that none of the things that are happening have anything at all to do with any part of the instrumentation: it is the design of the heater system which is at fault, but it is the instrument technician who will be expected to find out what is wrong.

The second system, shown in Fig. 11.5(b), is much less likely to give the same trouble. Condensate is discharged to a low pressure collecting system, without having to overcome the static head in the first system (Fig. 11.5(a)). Thus, the pressure in the coil can fall to almost atmospheric before the cyclical behaviour described above will set in; the range of process feed rates is then:

$$\frac{134 - 100}{101 - 100} = 34:1$$

or more than 10 times as great. If the condensate system cannot be altered to operate in this way, then steam at a higher pressure must be used (which would mean that the steam coil would have to be 'rated' for use at the higher pressure). If 10 bar steam pressure were used, for instance, the range would be:

$$\frac{184 - 100}{112 - 100} = 7:1$$

which is nearly three times the range possible with steam at 2 bar pressure.

Of course, had the desired temperature of the process feed been higher, say 110 °C instead of 100 °C, the problem of cyclical behaviour might never have been experienced, since then the range of feed flow rates would be:

$$\frac{134 - 110}{112 - 110} = 12:1$$

which would probably be quite adequate. Thus, such a problem may arise, not because of bad design but because a process operator has decided to change the process operating parameters.

The reader should learn from this simple example first to ask himself, when looking for the reason for bad control, is it possible for the control system to do what is being expected.

11.6 PLANT DESIGN FOR CONTROLLABILITY—DYNAMIC RESPONSE

Even if the sort of problem described above (which makes it impossible to establish steady-state, or equilibrium, conditions) does not occur, there are many ways in which control can be adversely affected by design or operation of the plant, without there being anything wrong with the instrumentation. This is because of the delays which occur in the process and measurement, as was shown in Chapter 8. Consider the system shown in Fig. 11.6, for instance.

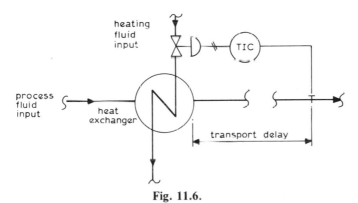

Fig. 11.6.

Heat transfer between the heating fluid and the process fluid, and also from the process fluid to the temperature sensor, will make the response of the process and measurement second or third order. However, in addition, further dead time will be added to this response (decreasing T_c/T_d and hence making control more difficult) by the 'transport delay' introduced by the distance the temperature sensor has been located downstream of the heat exchanger (Fig. 11.7). This distance may be large because the local indicating controller has been sited in a suitable position to be seen

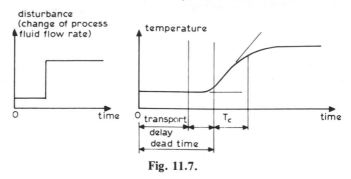

Fig. 11.7.

by operating staff, whilst the control valve and heat exchanger are in an elevated and relatively inaccessible location. The sensor controller distance is limited by the available impulse connection (which is fixed when the instrument is ordered—perhaps before design is completed) but the controller–control valve distance is not constrained in this way. Hence, all these factors may result in a considerable length of pipe between the heat exchanger and the temperature sensor. This is doubly unfortunate because, not only is control made more difficult under any conditions by the unnecessary addition of dead time, but this dead time itself will vary with the flow rate of the process fluid, which is probably a function of the plant throughput.

11.7 DYNAMIC NON-LINEARITY

The previous section showed how control can be made much more difficult by the unnecessary addition of dead time to the system response. It should be clear by now that the design of the plant equipment items is just as important for good control as the design of the controllers or final control elements. Dead time and lumped time constant which characterise the response are largely determined by 'residence time', i.e. the time that on average a small unit of flow 'resides' in a unit of plant. For instance, in the example given above, at any particular process fluid flow rate a small quantity will remain in the body of the heat exchanger for a given time (the residence time) depending on the capacity of the heat exchanger body and the process flow rate. If heat is being transferred from the heating fluid to the process fluid at a constant rate (depending on the temperature difference and heat transfer surface area and condition) then the rise in temperature of the process fluid passing through the heat exchanger obviously depends on the residence time (or capacity) of the heater. Thus, it can be seen that the size (and other aspects of the design) of the heater will determine the response of the system to control action. It can also be seen that, since residence time changes when the process flow rate changes, the response will also change, just as the dead time in the previous section changed.

It is very important to realise that the response of a system will change with throughput, and therefore control action must be retuned for optimum results whenever the throughput changes substantially. This phenomenon is known as 'non-linearity', a linear system being one in which the response is constant over the whole range of throughputs—a comparative rarity.

The reader will recall from Chapter 8 that the integral and derivative control action factors are dependent on the basic proportional action factor. Hence, if this is changed, the integral and derivative components of the control action change in proportion with the proportional action component. If, in the example in the previous section, throughput changes, the dead time and lumped time constant will both change approximately in proportion, and the response curve will change only in that it will be 'stretched out' along the time axis (i.e. it will not change in form). Under these conditions it is only necessary to vary the proportional band (gain or proportional action factor) of the controller to retune it for the new throughput. Controllers are available which have this facility, and a suitable non-linear control system is shown in Fig. 11.8 that can replace that shown in Fig. 11.6 under conditions where the throughput is expected to vary over a wide range.

In this system a computing relay, X, could be adjusted by trial and error so that as the throughput changes, the gain of the temperature controller is

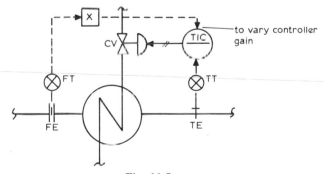

Fig. 11.8.

increased or decreased by an amount which alters the controller response just sufficiently for the loop response to remain approximately constant. There are in fact microprocessors on the market today which provide such a facility (see Section 9.9).

11.8 POOR CONTROL AND BAD MEASUREMENT

Consider, for instance, the case of flow measurement in a pipeline which does not necessarily run full (Fig. 11.9). All sensing elements must be

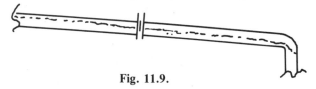

Fig. 11.9.

located in such a position that they are fully immersed at all times and in all circumstances (including shut down). Temperature measuring elements may not be properly immersed to the correct depth, and pressure impulse connections can be blocked. It is no use measuring the process variable in the wrong place and then expecting the control system to work properly (Fig. 11.10). Nor should pressure tappings for level measurement in tanks be made too close to the bottom of the tank if sludge or sediment is likely to gather there.

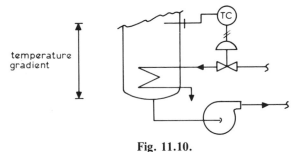

temperature gradient

Fig. 11.10.

The position of the control valve in the piping system is of great importance in most cases. It must never be placed upstream of a flow measuring element (see Fig. 11.11). It should not normally be placed in the suction of a liquid pump (Fig. 11.12). This is because the pressure is always lower in the suction. Two problems may arise from this fact: first as the

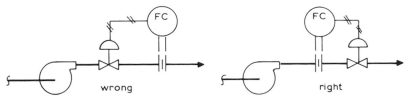

Fig. 11.11.

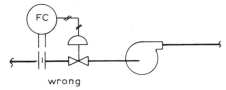

wrong

Fig. 11.12.

control valve closes it may reduce the pressure downstream, that is at the pump suction, to such an extent that flashing occurs in the pump, spoiling its performance and thereby interfering with control functions (and quite probably damaging the pump also). Secondly flashing may occur in the control valve itself, making its sizing and characteristics indeterminate. A nett positive suction head is always quoted for a pump, i.e. the minimum head pressure at the suction which will ensure that flashing does not take place. However, it is better, wherever possible, to locate the control valve in the higher pressure section of the pipework.

There are many ways in which measurement may be the cause of poor control; the instrument technician will have to learn by experience how to recognise them, and what to look for.

11.9 OBJECTIVES OF PROCESS CONTROL

Whilst the measurement and regulation of process variables is essential to control of the plant, there is a great deal more to the design of a control system which will make it possible for a modern process unit to be operated efficiently. In many cases operation without such a control system is not possible: modern processing units are often so complex that operation on the basis of human manipulation of all the process variable set points is out of the question. On the other hand, it must not be thought that the point has yet been reached that human influence is not required to operate the process units. In any modern plant there is a 'hierarchy' of control, with the human operator taking the most complex decisions whilst mechanisms take the simpler ones, such as when and how much to move the control valve stem in order to return the process variable to its desired value. In many cases, as has already been seen, control mechanisms decide how the desired value of a lower level controller should be altered to achieve a higher level desired value (master/slave cascade control). Increasingly today, digital computers are programmed to make decisions at a higher level than this; such decisions often involve changing the set points of several controllers in order to maintain some optimal processing condition, such as energy balance or product purity. Even without programmable computers, control systems have to be designed, which may incorporate many regulating 'loops', to carry out a given control strategy.

Whilst the design of measurement systems and the systems by which control is to be achieved is the responsibility of the instrumentation and control engineer alone, the design of the process control is not. Such design is not concerned with *how* control is to be achieved, but with *what* is to be achieved by the control system. Objectives must first be defined, process limits and constraints identified; it must be determined which process variables require to be and can be measured, and which can be manipulated. The measured and manipulated variables must be paired, the necessary feedforward/feedback, cascade, ratio or interactive regulating strategies identified, and the degrees of freedom of the process considered. Such design must be the joint responsibility of the process engineer and the instrument/control engineer; the former knowing best what is required, the latter what is possible.

Too often the control system for a process or plant is designed without due thought to the emphasis which should be given to, often conflicting, objectives. For instance, in times of recession it is often the case that a plant is operated below its maximum capacity, because the market demand is less than it was when the plant was designed. In such circumstances, the quantity which can be sold will depend on whether the quality and price are better than or worse than those of competitors. Therefore, the objectives will be to operate the plant in such a way as to maximise productivity (i.e. the quantity of product made for given inputs of raw material (feed) and energy) and/or product quality, so that the best product possible can be sold at the lowest price possible. On the other hand, in a boom situation, it may be possible to sell as much as can be produced, even though the quality is not as high as it could be. Whilst judgements as to which objectives are appropriate are the province of management, the design of the control

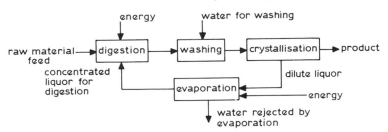

Fig. 11.13.

system must reflect these objectives, and often must be such as to provide as much flexibility as possible to cope with different sets of objectives.

Consider the block diagram of a chemical extraction process given in Fig. 11.13. The raw material from a mining process is digested (that is dissolved) in a liquid in order that other material (which does not dissolve in the liquid) can be removed. The product is then separated out from the 'liquor' by crystallisation, and the remaining liquid is recycled to digest more raw material. Energy is necessary to heat the digestion process and to concentrate the liquor left after crystallisation. If the objectives of control/operation are to satisfy a market where less can be sold than can be made (i.e. recession), then it is important that as much raw material is digested as possible for each unit quantity of liquor. Roughly the same amount of energy will be used to concentrate it in the evaporation stage no matter how little or much raw material is digested, and thus the cost per unit of product will be minimised. If on the other hand it is possible to sell however much is made, then it will be less important how much each unit costs, and indeed the additional profit from higher sales is likely to outweigh the slight reduction in profit per unit produced. In the first case the control system and operating techniques must aim to provide the maximum efficiency of digestion at the expense of throughput, whilst in the second case it is throughput which must be maximised even at the expense of efficient digestion.

The company making this product may find that they can sell it at a much higher price per unit if it is very pure. In this case control and operational objectives will be to maximise product purity even at the expense of both throughput and digestion efficiency, and possibly regardless of the economic climate. In practice, of course, the emphasis on the various objectives will change from time to time and will in any case be a combination of all these factors. For instance, it may be possible to sell only some of the product to the buyers of high purity material.

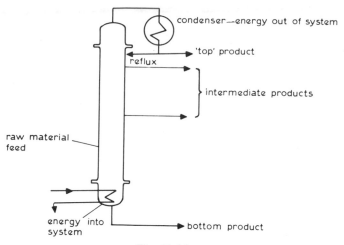

Fig. 11.14.

Distillation is one of the basic processes of petroleum refining (Fig. 11.14). Crude oil is separated into products which contain a high proportion of 'light ends' (the more volatile components) and those which contain a high proportion of 'heavy ends'. In general the top products are sold as petroleum and the intermediate as diesel or light fuel oil, whilst the bottom product is only suitable as fuel for industrial use. The market requirements and the 'quality' of the feedstock both change from time to time, and the control systems and operating techniques must be designed so that the distillation plant can produce more of one type of product and less of another as required.

To illustrate how differing objectives may affect the design of control systems, as well as plant, compare the processing requirements of a simple distillation process designed to produce 'top' product of maximum purity ('bottoms' probably being considered as waste product) and one designed to produce two products (top and bottom) of roughly equal values. Maximum recovery (i.e. maximum production of distilled products) is incompatible with minimal energy use. If one product is valuable whilst the other is essentially waste the lowest cost per unit of product is usually obtained by using as much energy as possible in order to obtain the maximum separation, since the energy cost per unit of productivity is likely to be less than the cost of losing valuable product not separated from the waste stream. On the other hand, if the value of the two product streams is roughly similar, the lowest cost per unit of production will be obtained by minimising the energy used, since energy costs are a very significant part of the total cost of production these days; the fact that a significant component of each product stream is the unwanted product will not in many cases affect the product sale price. There are cases, of course, where purity of product composition is important, regardless of the value of each product, and in such cases the correct objectives may be more difficult to define.

11.10 OBSERVABILITY AND CONTROLLABILITY

The parameters of a process are measured in order to determine how the process is behaving and there must be sufficient information for this purpose. If there is not, the process is said not to be observable and therefore cannot normally be controlled. For instance, in order to control the process of steam raising in a boiler, it is necessary to measure the pressure of the steam and the flow rate of the steam leaving the boiler, so that the inputs of water and heat can be regulated. In practice, the rise or fall of the level in the steam drum is often taken as a measure of the mismatch between the quantity of water entering and the quantity of steam leaving. If the level is static, this satisfies the requirement for 'mass balance'. Pressure is a measure of the 'condition' of the steam; condition in this case indicating the quantity of heat added to each mass unit of water to convert it to steam. The rate of heat input is dictated by the condition and flow rate of steam generated.

If the mass balance control (mass flow of steam generated per unit time/mass flow of water into the boiler per unit time) is based on measurement of drum level, this assumes that the mechanism for regulating the drum level operates perfectly, and as will be seen later this brings its own problems. Having considered the boiler plant itself therefore, from the point of view of the requirements of control it is necessary to consider the sub-units, such as the drum, to determine the needs of control. The selection, sizing and design of process plant (vessels, pumps, distillation columns, heat exchangers, etc.) are very much part of the design of any control system. The control engineer must therefore work closely with the process and other design engineers to establish control objectives, not only for the total plant but also for each individual piece of plant. These 'control objectives' are the critical requirements for good operation of the plant and the individual equipment items. Often, because of long delivery times, these requirements must be decided early in a design project, and the control engineer should advise the other design engineers of the constraints and requirements for good control as early as possible.

The basis of design of all process control systems must be the need to satisfy mass and energy balances in steady-state terms. In addition, recent increases in energy costs make it essential to regard minimisation of energy usage an objective of control. For instance, most of the energy wasted in distillation is due to incorrect control of the reboiler and condenser which, respectively, put energy into and remove heat from the process. The relationship governing the steady-state operation of a heat exchanger is given by:

$$Q = UA\,dT$$

where Q is the heat transfer rate, U the heat transfer coefficient, A the heat transfer area, and dT the log mean temperature difference between the process and the cooling fluids (Fig. 11.15). Control of the amount of

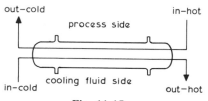

Fig. 11.15.

heat removed from the process can be effected therefore by manipulating any of the terms on the right-hand side of this equation, i.e. the heat transfer surface, the temperature of the cooling fluid (which amounts to manipulating the log mean temperature difference since the temperature of the process fluid is the controlled variable and cannot be manipulated) or the heat transfer coefficient (which is not normally feasible).

Water-cooled condensers normally used for this purpose are best controlled by 'tempering' the cooling water as shown in Fig. 11.16, using a recirculatory system in which the cooling water is circulated through the heat exchanger at a constant velocity: its temperature is regulated by manipulating the flow rate of the return, thus admitting more or less of the cold supply. The process fluid temperature is in turn regulated in cascade by manipulating the set point of the 'tempered' water. The response of the 'slave' controller will of course depend on the speed of circulation of the cooling fluid through the heat exchanger, which will in turn depend on the sizes of the pipes, the pump capacity and the residence time of the fluid in

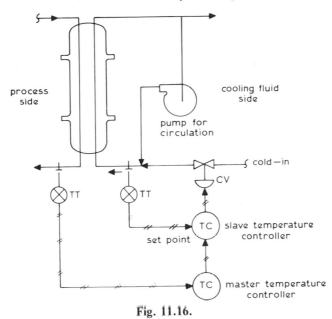

process side

cooling fluid side

pump for circulation

cold — in

CV

TT

TT

set point

TC slave temperature controller

TC master temperature controller

Fig. 11.16.

the heat exchanger. Thus, the control engineer must work with the process engineer, the piping engineer and the mechanical engineer in specifying this equipment, bearing in mind that the response required of the master control must be several times slower than that made possible by these design features of the slave loop.

'Accumulator' vessels are often provided in the process design, as in the distillation column reflux system shown in Fig. 11.17, in order to give stability to operation. Unfortunately, they introduce many problems into the design of the control systems by reason of the phase lag introduced into the transient response of the system. Nevertheless, the same capacity is necessary to provide 'surge' capacity (temporary flow rates greatly in excess of the throughput capacity of the heat exchanger) to deal with process upsets. Hence, system design is bound to be a compromise and again it is essential that the control engineer is involved in the specification of the process equipment and vessels from the outset.

In the system shown in Fig. 11.17 the composition analyser is used as the basis of a control loop which regulates the top product flow rate to give a required purity of specification. If this analyser detects an increase in the 'impurities', the associated controller will act to reduce the forward flow, so that in steady state more of the condensed 'overheads' will be returned to

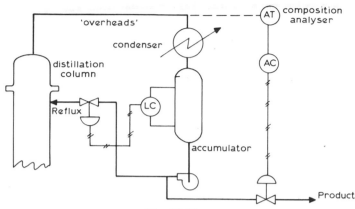

Fig. 11.17.

the column as reflux, thus increasing purity. Unfortunately, this increase in reflux suffers delay due to the time constant of the accumulator vessel—the reflux flow rate will only increase when the level rises in the vessel owing to the reduction of flow rate in the top product line. This delay will depend on the capacity of the accumulator, its shape (whether it is tall and slim or short and fat), and on the tuning of the level controller. This is typical of a system design which has been made by process engineers without the assistance of a control engineer, who would probably advise the use of feedforward control to overcome these difficulties as shown in Fig. 11.18.

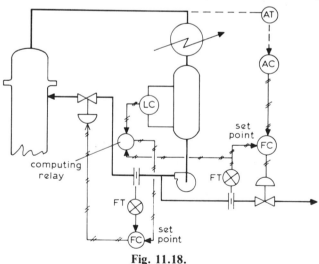

Fig. 11.18.

In this system any change of flow rate in the product line (resulting from the action of the composition analyser control) will be 'fed forward' to reset the flow control loop on the reflux line immediately. Any change in the level in the accumulator vessel will in due course further modify the set point of the reflux flow controller in order to satisfy the steady-state mass balance. The equation of the computing relay will therefore be

reflux set point = level controller output signal − product flow rate

with appropriate scaling and biasing (to ensure that the level controller integral term is approximately mid-scale value when the system is operating in steady state).

11.11 DEGREES OF FREEDOM AND 'PAIRING' OF VARIABLES

A common mistake in the design of complex process control systems is to ignore the rule that the constraints on a system can never be more than the degrees of freedom (less, but never more). The degrees of freedom are the variables (measured or not) which can be manipulated in order to operate the process. These variables will in most cases be paired with the most appropriate measured variables—for instance, in the previous section the process fluid temperature (measured variable) was paired with the mean temperature difference in the cooling water circuit (the manipulated variable). To illustrate the point, it will be obvious that for a boiler generating saturated steam, only one or other of the steam pressure and steam temperature can be manipulated, and to attempt to manipulate both will be to break this rule. It is not always so obvious, however, that the rule has, or has not, been kept, and a distinction must be made between steady state and transient degrees of freedom. For instance, in the previous section it was pointed out that the addition of an accumulator to the reflux system of the distillation process provided 'surge' capability; another way to look at this is that without the accumulator the sum of the product flow and the reflux flow must at all times equal the total overhead flow rate, whereas with an accumulator this constraint does not have to be observed transiently. The accumulator level controller is introduced to ensure that in steady state this constraint is observed. The feedforward action can then be tuned so that when the composition control loop causes a change in the forward product flow rate, the corresponding initial change in the reflux flow rate is greater than that dictated by steady-state mass balance. Subsequently, the level in the accumulator will fall because of the unbalance, and the level controller will modify the reflux flow rate to avoid the accumulator running empty and eventually (by integral control action) restore the desired value, thus satisfying steady-state degrees of freedom. 'Squared error' control action would allow small changes of level without significant control action, the control action factor increasing greatly, however, for large errors in level.

Once the degrees of freedom of the process system have been identified there will be a certain number of variables which must be measured (or analysed), and an equal number of (different) variables which must be manipulated in order to carry out the control strategy. Care must always be taken to ensure that they are 'paired' in such a way that each individual control loop manipulates the variable which most strongly affects the measured variable for that loop. If this is not the case, control will be poor if not totally ineffective, since control action taken in one loop will have a greater effect on some other measured variable than on that intended. Even if this rule is observed, it will sometimes happen that the effect of control action on other variables than that intended is very considerable; in such cases 'multivariable' control strategies are essential. Such interaction can be appreciated by considering the heat exchanger example in the previous section. If the flow rate of the process fluid is being manipulated in order to regulate some other measured value, such control action will inevitably influence the process temperature as will now be shown.

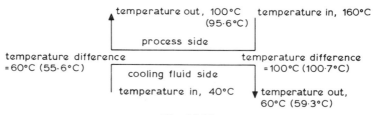

Fig. 11.19.

If the operating conditions are as shown in Fig. 11.19 with a process fluid flow rate of F, then the rate of heat transfer is given by

$$Q = 78 \cdot 3 \, UA$$

since the log mean temperature difference is

$$\frac{(100 - 60)}{\ln (100/60)} = 78 \cdot 3$$

If as a result of control action in the flow regulating loop the process flow rate is reduced 10%, then since U and A do not change

$$Q' = \frac{\mathrm{d}T}{60} Q$$

where Q' is the new rate of heat transfer and $\mathrm{d}T$ the new log mean temperature difference

$$\mathrm{d}T = \frac{(100 \cdot 7 - 55 \cdot 6)}{\ln(100 \cdot 7/55 \cdot 6)} = 75 \cdot 8$$

It can be seen, therefore, that the process outlet temperature will change from 100 °C to 95·6 °C as a result of a 10% reduction in the process flow rate, unless the temperature control loop acts to correct this error. Thus, the action of one control loop has resulted in a disturbance arising in another control loop. This is known as interaction, and the ratio of the steady-state change in the process outlet temperature, which would result from a given change in the process flow rate if the temperature control loop were not operating, is referred to as the steady-state open loop process gain between the manipulated variable (process flow rate) and the measured variable (process temperature). In the course of the system design these steady-state process gains must be calculated, and the measured and manipulated variables which show the strongest 'coupling' selected as the measured and controlled variables, respectively, of the single input/single output (SISO) control loops.

In extreme cases the coupling between one manipulated variable and a measured variable may be of the same order as that between another manipulated variable and the same measured value; in such cases a decoupling (or multivariable) control strategy may have to be adopted. This strategy consists of cross-connecting the outputs of the SISO controller in such a way that it manipulates both the manipulated (or controlled) variables: the control action factors are different for each manipulated variable, however, and the combined control actions are designed to give 'non-interacting' control. In the example above, for instance, the process flow rate controller output could be made to change the set point of the slave temperature controller in the opposite sense to the disturbance which is introduced by the change in flow rate, i.e. to raise the cooling water inlet temperature so that the steady-state drop in process temperature from 100 °C to 95·6 °C does not in fact take place. The control system would then be as shown in Fig. 11.20.

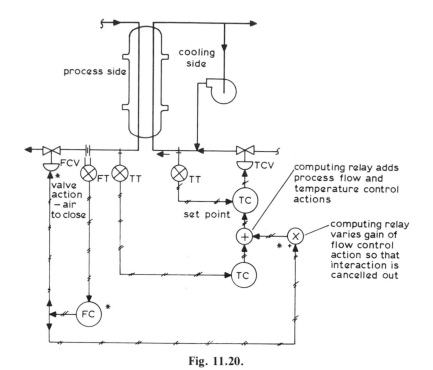

Fig. 11.20.

* *Note:* The 'sense' of the flow controller output signal will depend on the safety requirements (on pneumatic power supply failure) for valve operation. If the valve closes on increasing the signal (reducing the flow rate), then, since reduction of flow rate causes a fall in process temperature (interaction), the 'decoupling' control action is required to raise the cooling water inlet temperature in order to reduce the log mean temperature difference and thus counteract this interaction. Thus, the signal to the computing relay is of the correct sense in this case.

It should be borne in mind that the response of the flow control loop and that of the decoupling' temperature control action will be different, the latter depending on the rate of circulation of the cooling water through the heat exchanger, the former only on the speed of response of the control valve. It may therefore be expedient to limit the speed at which the flow control valve can respond to correspond with the speed of response of the temperature slave loop; in this way transient interaction between these two loops will also be avoided. It is clear from this that the transient response of the whole system is limited by the design of the heat exchanger.

In the case of very large and/or complex systems the pairing of manipulated variables with measured variables can be carried out systematically at the design stage, using a technique known as 'Bristols relative gain array'. A table is prepared as shown in Fig. 11.21, in which the manipulable (or control) variables are entered in sequence in the vertical positions, whilst the measured variables are entered in the horizontal positions. Thus, there is a space in the matrix for the steady-state open loop

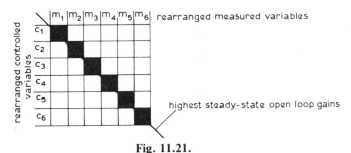

Fig. 11.21.

gain between any manipulable variable and any measured variable to be entered. In some cases it will be obvious that manipulating one variable cannot affect one or more of the measured variables, and in other cases it will be possible to calculate the steady-state process gain by methods similar to the above example. Once the table is complete, the variables are rearranged in such a way that the largest gains (regardless of sense) lie on the diagonal of the table (or array). The best pairing of variables can then be read off this diagonal.

The 'off diagonal' terms in the array, such as C_2/M_1 or C_5/M_2, represent interactions which are unhelpful to control. It is possible, having formed a full array, to gauge the quality of overall system control which can be expected by inspecting the terms in the array. For instance, if any of the 'off diagonal' terms are nearly as large as those on the diagonal in the same row, control is going to be very poor, as this will imply that a change in one of the 'controlled' or manipulated variables will affect some other variable almost as much as the one intended.

The relative gain array can be used as a design tool to select the best pairing of measured and manipulated variables, and so give the best design of control system possible using single loop controllers. The process requirements in some systems, however, make serious interaction between variables inevitable and in such cases it is possible to design a 'decoupling' element which will allow each controller to act through more than one final control element, in such a way that the total affect of variable manipulations through the final control elements used affects *only* the single measured variable of that controller. This is known as non-interactive or sometimes multivariable control. The following section presents a design study for a simple example of such a system, involving two measured and two manipulable variables. It will be noted that the design calculations even for such a simple system are quite extensive though straightforward. Since, however, the calculations are based on matrix algebraic methods it will be obvious that the design of decouplers for systems with large numbers of interactive loops will involve quite extensive calculation; such design calculations are, however, very easy to program on a desk top calculator or personal computer.

It should perhaps be mentioned, though it is beyond the scope of this book, that dynamic decoupling is also possible by this means. This can be readily understood if it is recognised that the rate of change of a variable can be regarded as a separate variable. For example, neither the direction nor rate at which temperature changes in a process has any connection at all necessarily with the instantaneous temperature. By including rates of change of measured variables as separate variables in the array a dynamic decoupler can be designed.

11.12 DESIGN OF A MULTIVARIABLE SYSTEM STEADY-STATE DECOUPLER

The following developments demonstrate the design of a steady-state decoupling system for a simple blending control system typical of the digestion 'liquor' system found in the Bayer process for producing alumina. Alumina is the raw material from which aluminium is produced by smelting and is itself extracted from bauxite ore by digestion in a caustic 'liquor' and subsequent crystallisation. After crystallisation the liquor is returned to the beginning of the process as 'old liquor' (OL). During the process water used to wash filters, etc., dilutes some streams of liquor, which are collected as 'dilute liquor' (DL) and blended with the OL to become 'strong wash' (SW) liquor. New liquor is produced in 'kiers'; this is more concentrated (in Na_2O) and is called 'kier liquor' (KL). The blend of OL/DL forming SW can be regulated and the blend of SW with KL can also be regulated, independently, giving two 'manipulable' variables, the *desired values* of which can be manipulated so as to regulate the concentration of the liquor in terms of 'free' (free radicals) soda (Na_2O) on the one hand and 'free' alumina (Al_2O_3) on the other. The optimal operation of the crystallisation process depends on regulating *both* these variables and so a control system is required which decouples the action of two conventional 3-term controllers to achieve independent steady-state regulation of both free soda and free alumina.

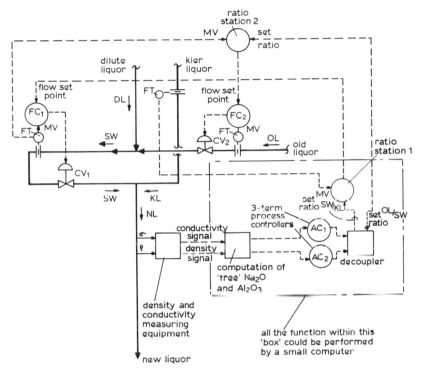

Fig. 11.22.

The diagram in Fig. 11.22 shows that the dilute liquor (DL) stream and the kier liquor (KL) stream are both 'wild', whilst the old liquor (OL) and strong wash (SW) (which is the sum of the OL and DL streams) are regulated. Since any control action applied to the SW stream through CV_1 must inevitably have an effect on the controller FC_2 in the OL stream, there is an obvious need for decoupling in this system. The interactions which need to be decoupled are a direct result of the process requirements and cannot easily be avoided in this instance.

The following shows how the relative gain array is determined from the process data:

	Units of flow	Al_2O_3 g/litre	Na_2O g/litre
New liquor (NL)	$(1 + a + b)$	135	140
Kier liquor (KL)	1	170	155
Old liquor (OL) ⎱ SW	a	75	145
Dilute liquor (DL) ⎰	b	100	100

from which:

$$\text{for } Al_2O_3 \; 135(1 + a + b) = 75a + 100b + 170$$

$$\text{for } Na_2O \; 140(1 + a + b) = 145a + 100b + 155$$

Hence $a = 0 \cdot 3400$ and $b = 0 \cdot 4175$.

Process gains

The first manipulable variable will be the ratio of the flow rates of SW and KL. Hence, the process gain: g/litre Al_2O_3 in NL divided by the percentage change in SW/KL ratio, is calculated as follows:

$$Al_2O_3 \text{ in SW} = [(75 \times 0 \cdot 3400) + (100 \times 0 \cdot 4175)]/0 \cdot 7575$$
$$= 88 \cdot 7863 \text{ g/litre}$$

$$Al_2O_3 \text{ in KL} = 170 \text{ g/litre}$$

$$Al_2O_3 \text{ in NL} = [170 + (88 \cdot 7863 \times 0 \cdot 7575)]/1 \cdot 7575$$
$$= 134 \cdot 9961 \text{ g/litre}$$

Assuming a -1% change in SW/KL ratio:

$$Al_2O_3 \text{ in NL becomes } \frac{170 + (88 \cdot 7863 \times 0 \cdot 7575 \times 0 \cdot 99)}{1 + (0 \cdot 7575 \times 0 \cdot 99)}$$
$$= 135 \cdot 1961 \text{ g/litre}$$

Hence a -1% change in SW/KL ratio produces:

$$\frac{100(135 \cdot 1961 - 134 \cdot 9961)}{134 \cdot 9961} = +0 \cdot 148 \% \text{ change in g/litre } Al_2O_3 \text{ in NL}$$

Therefore the process gain $= -0 \cdot 148$.

Similarly, the process gain: g/litre Na_2O in NL divided by the percentage change in SW/KL ratio is calculated thus:

$$Na_2O \text{ in } SW = [(145 \times 0\cdot3400) + (100 \times 0\cdot4175)]/0\cdot7575$$
$$= 120\cdot1850 \text{ g/litre}$$

$$Na_2O \text{ in } KL = 155 \text{ g/litre}$$

$$Na_2O \text{ in } NL = [155 + (120\cdot1850 \times 0\cdot7575)]/1\cdot7575$$
$$= 139\cdot9890 \text{ g/litre}$$

Assuming a -1% change in SW/KL ratio as before, Na_2O in NL becomes:

$$\frac{155 + (120\cdot1850 \times 0\cdot7575 \times 0\cdot99)}{1 + (0\cdot7575 \times 0\cdot99)} = 140\cdot074 \text{ g/litre}$$

Hence the process gain $= -0\cdot061$.

The second manipulable variable will be the ratio of old liquor to total strong wash flow rates.

The process gain: g/litre Al_2O_3 in NL divided by the percentage change in OL/SW ratio is calculated as follows:

The design value of this ratio is $0\cdot340/0\cdot758 = 0\cdot4485 = R$

$$Al_2O_3 \text{ in } SW = 88\cdot786 \text{ g/litre}$$
$$Al_2O_3 \text{ in } KL = 170\cdot000 \text{ g/litre}$$
$$Al_2O_3 \text{ in } NL = 134\cdot996 \text{ g/litre}$$

Assuming a -1% change in the OL/SW ratio:

$$R = (0\cdot99 \times 0\cdot4488) = 0\cdot44406$$

then Al_2O_3 in SW becomes:

$$\frac{75(0\cdot7575 \times 0\cdot44436) + 0\cdot7575 - (0\cdot7575 \times 0\cdot44436) \times 100}{0\cdot7575} = 88\cdot89 \text{ g/litre}$$

Hence Al_2O_3 in NL $= [(170 + (88\cdot89 \times 0\cdot7575)]/1\cdot7575 = 135\cdot041$.

Hence the process gain $= -0\cdot0331$.

For $R = 0$, i.e. -100% change, the process gain $= 0\cdot0331$. Hence this control action is linear. Similarly, therefore, the process gain: g/litre Na_2O

in NL divided by the percentage change in OL/SW ratio is calculated as follows:

$$Na_2O \text{ in } SW = 120 \cdot 185 \text{ g/litre}$$
$$Na_2O \text{ in } KL = 155 \text{ g/litre}$$
$$Na_2O \text{ in } NL = 139 \cdot 989 \text{ g/litre}$$

Assuming a -100% change in OL/SW ratio, R becomes zero. Hence:

$$Na_2O \text{ in } SW = [(145 \times 0) + (0 \cdot 7575 \times 100)]/0 \cdot 7575$$
$$= 100 \text{ g/litre}$$

$$Na_2O \text{ in } KL = 155 \text{ g/litre}$$

$$Na_2O \text{ in } NL = 155 + (0 \cdot 7575 \times 100) - 1 \cdot 7575$$
$$= 131 \cdot 2856 \text{ g/litre}$$

Therefore the process gain $= + 0 \cdot 062$.

It is now possible to form the relative gain array, thus:

	Ratio flow SW/KL	Ratio flow OL/SW
g/litre Al_2O_3	$-0 \cdot 148$	$-0 \cdot 036$
g/litre Na_2O	$-0 \cdot 061$	$+0 \cdot 062$

Taking the array for a two input/two output system as:

		Output to SW/KL Ratio Stn C_1	Output to OL/SW Ratio Stn C_2
Al_2O_3 control action	M_1	w	x
Na_2O control action	M_2	y	z

$$\begin{bmatrix} M_1 \\ M_2 \end{bmatrix} = \begin{bmatrix} w & x \\ y & z \end{bmatrix} * \begin{bmatrix} C_1 \\ C_2 \end{bmatrix}$$

The effect of any steady-state changes in C_1 and C_2 on M_1 are:

$$\delta M_1 = w\delta C_1 + x\delta C_2 \tag{1}$$

and similarly:

$$\delta M_2 = y\delta C_1 + z\delta C_2$$

Decoupling matrix

A second array is defined such that it enables a set of δC_n to be computed which will influence only one of the measured variables:

	δM_1	δM_2
δC_1	p	q
δC_2	r	s

$$\begin{bmatrix} \delta C_1 \\ \delta C_2 \end{bmatrix} = \begin{bmatrix} p & q \\ r & s \end{bmatrix} * \begin{bmatrix} \delta M_1 \\ \delta M_2 \end{bmatrix}$$

Then

$$\delta C_1 = p\delta M_1 + q\delta M_2$$

and

$$\delta C_2 = r\delta M_1 + s\delta M_2 \tag{2}$$

Combining 1 and 2:

$$\delta M_1 = w(p\delta M_1 + q\delta M_2) + x(r\delta M_1 + s\delta M_2)$$
$$\delta M_2 = y(p\delta M_1 + q\delta M_2) + z(r\delta M_1 + s\delta M_2)$$

Simplifying

$$1 = wp + wq\,\frac{\delta M_2}{\delta M_1} + xr + xs\,\frac{\delta M_2}{\delta M_1}$$

$$1 = yp\,\frac{\delta M_1}{\delta M_2} = yq + zr\,\frac{\delta M_1}{\delta M_2} + zs \tag{3}$$

The requirement that only one measured variable must be affected dictates:

and

$$\delta M_1 = 0 \quad \text{when } \delta M_2 = \text{some finite value} \tag{i}$$
$$\delta M_2 = 0 \quad \text{when } \delta M_1 = \text{some finite value} \tag{ii}$$

Applying (i) to (3), eqns (3) reduce to

$$1 = wp + xr$$
$$0 = yp + zr$$

and applying (ii)

$$0 = wq + xs$$
$$1 = yq + zs$$

which can be solved to give values for p, q, r and s. Thus

$$\begin{bmatrix} p & q \\ q & s \end{bmatrix} = \begin{bmatrix} z & -x \\ -y & w \end{bmatrix} * \frac{1}{(zw + yx)}$$

The decoupling matrix can thus be formed from the relative gain array:

$$\begin{bmatrix} p & q \\ r & s \end{bmatrix} = \begin{bmatrix} +0\cdot062 & +0\cdot036 \\ +0\cdot061 & -0\cdot148 \end{bmatrix} \times \frac{-1}{(0\cdot148 \times 0\cdot062) + (0\cdot061 \times 0\cdot036)}$$

$$= \begin{bmatrix} +5\cdot452 & +3\cdot166 \\ +5\cdot364 & +13\cdot014 \end{bmatrix}$$

Operation of decoupling matrix

The following illustrates the way the decoupled control action works. A small change in both Al_2O_3 and Na_2O content of the kier liquor has been assumed (one positive and the other negative) and the proportional control action (assuming unity controller gain) calculated to show that *both* errors are *simultaneously* reduced by approximately the same proportion.

Assume a change in KL composition from design to 168 g/litre of Al_2O_3 and 157 g/litre of Na_2O. Then NL contains

$$[168 + (0\cdot7575 + 88\cdot7863)]/1\cdot7575$$
$$= 133\cdot8453 \text{ g/litre of } Al_2O_3$$

and

$$[157 + (0\cdot7575 \times 120\cdot1850)]/1\cdot7575$$
$$= 141\cdot1264 \text{ g/litre of } Na_2O$$

hence the error in $Al_2O_3 = 135 - 133\cdot8453 = 1\cdot1547$ g/litre and the error in $Na_2O = 140 - 141\cdot1264 = -1\cdot1264$ g/litre. Then:

$$\begin{bmatrix} \delta C_1 \\ \delta C_2 \end{bmatrix} = \begin{bmatrix} 5\cdot452 & 3\cdot166 \\ 5\cdot364 & -13\cdot014 \end{bmatrix} * \begin{bmatrix} 1\cdot1547 \\ -1\cdot1264 \end{bmatrix}$$

$$= \begin{matrix} +2\cdot729 \\ +20\cdot853 \end{matrix} \text{ expressed as } \% \text{ changes in ratios}$$

Hence new ratio SW/KL $= (1 - 0.02729)0.7575 = 0.7373$ and new ratio OL/SW $= (1 - 0.20853)0.4485 = 0.3550$. Then:

$$Al_2O_3 \text{ in SW} = (0.3550 \times 75) + (1 - 0.3550)100$$
$$= 91.1246 \text{ g/litre}$$

and

$$Na_2O \text{ in SW} = (0.3550 \times 145) + (1 - 0.3550)100$$
$$= 115.9754 \text{ g/litre}$$

Hence:

$$Al_2O_3 \text{ in NL} = 168 + (0.7373 \times 91.1246) - 1.7373$$
$$= 135.37 \text{ g/litre}$$

and

$$Na_2O_3 \text{ in NL} = 157 + (0.7373 \times 115.9754) - 1.7373$$
$$= 139.59 \text{ g/litre}$$

and it can be seen that the new error vector is:

$$\begin{bmatrix} 0.37 \\ -0.41 \end{bmatrix} \text{ as opposed to } \begin{bmatrix} 1.1547 \\ -1.1264 \end{bmatrix}$$

The percentage reduction in each error is very nearly the same:

$$\begin{bmatrix} 68\% \\ 64\% \end{bmatrix}$$

thus demonstrating that the two control actions are almost totally decoupled.

11.13 DYNAMIC INTERACTION

The previous section showed how steady-state interaction can be avoided by good control system design, and how it may sometimes be possible to *avoid* dynamic or transient interaction by ensuring that loop responses are approximately the same by tuning. However, it is not always possible to achieve this as the process itself may have more than one response to the same control action, and these responses may themselves interact.

For example, consider once again a change of reflux flow rate and its effect on the operation of the distillation process taking place in a

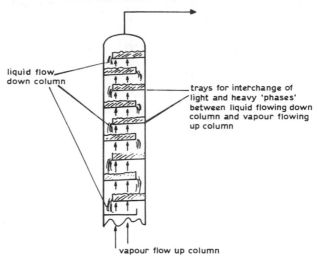

liquid flow
down column

trays for interchange of
light and heavy 'phases'
between liquid flowing down
column and vapour flowing
up column

vapour flow up column

Fig. 11.23.

distillation column having a number of trays (Fig. 11.23). Each 'tray' contains a small quantity of liquid in order to provide the residence time required for the interchange of light (more volatile) phases or components to the rising vapour and heavy (less volatile) phases to the falling liquid. Any change in the flow rate of the liquid flowing down, or of the vapour flowing up, will change the composition of the top product and the bottom product streams, but this change will be subject to the total delay represented by the many time constant delays of the individual trays in series, and thus to considerable dead time (depending on the size of the column and the number of trays this can be of the order of hours). However, the hydraulic response of the system—i.e. the change in liquid flow down the column after a change in reflux flow rate—is very much quicker. This is because the flow of liquid from tray to tray is regulated by weirs on each tray, and there is little if any residence time delay (change in flow rate off the tray is almost instantaneous after a change of flow rate onto the tray). The increased liquid flow down the column will have to be matched by an increase in vapour flow rate up the column if the composition of the bottom product is not to be seriously upset; yet this control action will precede, perhaps by hours, the change in composition at the individual trays, which can progress only slowly in cascade down the column. Thus, whilst this disturbance is propagating slowly down the column, a new disturbance in composition will start to propagate upwards from the base of the column, and disturbed composition is inevitable throughout the column for some time. It is essential that the control system design recognises such interaction *within the process* and that it acts in such a way as not to exacerbate it. One way that this can be achieved is to use a sampled data technique: the measurement is 'sampled' and the appropriate control output produced by a conventional SISO controller, then no further change in this output is permitted until a time has elapsed which is rather longer than the system 'settling' time which includes dead time. A mechanism for achieving this is shown in the diagrams in Fig. 11.24.

Even in the absence of dead time in the system, system responses can often interact to provide a very difficult control problem; a prime example of this is to be found in the drum level control of the modern water tube boiler. A boiler is always demand controlled, that is to say its function is to supply steam of a given quality when the process demands it. An increase in demand for steam requires a corresponding increase in the flow rate of feed water to replace the steam: however, in order to satisfy the steady-state mass balance the flow of water is basically regulated by the drum level control loop. The interaction occurs because there are two separate and unfortunately contrary responses to the increase in heat input which must also occur when steam demand increases in order to satisfy the energy balance. The first response, which occurs very rapidly, results from the physical fact that the water expands in the boiler tubes when the heat input rate increases; the capacity of the tubes is much greater than that of the drum and so the level in the drum rises rapidly at first. The drum level controller, seeing the level rising, acts to reduce the feed flow rate initially; however, expansion of the water is a finite and therefore transient response to a step change in steam flow demand, and very soon the combination of increased outflow of steam and reduced inflow of feed water results in the drum level beginning to fall at an accelerating rate. This is the steady-state response to the increased demand and unless the control system is so designed that it is wary of the initial transient response the level in the boiler drum will fall so rapidly that there will be no water in the drum before the feed water valve (which is often large) can open enough to check the fall. The solution to this problem is a combination of system design and adaption of the standard control actions (see Fig. 11.25).

Feedback regulation of the drum level is provided by a cascade system comprising a master level controller and a slave flow rate controller. Feedforward control is added by a flow rate controller on the steam flow, which, together with the flow rate controller on the water flow, constitutes a ratio control system. Steady-state dominance of the level control is ensured

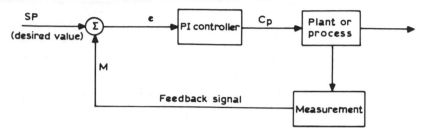

A) Conventional feedback control

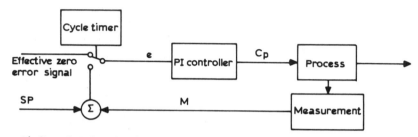

B) Sampled data feedback control

(i)

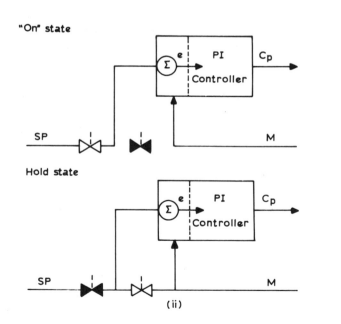

(ii)

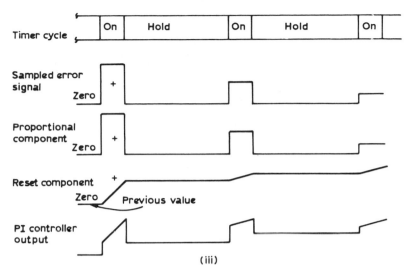

(iii)

Fig. 11.24. (i) The feedback signal in conventional control (A) is compared in a summing junction with the set point: the resultant error, e, directly feeds the controller. In analog sampled-data control (B) the controller operates on a sample of the measured error signal during a brief period determined by the cycle timer, and then holds its existing output signal when the timer connects its input to an effective zero signal. (ii) When the desired setpoint value, SP, and the measured variable, M, are briefly connected to the respective input ports leading to the summing point, the controller receives a sample of the actual error signal in an 'on' state. When switch action connects its inputs together, the controller receives an effective zero error signal and enters the 'hold' state. (iii) The automatic reset control function of the two-mode controller, third line down, displays a special function by holding the response to the actual error signal for the duration of the 'hold' period.

by the fact that the steam flow rate controller does not provide integral control action, whereas the level controller does. In order that the level controller will substantially ignore the initial rise in drum level, caused by expansion of the boiler water, *inverse* derivative control action is added to the proportional and integral actions: as its name implies, inverse derivative control action reduces the proportional action to an extent relative to the rate of change of the measured variable (level in this case). Thus the system ensures that when the steam flow rate increases, the water flow rate is immediately increased despite the rise in level due to expansion (the drum must be designed to accommodate this 'swell'), and that after this transient response has died away control of drum level dominates the water flow rate, ensuring that in steady-state the level will be at the desired value.

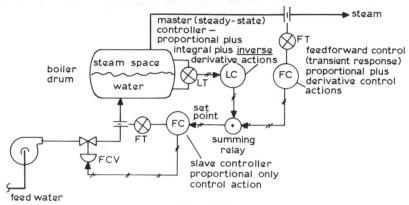

Fig. 11.25.

11.14 INSTABILITY

It has already been stated that process plant is normally designed to have as much self-regulation as possible; however, there is one group of processes which cannot be so designed—exothermic reaction processes. Such a process is open loop unstable, that is to say if it is not controlled in some way it will 'run away' to some limiting state, perhaps even explode. This is because any rise in temperature causes the process to produce more heat and, hence, raise the temperature still further. The control system must increase the rate of heat removal when the measurement system detects a rise in temperature, but whether the closed loop system will be stable or not will depend on whether the measurement system response is fast enough and whether the control action can be applied fast enough. If these responses are too slow the reaction temperature will increase faster than the control system can deal with it, and the closed loop system will also be unstable. Such reactions take place in jacketed vessels, with cooling water circulating through the jacket, and response to control action (increasing the flow rate of the cooling water, or reducing the inlet temperature) is subject to the time constant delays always associated with heat transfer through vessel walls, as well as delays due to mixing within the process materials inside the vessel. Temperature measurement, too, is subject to heat transfer delays. Where there is a vapour space inside the reactor vessel and the reaction products are volatile (such as a polymerisation reaction), a pressure sensor can detect increase in reaction rate more quickly than a temperature sensor, and a cascade loop as shown in Fig. 11.26 may provide

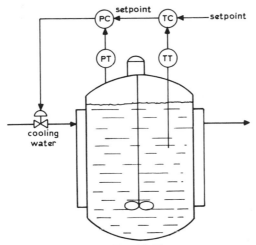

Fig. 11.26.

fast enough measurement response. However, the problem of response to control action is largely a matter of the design of the vessel jacket, cooling system and mixing equipment. For instance, the greater the temperature difference possible between the cooling fluid and the process material and the larger the effective heat transfer surface, the greater the control action that can be applied and therefore the faster the response possible. The capacity of the jacket will add a capacitive/resistive delay to the heat transfer process and should therefore be as small as possible. However, equipment decisions of this sort are often made early in the project design phase before a control engineer has been able to evaluate the constraints.

The rate of reaction is proportional to the temperature at any time, and writing this mathematically

$$WC_p \frac{d}{dt} = t$$

where t is the temperature, W the weight of process material, and C_p is the specific heat of the process material; or in operator form

$$WC_p pt = t$$

Replacing the operator p with the Laplace operator (to obtain steady-state as well as transient response) the transfer function is

$$\frac{1}{WC_p s} \quad \text{or} \quad \frac{1}{WC_p}\left(\frac{1}{s}\right)$$

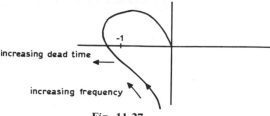

Fig. 11.27.

In other words the *open loop* response to a disturbance in t is given by

$$\frac{1}{WC_p}\left(\frac{1}{s}\right)t$$

The mechanism of heat transfer will contain two capacitive/resistive delays, one for transfer of heat from the process material in the reactor vessel through the metal wall of the vessel into the cooling water, and the second due to the capacity of the jacket delaying changes in the mean temperature difference between cooling water and process material, and therefore delaying the change in heat transfer rate. There will also be some dead time due to transport of cooling water, mixing in the process and other causes. The transfer function will be of the form

$$\frac{e^{-Ls}}{(T_1s+1)(T_2s+1)}$$

Similarly the transfer of heat through the wall of the thermowell into the temperature sensor will add two more capacitive/resistive delays, making the total transfer function for the process, heat transfer and measurement

$$\frac{1}{WC_p}\cdot\frac{e^{-Ls}}{s(T_1s+1)(T_2s+1)(T_3s+1)(T_4s+1)}$$

The Nyquist diagram for this is of the form shown in Fig. 11.27 where it can be seen that encircling the -1 point can hardly be avoided. Note that $1/s$ in the transfer function adds a $90°$ phase lag at all frequencies. The importance of minimising dead time can be clearly seen from the Nyquist diagram.

11.15 RANGEABILITY

There is very little point in designing a control system to manipulate the right process variables in the right way, if in fact the variables cannot be varied over the full range required. Whilst this may seem obvious it is in fact

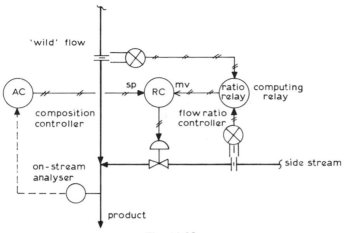

Fig. 11.28.

too often overlooked in the design of control systems which incorporate more than one 'loop'. For example, consider the blending system shown in Fig. 11.28. The flow coming forward from a previous processing unit has a 'wild' composition, i.e. its composition varies in a random fashion with time. A side stream of different composition is blended with the wild flow to achieve the required specification. The flow rate in the 'wild' stream may vary as well as the composition, and the flow rate required in the side stream will be a function of the compositions in all three streams and the flow rate of the wild stream.

The ratio of the side stream flow rate to the wild flow rate is maintained by the ratio controller so that changes in flow rate in the wild stream do not disturb the composition of the product. The analyser controller resets the set point value in the ratio controller (cascade) to maintain the product composition by feedback control. The ratio of flows required is a function of the composition of all three streams and can be defined thus

$$A_p(Q_w + Q_s) = A_w Q_w + A_s Q_s$$

where A is the composition (in suitable units) and Q is flow rate. The subscripts refer to the streams. Hence

$$A\left(1 + \frac{Q_s}{Q_w}\right) = A_w + A_s\left(\frac{Q_s}{Q_w}\right)$$

or

$$(A - A_s)\left(\frac{Q_s}{Q_w}\right) = (A_w - A)$$

or

$$\frac{Q_s}{Q_w} = \frac{(A_w - A)}{(A - A_s)}$$

Thus, it can be seen that if Q_w (the flow rate in the wild stream) increases, Q_s the manipulated variable must also increase. It can also be seen that if A_w (the composition of the wild stream) is close to the desired composition A, the ratio of flows will be small; if very different the ratio will be large. Finally, it can be seen that if A_s (the side stream composition) is close to the desired product composition, the ratio of side stream flow rate to the wild stream flow will be large. Thus, at one extreme the side stream flow rate (the manipulable variable) will be very large if side stream composition is close to product composition, wild stream composition is very different from product, and wild flow rate high. Alternately side stream flow rate will be very low if these factors are reversed. The rangeability required in the side stream must be carefully assessed early in the design because it is quite easy to find that it is not practicable, in which case it will be necessary to review the process design. It must be appreciated that this is not something to do with the control system design except that it may not be possible to design a suitable control system: other designers are unlikely to realise this and will probably blame the control system designer even though the decisions leading to such a state of affairs were not his.

CHAPTER 12

The Modern Process Control System

12.1 ARCHITECTURE OF A PROCESS CONTROL SYSTEM

In the early part of this century the human operator of a process plant had only simple measurement devices (such as pressure gauges, or temperature gauges mounted directly on the process pipe or vessel) to assist him in *regulating* the process variables. He spent his time walking round the plant, adjusting the position of a throttling valve here or there, in order to keep the value of pressures, flow rates and temperatures as close as possible to the *desired values*. There was little scope to change these desired values, processes were generally simple and crude, plant small and operation essentially steady state. Early control mechanisms (often referred to as 'regulators') were essentially mechanical mechanisms which sensed the movement of a diaphragm, Bourdon tube or bi-metallic element, and operated the stem of a control valve. Such mechanisms were developed in order to relieve the operator of some of the drudgery of his work, make it possible for him to operate larger plants and, incidentally, make it easier for him to change the desired values.

The development of pneumatic transmission of measurement signals in the 1920s and 1930s made it possible to collect into one 'central' location all the indicators, recorders and other equipment required for the operation of quite large plants, and, incidentally, make the operator's job more comfortable and sociable. The regulator mechanisms themselves had by this time developed into pneumatic servo mechanisms, making it possible (though not necessarily desirable) for these, too, to be located in the central control room, where they could be readily tuned and where the desired values could most easily be changed.

During and after the Second World War, as process plants grew larger, so the control panels in these central control rooms grew very large indeed, and two of the disadvantages of centralisation became apparent:

(i)   The quantity of information displayed by large numbers of indicators and recorders was too great for human comprehension.

(ii)   The inevitably increasing distance of the controllers (regulators) from both the point of measurement and the point of regulation (the control valve) became such that the signal transmission introduced significant delay into the feedback control loops to the detriment of the quality of control.

The development of electronic analog signal transmission in the 1960s (delayed in many industries by the danger of electrical energy in explosive and flammable atmospheres) solved the second problem, but did nothing to cure the first. Attempts were made to cure the first problem by introducing high density displays and operation 'by exception' by which it was meant that the operator's attention was drawn to the display of a variable only when it was significantly different in value from its desired value. Such attempts were not very successful and, in addition, the capital expenditure on huge quantities of cable and pneumatic tube was becoming excessive. The development of local regulating mechanisms into single input/single output (SISO) controllers had meant that the development of control systems design had been based on these universal components, rather than on more custom-built control system design. However, the fact that any complex control system such as feedforward, interactive, or even cascade or ratio control, required 'hardwired' or piped interconnections between individual controllers had long been a brake on the development of control system design, since the drawing board design of a process control system could only be altered when the plant was shut down (a rare occurrence in some industries).

The application of digital computers to process control in the 1960s did not at first solve any of these problems. Computers of that era were large, very expensive and much less reliable than today, and their use could only be justified if a single computer could replace a large number of analog SISO controllers (say 100 or more). Direct digital control, DDC as it was called, raised another serious problem; security or availability of the control system became an all or nothing affair. Control systems based on essentially independent SISO controllers could afford to lose one or two controllers by reason of equipment malfunction, but not the whole system. Computers were alternatively used in a 'supervisory' role (or set point control), in which the analog SISO controllers were retained, but this restricted their role to optimisation of the set points (otherwise the operator's job) and the considerable cost of the computer was added to the already high cost of conventional analog centralised control.

The development of the microprocessor and large scale integrated electronic circuits has made possible the development of 'distributed intelligence' control systems and thus overcome the crippling disadvantages of the centralised intelligence of conventional computers for process control. It has in the last few years become possible and economic to use multiple (micro)processors to construct control systems with an architecture which overcomes the 'all or nothing' problem of computer availability, whilst at the same time providing facilities for the engineer to reconfigure the interconnections between SISO controllers—the control system structure—*whilst the plant is operating*. At the same time it has become possible, using the data processing capability of digital computers, to solve the problem of displaying large amounts of data for the operator in such a way that he can make use of it. By distributing the 'intelligence' of the system it is also possible to locate the analog/digital interface close to the point of regulation and the point of measurement, thus greatly reducing the amount of cabling required, since the digital signals can be multiplexed serially over a single communication channel.

Paradoxically, it is the combination of 'integrated control' with distributed intelligence which has finally made possible a rational architecture for process control systems. The modern instrumentation system is just that, an integrated system rather than a collection of components which are connected together by simple constructional methods on site in accordance with rather rudimentary 'instrument diagrams' and cable schedules, involving point to point wiring or piping. Data is generated by transducers in conjunction with sensors usually mounted close to the point of measurement on the plant. At the present time transducers usually generate an analog signal or a pulse train signal (fluid flow by turbine or PD meters). Digital operation has not generally been applied to transducers for reasons which are at least partly historic; there is little commercial advantage as single pair cables are required in either case, measurement points being distributed widely over the plant. Once a number of such individual measurement signals have been brought together in some local gathering point, however, the cost of a single pair cable instead of very expensive multicore cables required for analog systems represents a very large capital saving indeed (perhaps 15% to 20% of the total instrumentation cost). Thus, the modern instrumentation system has a data 'highway' or 'bus' to distribute data to and from the central station and outstations of the system: this system operates by time division multiplexing of data packages using telecommunication and computer techniques. Analog signals from plant measurements are converted to digital form and digital control signals to analog form at local outstations, usually in safe areas so that the principles of intrinsic safety can be applied to the local analog signals. Indeed, there is no reason why these local signals cannot be pneumatic, since reliable pneumatic scanning valves are available which allow rapid conversion of analog pneumatic signals to sampled data digital signals in a single piece of equipment. The architecture of the communication bus which connects up the central installation with the outstations is obviously of considerable importance.

12.2 MICROPROCESSOR-BASED CONTROLLERS

The operation of microprocessor-based controllers was introduced in Section 9.9. In effect, it is today economically feasible to devote a small microcomputer system to the tasks performed previously by conventional analog and pneumatic controllers as described in Chapter 9. Not only these tasks but others, such as computations of algebraic functions of several measured value signals and discrete sequential control, can be carried out by a universal 'controller' costing no more than the much more limited analog controllers of the past. This capability is achieved, of course, by conversion of measured value signals from analog to digital form and for this reason the modern electronic instrumentation system comprises a number of functional blocks one of which is the input/output (I/O) system.

Digital signal processing has certain advantages over analog processing. These advantages stem from the fact that digital computation is very much more accurate than analog and also that digital computers can 'time share' tasks whereas analog computation must always take place in parallel because data cannot be stored. Thus, not only can the microcomputer, which is the basis of each 'controller', compute each control action—proportional, derivative and integral—separately, but it can also calculate *accurately* the sum of two signals or the ratio of two signals for ratio control. The same controller can carry out logical relationships to perform switching operations and discrete sequence control (batch operation) and can readily respond to on-off or switching inputs. It is easy to limit, or stop and start integral control action as the control actions are generated separately; thus, integral saturation can be totally overcome, which is virtually impossible with analog controllers because of control action interaction. Special control actions such as 'squared error' control for non-linear processes are simple to program.

Because microprocessor-based controllers are 'software programmable', unlike their hardwired analog predecessors, it is easy to change cascade or ratio multicontroller systems even while the plant is operating. Where two controllers are switched in and out during different periods of control, requiring integral tracking (see Section 9.7), this and bumpless transfer (Section 9.6) functions are easily incorporated as standard features.

One other advantage of digital computation is that the controller output can be in the form of a 'pulse stream' to raise/lower an electrical operating element or to drive a stepper motor. These alternatives to the conventional analog control output provide much greater flexibility in the type of 'final control element' drive which can be used, particularly where electrical equipment is concerned.

One of the advantages of digital computation, already mentioned, is the possibility of time sharing tasks (depending on serial rather than parallel computation and the existence of data storage–memory facilities). The modern LSI electronic chip technology has reached the state where a single microprocessor system can in fact 'share' the tasks which would normally require several, even tens of, conventional SISO controllers. Thus, it is possible now to buy systems in which single units act as though each were 6, 8 or more SISO controllers. The advantage of such a unit is that inter-controller connections to implement cascade, ratio, tracking functions, etc., become merely internal software and can be changed by reprogramming even more easily than is the case with single controllers which are microprocessor based. The disadvantage is that all 6 or 8 'controllers' fail as a unit, so such units need to be specified with care and due consideration for the implications of failure.

The term 'split-architecture' has been coined in recent years to describe a system architecture in which the controller and the displays are located in widely separated locations. The advantage of split-architecture is that the analog signal transmission distance, which of necessity involves two cores (wires) per measurement, can be minimised by locating the controllers and input/output units in a 'local' control room adjacent to the plant transducers. Onward transmission of display data to a centralised control room, located (in the case of a large refinery, for instance) at considerable distance from several such 'local' control rooms, is effected over serial telemetry links (often a single pair of 'cores') in digital form, thus saving considerably on the cost of cabling. This feature, more than any other, has heralded the demise of pneumatic large-scale systems, although there is no reason why the analog signal connections from local control rooms cannot still be pneumatic using high speed pneumatic 'scanning valves' which are, surprisingly, very reliable.

12.3 THE 'DISTRIBUTED CONTROL' SYSTEM

It has already been shown that the introduction of digital computing into instrumentation systems provides the opportunity to economise on the massive cabling requirements of earlier systems. To do so the analog signals must be converted into digital form at the nearest practical point to the plant transducers; usually a local control room in a 'safe' area (where toxic or explosion risks exist near the plant). Once the measurement signals have been converted to digital form they can be stored in solid-state memory and multiplexed for *serial* telemetry over a data link. The term 'distributed control' has been coined to describe such systems which depend on distributed processing of the plant measurement signals and control signals. It is therefore the signal processing or I/O (input/output) units which must be distributed to local 'control rooms' in such systems. If the controller functions are also devolved locally then it is a split-architecture system also, but there is no reason why this should necessarily be the case, and indeed it is not the case in all 'distributed' systems. The controller functions can be incorporated into units mounted in a central control room rather than in a number of local control rooms, as indeed was the case in many early 'DDC' systems in which one central computer (usually a mainframe or powerful minicomputer) performed all the functions of perhaps 200–300 controllers on a time share basis. The term 'distributed control', therefore, is somewhat unfortunate and misleading, and should be interpreted as meaning 'control systems with *distributed* signal processing'.

The architecture of the signal or data link is very important in this type of system, as any failure must inevitably affect more than one SISO loop. One reason for the split-architecture configuration, in which the control functions as well as the signal processing are distributed to local control rooms, is to preserve 'single loop integrity', and it is usual to provide some form of alternative display system in the local control room in order that operators can, in an emergency, operate the plant locally. However, a properly designed 'data link' should have enough 'redundancy' so that the statistical probability of its failure is extremely small. Statistical probability of failure, expressed as mean-time between failures (or MTBF) is *not* an equivalent concept of plant security to 'single loop integrity', which depends on the eminent practicability of replacing a single (standard) SISO controller as soon as it fails. However, data link architecture should today be almost immune to total failure if properly designed on principles of redundancy.

There are essentially three possible data link architectures as shown in Fig. 12.1—star, ring and multidrop. The actual connecting cables between units of the system are in fact no more vulnerable to failure than the multicore cables (two cores per signal) of earlier systems; mechanical damage is as likely to happen to the one as to the other. As these cables are almost certainly a single pair of wires, there is likely to be little real saving in most cases in the alternative routings implied by star, ring or multidrop configurations, though this may not always be the case. In this respect the ring configuration does offer an advantage in that one break in the ring can be tolerated if the system is designed correctly. The real security problems arise from distortion of digital signals (see Section 7.12) and failure of the input/output equipment which converts analog signals to digital form and multiplexes its transfer over the data links. Redundancy, therefore, is likely to mean duplication of these parts of the equipment and some designed-in method of comparing the received and decoded signals. In extreme cases, such as nuclear reactor controls, triplication of such systems provides the opportunity for a two out of three 'routing' system. If one set of equipment fails there is only a very slight possibility that one of the remaining two systems will fail simultaneously; so slight as to be discounted completely. Thus, the remaining two systems must agree and the failed unit can readily be identified and a warning generated. For most industrial purposes this degree of integrity is both too expensive and unnecessary.

12.4 DATA INTERFACE AND BUS

The design of the communication interface and bus will depend on the nature of the data transfers required by the particular system architecture. If, for instance, split-architecture is adopted so that control functions are devolved to the local gathering stations, the bus will have to carry data between the outstations (for cascade or ratio control, for instance). In some systems redundancy is built in by designing it so that one outstation can take over the control functions of a neighbouring failed outstation temporarily; such design features will obviously make heavy demands on the communication system.

In order to transfer digital data between two equipment items there must

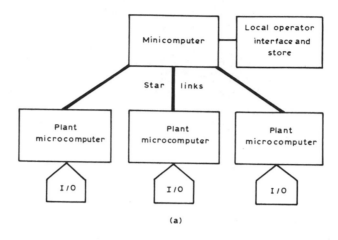

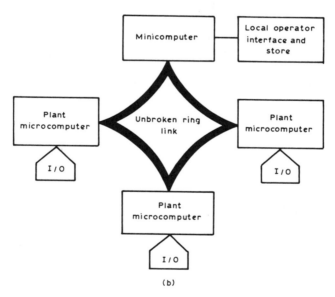

Fig. 12.1.   (a) Star configuration; (b) ring configuration.

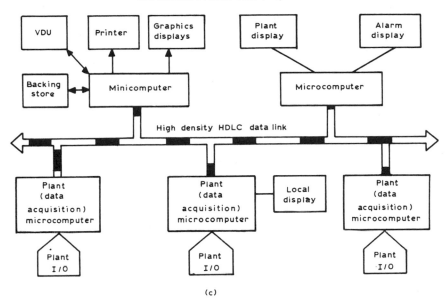

(c)

Fig. 12.1—*contd.* (c) Multidrop configuration.

be a set of rules, or 'protocol', to enable one to respond to the other and carry out different functions, such as, receiving or sending data, organising data 'packages' ready to send, decoding addresses or determining bus availability. The bus itself may be merely a twisted pair or single coaxial pair cable; it is the interfacing equipment at each termination point which has to be designed to implement the protocol. So-called standards for communication links are often little more than definitions of the protocol.

An example of a simple standard protocol is the common RS 232 link, which was designed for minicomputers to transfer data to and from peripherals, such as printers or remote terminals, but which is adequate for the transfer of reasonable amounts of data between one central equipment item and a number of outstations, each with its own dedicated link to the central equipment (star configuration). Data are transmitted in asynchronous mode serially over a single pair, character by character. Each character is represented by seven or eight 'bits' (marks or spaces) and a mark is represented by a voltage level between $-3V$ and $-25V$, a space by $+3V$ to $+25V$, so that zero voltage indicates no transmission. The rate of transmission can be between 50 and 20 000 'baud' (bits per second) which together with the wide voltage level limits gives high immunity to noise.

Separate control or 'handshaking' lines are used so that the central equipment can control the start and finish of a message. Start and stop bits and parity bits are added to the characters.

Most instrumentation systems will require a much higher rate of data transfer than could be handled by such a simple protocol; also it is likely that data transfer between outstations without involving the central equipment will be required. Appropriate protocol applied to ring and multidrop communications systems will have to include addresses of each message; the message 'packages' will have to be restricted in size also. In a ring system data are passed round the *endless* bus inside a never-ending stream of 'data slots', into which 'data packages' can be placed if vacant, or from which they can be taken if the address is correct. The system thus operates like one of those continuously moving elevators one sees at some building sites. A 'package' starts with a special bit which indicates the presence or absence of data. All stations will in turn read the initial bit and the address (if data are present) and will then either accept the message or retransmit it to the next station. Eventually any message must reach its destination, unless an error occurs, but if there are a large number of outstations it may take a long time, particularly if the rate of data transfer is close to maximum. For a system such as an instrumentation system in which there are strict time constraints (for sampled measurement data, for instance), the ring configuration, whilst it does provide a means of communication between outstations, is clearly not ideal.

A multidrop system differs from a ring system in that there is no one simple route between outstations. The risk of 'collision' dictates that only one station can be allowed to send data at any time. This can be achieved either by having a 'traffic regulator' which controls all data transfers (not necessarily the central equipment) or by designing a protocol, which recognises the collision risk and provides a set of rules, and functions initiated in accordance with the rules, which enable the communication system to 'free run' as does the ring system. Thus, each station would check, right at the beginning of transmission, for collision and would wait for an interval before continuing: the interval could be different for each station, thus establishing priorities. Unlike the ring system, each station in a multidrop system has an equal opportunity to transmit, but the protocol will have to limit message lengths to ensure that sampled data considerations are met.

A simple communication system (and, hence, a small and probably relatively inflexible instrumentation system) can be implemented using the star configuration and a protocol such as RS 232, the data transmission being entirely controlled by the central equipment which may be the only 'intelligent' item in the system. However, it can be seen from the foregoing that, as the system gets larger, transmission distances longer and the number of outstations increases, the protocol of the communication link must become more complex and intelligent. Each outstation in a ring or multidrop system must be able to store data ready for transmission or just received, organise its transmission and in general act independently of the functions of the outstation itself. The equipment required to do this is the communication system (the link is usually a simple pair of conductors); this is designed to be constructed from standard LSI 'chips' designed for the telecommunications and computer markets. In some cases microprocessors may well be used to implement the timing and logical switching functions necessary to fulfil the requirements of the interface devices, as these provide flexibility to program requirements which are special to the instrumentation rather than the telecommunication field, for instance.

To summarise, the communication links between local instrumentation installations close to the plant and modern centralised control and operational display centres have evolved from nothing more than a (very expensive) collection of cables to a free running and very complex communication system with many of the features of the national telephone system. More and more the communication system serves the needs of the other parts of the system rather than passively interconnecting them. Greater flexibility of function and expansion in the instrumentation and control system depends to a large extent on the design and complexity of the data communication system, which has now assumed the same *functional* importance within the total system as either the measurement or control systems. Perhaps more than anything this illustrates what is meant by the 'systems approach' to design.

12.5 DATA SECURITY

The effect of 'noise' on signal transmission has been discussed in Sections 7.9 and 7.12. Noise introduced into the data links or highway can result in serious degradation of the total system. This is the more so because the measured data received at local stations from parallel analog channels are, after conversion to digital form, transmitted serially at high speed. The capacitance, resistance and inductance of the communication link, as well as electrostatic pick-up, will all have an important bearing on the integrity of the data transfer. Redundancy in the data itself, i.e. additional bits added to the actual message and address in order to facilitate the detection of errors, provides security against such degradation. In the extreme case, each message can be retransmitted back to the originating station by the receiving station and checked to see that it has not been changed by the transmission process. However, this degree of redundancy is rarely acceptable or necessary. In the simplest case a single bit known as a 'parity bit' can be added or not by the transmitting station so as to make the total in the message either odd or even. There is a direct trade off between the degree of message redundancy and the probability that any error will be detected. A system with high redundancy can not only provide a good error detection but also enable error correction to be achieved without the need for retransmission of the data. Obviously, therefore, the design of the data transmitting and receiving equipment, as well as the cable link itself, is of vital importance to the performance of the entire system. The 'intelligent' interface, which is essential to the multidrop configuration, despite adding considerably to the system complexity, does provide the means to apply more secure methods of error detection and correction.

In addition to noise and cable characteristics, data transfer errors can arise from malfunction of the equipment itself. To detect such malfunctions self-diagnostic routines are programmed into the operating software of the microprocessors which constitute the basis for the equipment units. Again the degree of complexity increases with the degree of integrity required and there is always a practical limit. However, it can be seen that the whole approach to equipment availability is different from that conventionally practised which depends on back-up and spares to cater for quite frequent unit failures. It is not possible to design integrated electronic systems for this approach, if only because it is not a simple matter to determine that a fault has occurred, let alone what it is or where in the system it has arisen. Nevertheless, with good design, system integrity can be such that equipment availability is 100% except for total power failures or catastrophic damage.

One of the sources of noise from which it is most difficult to protect the system is the power supply: any rapid switching of power anywhere on the plant (such as the operation of a motor contactor) is liable to cause 'spikes' of considerable voltage and power level in the power supply system, which can all too easily find their way into the digital data highways of the instrumentation system. In fact, it is one of the main disadvantages of such digital systems that they are much more susceptible to errors arising in this way than an analog system: this is because the 'spikes' simulate the sharp change in voltage levels that go to form a good bit in a digital parameter.

The safest solution to the power supply noise problem is to install an uninterruptable power supply (UPS), consisting of batteries charged continuously from the AC mains supply, and used at the same time to generate the required equipment power supply levels. However, this is an expensive solution and is not always justified. Other precautions against entry into the instrument systems of noise from heavy electrical switchgear via the common power supply are possible. Line filters, which store energy in first order CR circuits (see Section 8.16) and release it more slowly over a very short time interval within the period of the supply, will 'spread' the energy in a spike and thus reduce its potential effect on digital circuitry. Successive line filters may be used, but even then, such is the intensity of some spikes that errors will still be induced in digital circuitry in some cases. The use of 'isolating transformers' as a barrier to spikes is now recognised as essential in most systems.

An isolating transfer is not there essentially to vary the supply voltage, but simply to provide a barrier to 'normal mode' transmission of noise energy, and by good design to greatly reduce the transfer of common mode energy. (Normal mode is the name given to energy transfer by flow of current in a circuit, whilst common mode is the name given to the transfer of energy by induction, capacitance or electrostatic means from one circuit to another.) A normal transformer, whilst completely preventing normal mode transfer of energy, is designed for efficient transfer of common mode energy at power supply generation frequency. Most of the energy in a spike, however, occurs at very much higher frequency than the generating frequency, and so it is possible to design an isolating transformer to reject this energy whilst accepting the 'legitimate' power transfer. This is achieved by incorporating a screen between the primary and secondary windings of the transformer: the capacitance between this screen and the primary winding is sufficient to provide efficient energy transfer for the high frequency unwanted energy by capacitive coupling, whilst being very in efficient in this respect with respect to the very much lower frequency mains supply energy. The screen is connected to ground and thus 'shunts' the unwanted power in the spike harmlessly to earth. The ground connection *must* be isolated from the normal plant earthing system, as on typical process plant there can exist large (several volts) differences between earth or ground potential at different locations; if the screen is connected to the normal ground, therefore, current can flow owing to such differences, introducing normal mode noise back into the instrumentation system and negating the barrier effect of the transformer. In special cases additional 'box' screens are provided around each winding of the transformer to further increase the 'shunting' to ground effect. In general, separate isolating transformers should be used wherever signal lines are connected to substantially different earth (ground) potentials. Such isolating transformers can reduce common mode noise transfer by as much as 140 dB (10^7:1) which, although it sounds impressive, may be necessary to protect against such transients, as are caused by oil burner ignitor switching, lightning strikes or high power radio transmissions.

Line filters and isolation transformers can reduce the effect of spikes or transients on digital circuits, but will do nothing to mitigate the effect of 'brown-outs' or 'black-outs' in the mains supply. 'Brown-outs', or the temporary reduction of generator voltage to levels which cause malfunction in the digital instrument system circuits, can be obviated by providing regulator devices which sense the voltage change and compensate so that the output to the digital circuits is unaffected. Of course the response of such 'regulators' is very slow compared to line filters or isolation transformers, and the function of the two is quite different. 'Black-outs', or the total or near total cessation of supply, can only be compensated for by the provision of a UPS or by designing the circuitry to shut down in an orderly fashion on loss of supply and start up without corruption on restoration of supply. The operation of digital circuits is today so fast that this is a perfectly reasonable design criteria, and 'watchdog' circuits to achieve such 'orderly shut down' are now common practice.

12.6 DISPLAY AND RECORDING

Apart from distributed signal processing the modern process control and instrumentation system utilises a computer-based display and data recording system which is as radically different from the traditional control panel instrumentation as the data transmission system is from earlier analog systems. However, it should be recognised that, apart from a common dependence on digital rather than analog operation, the two developments—signal processing and transmission, on the one hand, and display recording, on the other—are totally separate.

The modern display system depends entirely on the 'graphics' capability of modern computers. Diagrams of the process plant in the form familiar to process engineers and operators as flow diagrams and instrument diagrams, allow digital or analog displays of process variables to be related to process operation. New displays for other areas of plant can be constructed by the computer on the VDU (visual display unit) screen in a few seconds, so that each display can be just as comprehensive as the system designer or process design engineer may decide is appropriate for good operator control (it is still the plant operator who sets the desired values). In practice, overviews and more detailed 'local' views are usually provided. Such displays are usually 'programmed' by the user or plant designer using a special keyboard containing many 'function keys'. This is because the process design may not be finalised until long after the contract for the instrumentation system is placed, and also so that post-design changes can be easily incorporated into the displays.

Whether the system is split-architecture or not, the set points of all controllers and control action settings are always under the control of the operator or instrument technician, who can change these values from the control panel using the same or a separate keyboard. In addition, there is usually an 'engineers' keyboard which enables interconnections such as cascade, ratio or tracking connections to be changed so that the overall control scheme can be altered even whilst the plant is operating. Often a separate VDU is provided for this purpose.

There are several reasons for providing the means of recording some plant variables. It may be essential for good observation to observe trends in a variable over a period of hours or even days. Such 'trend' recording is particularly necessary during the initial operating period of a continuous process plant. Often in the past 'dedicated' analog recorders have been provided in the design which are only really used at start up. The modern computer-based graphic system again utilises the memory capability of digital data processing and the VDU to display trends of any variable as required. In addition, by storing sampled values of any variable it is possible to display records on an 'historic' basis: such data is often 'dumped' onto 'floppy disc' memory at the end of each day so that historic displays are possible long after the period of operation. This facility to store historic data is a very considerable and important development, since it is possible to analyse long-term developments in the process operation. It makes possible the application of management techniques to process operation (as opposed to closed loop control), using computers at a 'higher hierarchical level' either to instruct operators to reschedule the plant set points or to directly alter them in 'supervisory mode' control actions.

An important feature of any process control instrumentation system is the provision of alarms and discrete indications to attract the process operator's attention when particular plant measurements exceed or fall below certain critical values. The provision of such detection points in the centralised display/recording system is essentially very easy except for one thing—the detection of 'first-up' occurrences! The computer system carries out a routine 'scan' of all such parameter values on a cyclical basis, but it is often the case that critical detectors are connected directly into trip devices which act to cause sudden closing of a value or stoppage of a pump drive when the critical value is exceeded. These 'fault trip interlock actions' sometimes cause other variables to exceed or fall below critical values, and, unless the computer scanning system is fast enough, it may not afterwards be possible to determine which plant measurement actually initiated the sequence of fault trip actions which result. As it may be vital to know this, the alarm and shut-down systems must be defined and specified to the equipment manufacturer very carefully indeed. It may be necessary to use a separate equipment system altogether for some of the most critical alarms and trips.

12.7 'SMART' INSTRUMENTS

The signals from individual transducers located close to plant equipment are usually transmitted in analog form to some local gathering station if not to the control room. This is because each transducer is separately located and requires at least a single pair cable whether signals are in analog or digital form: there is no economy of cabling possible by going over to digital signal transmission at this point in the system. Moreover, analog signals are simpler to generate and less liable to corruption from 'noise'.

With the advent of very large scale integration of electronic circuits it is now feasible to produce transducers with quite complex digital signalling capabilities, including error checking to combat the noise problem, just as cheaply as analog signalling. The advantage of this is that 'smart' instruments can be produced at an economical price which can send and receive not only measurement data, but also calibration and maintenance data. To achieve this the separate 'messages' involved will 'time share' the communication channel (still a single pair). As a result, future systems will have the facility to monitor the calibration 'drift' of transducers and even important operating parameters such as temperature, to provide much more reliable performance.

12.8 SUPERVISORY CONTROL

As was mentioned in Section 12.6, the ability to store historic data makes it possible to analyse plant operation over long periods and to apply the results of such analyses to improve operation of the process. Given a mathematical model of the behaviour of the process, it will be possible to determine, a priori, a new set of set points, which will be near optimum, to meet some new processing or marketing requirements. A computer can be used to implement such supervisory or set point optimisation schemes and the results of its computations can readily be used to change the controller set points.

There are many definitions of supervisory set point control; it all depends on the objectives. In industry these objectives will always be concerned directly with optimising either profits, quality or quantity in some way. However, there are very wide variations in the requirements of a control system which will achieve or help the operator to achieve such objectives. It may be most important to optimise response at start-up or shut-down as in discontinuous rolling. In chemical and oil processing it is traditional and very necessary to design the plant units so that operation is highly stable and, hence, advanced control is likely to imply the scheduling of multiple set point changes to reflect optimal changes in *steady-state* operation to meet changing production or market requirements. Thus, if the feed quality to a cat cracker changes (supply side disturbance) the computer will calculate a new set of operating parameters, such as:

(i)   feed enthalpy,
(ii) catalyst/oil ratio, and
(iii) space/velocity ratio.

and the new controller desired values required to achieve these operating parameter values.

Similarly, if the criteria of optimality changes (demand side disturbance) because of operating or market requirements, the computer must again calculate a new set of controller-desired values.

The computer system required will include in its application software some or all of the following programs:

1.   Process model comprising sets of linear equations and first order interaction relationships which 'describe' the process chemistry.
2.   Process equipment model comprising a set of equations defining the mechanistic operation of the plant and equipment items.
3.   An adaptive routine which will compare performance parameters, calculated from plant measurement recorded variables, with the equivalent parameter values estimated by the process model, and make correction to the coefficients of the latter.

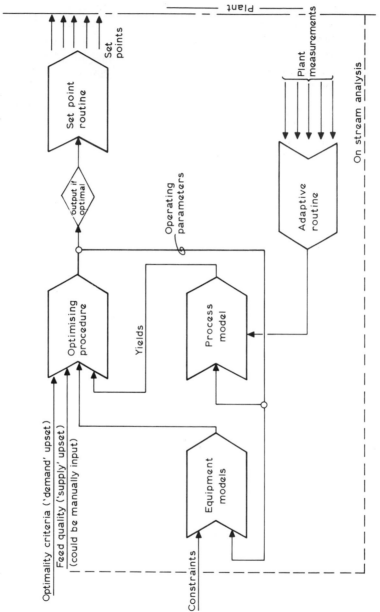

Fig. 12.2.

4. An optimising and set point routine which will use suitable mathematical techniques to compute the optimal set of controller-desired values for any given set of operating conditions. The routine will have to take due account of operational limits set by management or supervision and also of the limits of operation of the plant equipment items. It will therefore operate interactively with the two models (1 and 2).

The block diagram in Fig. 12.2 illustrates the interactions between these software elements. Closed or open loop operation is possible and the adaptive routine could be omitted for a 'stationary' plant (i.e. one which does not change its characteristics as heat exchanges become fouled or catalyst ages, etc.). The degree of complexity of the models and the optimising procedure is also a matter of judgement in respect of each and every application.

Index